# The Human Capacity for Transformational Change

Pressures for transformational change have become a regular feature of most fields of human endeavour. Master thinkers and visionaries alike reframed existing divisions as connecting relationships, bringing together as dynamic systems the supposed opposites of parts and wholes, stability and change, individuals and society, and rational and creative thinking. This reframing of opposites as interconnected wholes led to a realisation of the power of a collective mind.

This book offers ways and means of creating the synergies that are crucial in influencing desired transformational change towards a just and sustainable future. It describes how and why our current decision-making on any complex issue is marked by clashes between the different interests involved. More optimistically, the book pursues ways of bringing together government, specialised and community interests at the local, regional and personal scales in a collective transformation process. Practical examples signal the emergence of a new knowledge tradition that promises to be as powerful as the scientific Enlightenment.

Written in accessible language, this book will be insightful reading for anyone struggling with transformational change, especially researchers, students and professionals in the fields of administration, governance, environmental management, international development, politics, public health, public law, sociology, and community development.

**Valerie A. Brown** is Director of the Local Sustainability Project, Human Ecology Program, Fenner School of Environment and Society, Australian National University, Emeritus Professor of Environmental Health and author of over 12 books and 110 refereed journal papers on collective thinking and the collective mind.

**John A. Harris** is a university academic, outdoors educator and collective action researcher with the Local Sustainability Project and Alliance for Regenerative Landscape, Agriculture and Social Health in Australia.

'This refreshing, stimulating, indeed brilliant book helps move the concept of "collective mind" out of the realm of speculative philosophy and into the practical work of changing the world. We humans must think together, across our wide diversity, to deal with the great challenges before us.'

*Alan AtKisson, writer and international consultant, Director, AtKisson Group*

'This is a truly amazing – bold, audacious – intellectual enterprise that hopefully will become a mandatory text for discussion and study in the academy as well as for use in community development and planning.'

*Caroline Ifeka, consultant anthropologist, Nigeria and London*

'This brilliant book leads to a vision of the world which is neither a dystopia (a prediction of gloom and disaster), nor a utopia (a model of impossible perfection). Rather, it leads to a future of a way to live that works in practice.'

*Wendy Rainbird, environmental educator, policy advisor,*
*and Landcare administrator, Canberra Australia*

'In *The Human Capacity for Transformational Change*, Brown and Harris have elegantly made accessible the processes that shape human existence and our collective influence on today's world. They nicely deconstruct how different ways of thinking inform the broad policy directions that serve our current global trajectory.'

*Colin L. Soskolne, University of Alberta Canada; Vice-President Executive*
*Committee Society for the Advancement of Science in Africa*

'This is an important and thought-provoking guide to navigating that complex reality and imagining, together, a world transformed. Brown and Harris draw on the best of our transcendent impulses, grounded in good science and an understanding of complex social phenomena to propel us to the next phase of human existence.'

*David Waltner-Toews, University of Guelph, Canada;*
*founding president of the Network for Ecosystem Sustainability and Health*

# The Human Capacity for Transformational Change

Harnessing the collective mind

**Valerie A. Brown and John A. Harris**

LONDON AND NEW YORK

from Routledge

First published 2014
by Routledge
2 Park Square, Milton Park, Abingdon, Oxon, OX14 4RN

and by Routledge
711 Third Avenue, New York, NY 10017

*Routledge is an imprint of the Taylor & Francis Group, an informa business*

*British Library Cataloguing in Publication Data*
A catalog record has been requested for this book

*Library of Congress Cataloging-in-Publication Data*
Brown, Valerie A.
The human capacity for transformational change : the future of the
collective mind / Valerie A. Brown, John Harris.
pages cm.
Includes bibliographical references and index.
1. Sustainable development. 2. Environmental policy. 3. Environmental
management. 4. Human ecology. 5. Social change. 6. Power (Social
sciences) I. Harris, John A. II. Title.
HC79.E5B77 2014
338.9'27--dc23
2013037342

ISBN13: 978-0-415-53990-6 (hbk)
ISBN13: 978-0-203-10787-4 (ebk)

Typeset in Times by Saxon Graphics Ltd, Derby

Printed and bound by CPI Group (UK) Ltd, Croydon, CR0 4YY

# Contents

**PART III**
**Changing worlds**                                          197

# Figures, tables and boxes

**Figures**

## Tables

## Boxes

# Foreword

## Transcending diversity: harnessing the collective mind

*Only when difference has its home, when the need for belonging in all its murderous intensity has been assuaged, can our common identity begin to find its voice.*

M. Ignatieff, *The Needs of Strangers*

This volume by Valerie Brown and John Harris is a necessary antidote for the despair of global fragmentation. Drawing on disparate thinkers ranging from Charles Darwin, Norbert Wiener, and James Lovelock to Pierre Teilhard de Chardin, Gregory Bateson and Christopher Alexander, they invite us to consider another possibility – neither a utopic nor a dystopic state, but a world transformed, pliable, utopian in attitude and thought, but grounded in the evident uncertainty in which we live out our lives. The criteria the authors used to select these thinkers were that

> 'their transformative ideas contributed to a new understanding of how the world works; second, that the development of their ideas includes the full range of questions that shape the human mind; and third, that their ideas lead to a fresh tradition and a shift to an era of collective thinking'.

That Brown and Harris can accommodate these apparently contradictory perspectives in one global vision is a testament to their robust imagination and their understanding of the complex and difficult challenges we face. It is a hopeful book, and a necessary one, identifying the transformational changes that can take us from a world where humanity vacillates between destructive difference and brutal tyranny to a world where a home for difference makes us all feel, ultimately, at home.

As Brown and Harris note, this kind of complexity requires us to acknowledge multiple legitimate, and often apparently irreconcilable, perspectives in the world – and to go beyond. Even as scientists have been quick to espouse diversity in the natural world, they have fought against cultural and epistemological diversity. Yes, there were multiple ways of looking at the world, but twentieth century reductionist science trumped all of them. Thus even the acknowledgement that the reality in which we dwell might be open to multiple interpretations is a new challenge for science, in which the facts are uncertain, values are in dispute, the decision-making stakes are high, and there is a sense of urgency that decisions be made (Funtowicz and Ravetz, 1993; 2008). To deal with issues of sustainability, it was no longer sufficient to give everyone a good education in natural sciences. There was a need to expand the peer group, and to accommodate a much wider range of modes of constructing knowledge about the world than is common in 'normal' science. This post-normal scientific inquiry required collaborative learning and knowledge integration, in which expertise is collective. Difficult as the practice of Post-Normal Science might be, even this was not enough to move us forward.

While the arguments in favour of this Post-Normal Science are compelling, they give no guidance as to what kinds of questions we might ask once we begin to gather these multiple perspectives. So we have everyone around the table: what now? Are we merely negotiating personal interests, or do we have a collective responsibility that transcends the need to converse across our various boundaries? Having come from our particular places with our particular histories and ways of understanding, do we have some responsibility to converse and think, *collectively*, about our future? Here again, Brown and Harris articulate a series of questions on ethics, aesthetics and empathy that can help us move beyond arguments about boundaries, power and exclusivity.

As biological beings that are part of a biosphere, our collective survival requires not only that we account for multiple human perspectives but also (insofar as knowledge and empathy allow us) the perspectives of multiple species. And if global sustainability implies a global narrative, what might that look like? After centuries of brutal religious and ideological tyrannies, each laying claim to special knowledge (the utopias and dystopias Brown and Harris so rightly set aside), we shy away, in rightful fear, from yet another claim to what will – what should – transpire. We cannot know what it is.

If the tensions we face were only a systemic tug between the part and the whole, we might, in principle at least, solve some of these problems through some combination of complexity theory and cross-cultural dialogue, perhaps using references to mythologies and common symbols. The notion of sustainability, however, introduces a temporal dimension in which complex systems change, flip, and recreate themselves in a manner that is rendered invisible in many discussions of complex systems (Hayles, 2000; Raez-Luna, 2008). Thus, the diverse social-ecological systems are themselves transforming over time, so that exactly what is dialoguing or being preserved is not always clear.

When a plurality of perspectives is viewed as a mutual accommodation within a sense of global community, or within a liberal-democratic technocratic framework (which is where many of these ideas have been given their modern voice), then the task of doing Post-Normal Science is difficult, but is essentially reasonable and civilised. In the world in which we live, however – the world of power and culture, of injustice and imperialism – each of those perspectives may protect its own vision of reality with 'murderous intensity'. Thus our greatest challenge in our learning journey to the future may not be to find a technical solution to the energy or diversity 'problem', but to find a home for difference, even as we find a voice for a common destiny, to weave an unknown collective narrative from our many stories, without losing the many particularities.

On the one 'invisible' hand, we (especially those members of the privileged economic minority) are presented with unprecedented opportunities to further personal growth and experience within a global shopping mall of cultural values. On the other, we find limits to the satisfaction those choices offer because we lack a meaningful frame of reference which can inform us that we have made the right choice (Ignatieff, 1984). As Leonard Cohen aptly puts it in his poem/song 'Closing Time' it 'looks like freedom but it feels like death'. The unfolding world, however, is not a dichotomy. It is a complex conversation among billions of beings, and the current chaotic instability may be seen as the birth pangs of a new world, a world of collective human thinking and endeavour.

In framing the possibilities of this new, open-ended narrative, Brown and Harris turn to Teilhard de Chardin (1959). Observing the millennia of transformations that, after Darwin, we have come to call evolution, Teilhard de Chardin suggests that humans have moved from the biosphere to the noosphere (literally, an envelope of thought that surrounds the globe). We are self-reflexive, not only knowing, but knowing that we know. Some now interpret the Internet or World Wide Web as evidence of Teilhard de Chardin's ideas. Place and ethnic group can be transcended by identifying our human place as the entire globe.

In this transformation, as in all such prior changes (which Brown and Harris acknowledge), there is the danger that such a grand narrative can again be usurped by those who believe that this process requires some guidance from economic, religious and political elites who have the 'correct' understanding of what is really happening. This usurpation can take place in the household, village, neighbourhood, culture... at any scale. Ignatieff's caution that we must find a home for difference should not lose sight of the local in a struggle to find global solutions. The historical identification with place is somehow transposed in hierarchical levels from a village locale or ethnic community to our global home. This long march through the nested hierarchy is daunting, with the stakes considerably higher than they have been, now that the future viability of Earth as a planet hospitable to human life is at stake. There is, then, a conversation here, a necessary tension, and a role for people of good will and wisdom to act.

If every individual acted in a totally autonomous fashion, a diversity of ideas and behaviours might result, but we also would have no society benefiting from that diversity, and from which future individuals might benefit. If every farmer tied up all resources in diversity as an insurance policy against future exigencies, then productive efficiency would suffer. In this case, diversity is a conditional rather than an absolute good. At the other end of the argument, that is, that Earth could function very well with little diversity (fewer species), lies the absurd notion that one or two (or even several hundred) life forms could perform all the intricate, interwoven life-processes that make this planet hospitable to primate mammals such as ourselves.

Communities, ecosystems, and ultimately the entire biosphere need some diversity in order to adapt and survive, but not so much that they become gridlocked with information overload. In terms of C. S. Holling's figure eight model of ecosystem dynamics and its various manifestations (Holling, 1995), whereby the system passes through phases of exploitation, conservation, release, reorganisation and conservation again, one might argue that too much diversity in structures and functions tends to tie the system up in a conservation mode and thus predispose it to major collapse; too little diversity puts major constraints on the possibilities for reorganisation, since it means there is a paucity of resources to exploit.

As diversity increases, new orders/organisations emerge to contain the diversity and give it meaning; that way, creative sources for future adaptation are protected and available for future needs. There is a continual interplay between diversity at one scale (individuals) being contained within, and being necessary for, unified classes at larger scales (family groups), which themselves constitute diversity at another scale (community). The tendency of those larger units is necessarily to dampen internal disorder or chaos that may accompany the urges to diversify (Bella, 1994).

The need to maintain the potential for future individuals to flourish is one of the constraints on their current capability to do so, and one of the issues that surely must arise at the multi-perspective community table. Communities remind us that the future counts and thereby exerts temporally backward pressure to ensure continuity. That is, by promoting the flourishing of communities as communities (with a parallel argument being made for multi-species eco-communities) we may be constraining the options for individuals living now, while keeping options open for future individuals.

Thus, although diversity is good, it presents serious challenges for our quest to generate a resilient and viable future for people on this planet. Solutions to some of those challenges rely on incorporating scale and context into our understanding while recognising that diversity is inextricably linked to notions of unity. There is a kind of dance here, between the systems and the stories, the individuals in families in communities in global networks, the seeds and trees in each place, conversing across shifting physical boundaries in a changing planet. Even as we nurture our collective mind through global communications, our future unfolds in connecting and re-connecting people to place, and nurturing their sense of self through the authentic experience of belonging to and caring for something material and permanent. The revival of communities of place must be significantly different from those of the past when ethnicity, culture, and territory formed the basis for racial imperialism. Instead, the communities of place we need are those where diverse communities of interest, emerging from different cultural histories coexist and enrich each other in multiple and emerging forms, recognising their fundamental dependence on each other.

Here, as elsewhere, Brown and Harris point to signs of hope – transformational movements from Transition Towns and Healthy Cities to the World Social Forum all 'seeking a world inspired by the rich contributions stemming from the differences that create a society'. These groups, they assert, are 'committed to transformational change being open-ended, interconnected and collaborative, valuing uncertainty and diversity'. These kinds of developments can be juxtaposed against complementary movements not necessarily reliant on ideas of community, where attempts are being made to establish and enforce universal standards in human rights and environmental integrity or health (e.g. Rapport 1998; Westra 1994; Manuel-Navarrete *et al.* 2008).

The new goal is to develop a code to which all humans can relate, one that addresses the needs we have in common as humans (Ignatieff, 1984).

We live in a fine line between self and other, local and global, ecosystemic unfolding and invasive species, tyranny and anarchy, hegemony and fragmentation. These tensions will never be – and probably should never be – resolved. From a bio-medical viewpoint, only death reflects the resolution of all tensions. A sustainable, healthy human community will be one where we act on the faith that there *is* a common narrative, a common, global journey, but that this commonality is not predetermined and only becomes visible as we tell it; it is an emergent tapestry of tales told from many perspectives, rooted in a common reality whose nature and dimensions we can perhaps, in solidarity, collectively, and only collectively, discern.

Val Brown and John Harris have given us an important and thought-provoking guide to navigating that complex reality and imagining, together, a world transformed.

David Waltner-Toews
Professor Emeritus, University of Guelph, Canada
September, 2013

Acknowledgement: Thanks to Ellen Wall for many hours of discussion

## References

Bella, D. A. (1994) 'Organizational Systems and the Burden of Proof'. Paper presented at the symposium Pacific Salmon and their Ecosystems: Status and Future Options. University of Washington, Seattle, US.

Funtowicz, S. O. and Ravetz, J. R. (1993) 'Science for the Post-Normal Age', in *Futures* 25: 739-755.

Funtowicz, S. O. and Ravetz. J. R. (2008) 'Beyond Complex Systems: Emergent Complexity and Social Solidarity' in *The Ecosystem Approach: Complexity, Uncertainty, and Managing for Sustainability*, Waltner-Toews, D., Kay, J. and Lister, N-M. (eds.). New York: Columbia University Press, pp. 309–322.

Hayles, N. K. (2000) 'Making the Cut: The Interplay of Narrative and System, or What Systems Theory Can't See', in *Observing Complexity: Systems Theory and Postmodernity*, Rasch, William and Wolf, Cary (eds.). Minneapolis, US: University of Minnesota Press, pp. 73–85.

Holling, C. S. (1995) 'Sustainability: The Cross-Scale Dimension', in Munasinghe, M. and W. Shearer (eds.) *Defining and Measuring Sustainability.* The United Nations University and the World Bank, pp. 65–75.

Ignatieff, M. (1984) *The Needs of Strangers.* New York: Penguin Books, p. 156.

Manuel-Navarrete, D., Dolderman, D. and Kay, J. J. (2008) 'An Ecosystem Approach for Sustaining Ecological Integrity – But Which Ecological Integrity?', in *The Ecosystem Approach: Complexity, Uncertainty, and Managing for Sustainability*, Waltner-Toews, D., Kay, J. and Lister, N-M. (eds.). New York: Columbia University Press, pp. 335–44.

Raez-Luna, E. (2008) 'Third World Inequity, Critical Political Economy, and the Ecosystem Approach', in *The Ecosystem Approach: Complexity, Uncertainty, and Managing for Sustainability*, Waltner-Toews, D., Kay, J. and Lister, N-M. (eds.). New York: Columbia University Press, pp. 323–34.

Rapport, D. (1998) 'Ecosystem Health: An Integrative Science', in *Ecosystem Health,* Rapport, D., Costanza, R., Epstein, P. R., Gaudet, C. and Levins, R. (eds.). Oxford, UK: Blackwell Science, pp. 3–50.

Teilhard de Chardin, P. (1959) *The Phenomenon of Man.* New York: Harper & Row, p. 320.

Waldegrave, C., Tamasese, K., Tuhaka, F. and Campbell, W. (2003), *Just Therapy – A Journey.* Adelaide, Australia: Dulwich Centre Publications.

Westra, L. (1994) *The Principle of Integrity: An Environmental Proposal for Ethics.* Lanham, Maryland, US: Rowman & Littlefield Publishers, Inc.

# Acknowledgements

The authors would like to acknowledge the many people who have contributed so much to this book over so many years. As well as all the collective minds drawn on in the book, we would like to thank the following people for believing in the project and acting as readers and critical friends over the years: Erica Fisher, Jackie Ohlin, Wendy Rainbird, John Schooneveldt, and Colin Soskolne. Their comments have influenced us a great deal while they are not to be blamed for our mistakes. It has been great working with them as a collective mind.

Sources of inspiration have been many. Our students in environmental and human ecology courses at the Australian National University, the University of Western Sydney, and the University of Canberra have given us insight into a collective future. For Valerie, whole-of-community development in communities in Asia, Nepal, Europe and around Australia, and a residency at the Rockefeller Foundation Bellagio Centre in 1999 opened up the links between the past and the future, and between the world of ideas and the world of practice. For John, ecological systems projects in Papua New Guinea and Vietnam and environmental education in Australia, and North and South America helped ground a passion for the natural environment. For both of us, the Human Ecology Forum at the Australian National University brought together researchers, practitioners, community change agents and collective thinkers almost every week for over 30 years.

Our families have provided a wellspring of personal support. Their existence reinforced the importance of utopian thinking in maintaining the hope of a harmonious future. For John, the companionship and advice of Jane, and of Craig and Stephen and their young families of Brooke, Ellie, Grace and Scarlett helped in focusing on that future. For Valerie, over 50 years of linking the worlds of politics and research with Wallace Brown, and the spur of needing a better world for Sarah, Christopher, Elliot and Amon kept the dream of collective thinking alive.

Our editor Paul Wallace has done a marvelous job in working with us on the clarity and accuracy of the text. Earthscan from Routledge have been supportive publishers and we would like to thank Jonathan Sinclair Wilson and our editors Khanam Virjee, Helena Hurd and Helen Bell. Finally, we would like to welcome and thank our readers. Collective thinking can only emerge from within a collective mind.

Valerie A. Brown and John A. Harris
Canberra, 2013

# Part I
# Changing minds

# 1 Living with transformational change

## A future for the collective mind

**Synopsis:** present unregulated changes to the state of the world are only the latest in a long series of transformational changes to the planet. The current changes are being driven by human actions that in turn arise from human systems of thought. The collective thinkers who have been selected as shaping the present are Charles Darwin, who recognised that constant evolutionary change includes human minds; James Lovelock, who identified the self-organising systems that link people and planet; and Norbert Wiener, who found that electronic computers could act as extensions of the human mind. This has become the narrative that frames today's thinking. Visionaries that followed them foretold how humanity could live in a humane, sustainable world influenced by a collective mind. That collective mind has spread throughout the world with some fascinating consequences.

## Context of the change: time and place

It is a surprise to find that the current era of transformational change is being treated as if it were a one-off event. Past global upheavals confirm that global transformational changes happen at regular intervals. Our planet was once full of lumbering, small-brained, large-boned creatures called dinosaurs, living in forests, eating giant ferns and cone-bearing trees, and each other. The next moment, geologically speaking, they were gone.[1] Earth is now being paved with concrete and asphalt by agile, large-brained, small-boned humans that grow their own food in plots, move about in metal boxes, and attempt to manage the planet. This era of change could go in either direction, towards human extinction or towards a humane coexistence with the other living systems of the planet.

With each era of change comes a different image of the world. In the past, Earth was believed to be flat, have a fixed beginning and end, and be at the disposal of distant gods. Now we see the world as a minute ball in an infinitely expanding universe and in the grip of drastic human-generated changes. Whatever the current thinking, the hope for a better future remains part of the human condition, as reflected in the words of a turn-of-the century poet:[2]

**To a poet a thousand years hence:**

2
I care not if you bridge the seas,
Or ride secure the cruel sky,
Or build consummate palaces
Of metal or of masonry.

3
But have you wine and music still,
And statues and a bright-eyed love,
And foolish thoughts of good and ill
And prayers to them who sit above?
                *James Elroy Flecker 1884–1915*

Worldwide, people remain confused about how to respond to the changes that they see occurring and feel are enveloping them. One moment the world is united by admiration for a moon walk and the next sharply divided on the use of nuclear power. Our grasp of technology has led on the one hand to a rapid increase in population, resource consumption and pollution, and on the other it has enabled us to live longer, and given us instant global communication and great cities. The magnitude of the human influence on the Earth has led to the current era being called the Anthropocene (*anthro* being Latin for human) and the planet the Anthroposphere.[3] These titles recognise the influence of the human mind on the state of the planet, while accepting humankind's continuing interdependence with the living and the non-living world.

Within the larger question of what sort of a world do we as humans hope to inhabit comes the need to answer a range of other, dependent questions. These are the questions that determine human action to shape the future: the sum of introspective, physical, social, ethical, aesthetic, sympathetic and reflective questions that collectively direct the human mind. With the hope of living in a humane and sustainable world:

- What are the assumptions of the person doing the thinking?
- Is it physically possible to achieve a sustainable planet that will support us humans in our chosen lifestyles?
- Is it socially accepted that all members of a society can contribute their full potential to their hoped-for future?
- Are there ethical principles that hold that all members of a society should respect each other and their supporting environment?
- Is it aesthetically satisfying for all people, no matter what nationality, culture or creed, to live in a harmonious relationship with their environment?
- Is there a sympathetic understanding between the different interests in the same society and among different societies?
- What is the core message of the answers to the set of questions?

To answer all these questions in relation to any event connected with change flies in the face of previous practice.[4] The dominant mode of inquiry has been to reduce the matter to be investigated to one question at a time, to draw on physical evidence wherever possible, and to search for an expert to help find the answer. This way of thinking has been the backbone of the scientific era that has shaped Western thought over the past 300 years. The transformational change that originally led to the scientific era was called the Enlightenment, from the light thrown on the workings of the physical world. That era began with the seventeenth century mathematician René Descartes asking 'How do we know what we know?' and coming up with the famous conclusion that 'I think, therefore I am'.[5] Following this maxim of Descartes, people came to believe that it was possible to separate the mind from the body and one mind from other minds.

This line of thinking extended to the point where the thinking mind was regarded as separate from the physical brain. This supposed separation between the mind and brain has been rejected with the emergence of the present interest in the collective mind. The new multidisciplinary field of neuroscience has used electronic tools to document the plasticity of the brain, with its amazing capacity to combine multiple ways of knowing.[6] Thinking capacity is found to be generalised across the whole brain, with 95 per cent of thinking taking place in other-than-conscious zones, the zones of imagination, intuition and belief.[7] This finding matches the common sense recognition that objectivity is a science-era device. No human being (except perhaps those who are autistic) can think purely objectively along a single pathway. The multiple ways of thinking extend even to the many types of intelligence every one of us humans can access, as Howard Gardner has demonstrated in his work on multiple intelligences.[8]

The quest for the innate source of human thinking and human identity continues. There is the tale of the king who ordered that a child be reared inside a well to see what language it would speak when it came up. This tale echoes the real life experience that any human being reared in isolation until they are seven years old will never fully learn to speak or to respond to others. Interaction between people is fundamental to human existence: children left isolated in orphanages fail to thrive; deaf and blind Helen Keller became a gifted author and public speaker after her devoted carer found a way to release her from her mental isolation.[9] The belief in objectivity, central to science, ignores the lived experience of any group of people who share a time and place and hopes and fears about a common future. Science itself is a community of practice in which the members speak their own language and share a common experience.

The mastermind of the Enlightenment, Isaac Newton, developed the laws of physics that followed a straight cause-and-effect pathway. The law that stated 'every action has an equal and opposite reaction'[10] led to some of the miracles of mechanical technology. This interpretation of the way the physical world works has now been superseded by Einstein's interpretation of the world as a matter of relationships between energy, time and space.[11] This shift in thinking has allowed us humans to experience a curtain of flight around the planet, the energy of the atom and global communication via the World Wide Web. It has also allowed consideration of all events as dynamic relationships, rather than fixed moments in time.

Both the social and physical worlds have been exposed to these fresh levels of thought, not only separately, but also through the interactions between them. The discoveries of James Lovelock on the self-organisation of the physical world[12] and of Gregory Bateson on the self-organisation of the social world[13] come together in a systems-based interpretation of the world. A self-organising system is one which emerges from times of chaos, directed by its own organising principle and internal purpose.

Ideas of a collective world are being heralded with the emergence of collective nouns for the planet. The name given to the planet as a single self-governing organism is Gaia, after the Greek goddess of the earth.[14] The name given to the planet to mark the collective social impact of one species is the Anthroposphere. For clarity, throughout this discussion of the collective era of transformational change we will use the word 'planet' when referring to the site of physical changes and 'world' when referring to the interaction between physical and social changes.

To draw on the full capacity of the human mind and so reach a comprehensive understanding of the current era of transformational change requires answers to all of the questions presented above. To do this requires access to the physical, social, ethical, aesthetic and sympathetic elements of thought, going beyond the scientific era that has restricted the elements to the physical and the social. Even more challenging, the various answers need to be brought together in a synergy in which there is a leap forward beyond the capacity of any one contributor, achieved only by combining them all. Such a leap will require access to the thinker's lived experience, deep emotions and cultural consciousness, as well as their independent observations. From a writer who helped launch the self-help movement over a century ago:[15]

> Deep within man [sic] dwell those slumbering powers; powers that would astonish him, that he never dreamed of possessing; forces that would revolutionise his life if aroused and put into action.
>
> *Orison Swett Marden 1908*

It may be one mind or it may be many minds that bring the answers to our diverse questions together. In either case, a synergy arises from reflecting on all of the answers. The outcome is a different and more effective understanding of the issue than any one type of question can supply by itself. In the present era of near-chaotic global change, the first thing a collective mind is asked to interpret is the nature and direction of the transformational change in any particular setting. An increasing number of helpful thinking tools are emerging, making the task of answering the full suite of questions simpler. Here, among other ideas, we consider the sand-pile game, the tale of the sorcerer's apprentice and the possibility of a Transformation Science.

## The sand-pile game

When transformational changes affect a whole society, the future is not the same as the past: tomorrow is not the same as yesterday. It may take some time before those affected can look back and see how much things have changed. Alexander Graham Bell's telephone had a far greater long-term effect on communication than Skype. Photographs of Earth as a blue ball in space (Figure 1.1) gave people a sense of the planet as their only home. This was a change in the perception of reality as great as Ferdinand Magellan establishing that Earth is round. A transformational change in thinking is a sea change in the way people believe things are.

Rather than trying to avoid the inevitability of transformational change, it seems preferable to try to understand it. It has become fashionable among those studying transformational change to liken it to a sand-pile game.[16] In a sandpit or

*Figure 1.1* NASA photograph of Earth 'The Blue Marble' was taken on 7 December 1972, by the crew of the Apollo 17 spacecraft en route to the Moon at a distance of about 29,000 kilometres (Wikimedia Commons)

sandbox, a player piles up a cone of dry sand as high as it can go. At some moment, adding just a few grains of sand can start a series of large or small slips and the cone of sand takes a new shape. Multiple attempts to predict what the new shape will be confirm that prediction of that shape is impossible. While the initial change may have been external, the systemic change has been spontaneously generated from within the system itself.

Implicit in the sand-pile story is that critical changes are always inherent in any system. One small change in a physical or social environment can release large and unpredictable effects in the entire system. An example of this innate unpredictability in the physical environment is the earthquakes that result from the movement of Earth's tectonic plates. The movement of the plates can be predicted, but not the earthquakes. Examples of unpredictability in the social environment are the world wars of the twentieth century and the global financial crisis of the twenty-first century. People with larger perspectives had predicted the instability in the system itself, and yet everyone was surprised and shocked by the outcomes. While it may be possible to expect and to try to influence transformational change, once it is set in motion it is impossible to avoid it or to accurately predict its course. There is no going back, there is only working with what is and what could be.

## Peak of the change

For most of the past three centuries that have made up the scientific era, there has been an expectation that experts could determine and manipulate what happened in transformational change. As the world has discovered, nothing could be further from the truth. There is now a widespread acceptance that any major change involves both social and environmental systems in a mutual interaction with highly unpredictable feedback loops. The options for change can be predicted and the outcome prepared for, while accepting that there can be no certainty. Ways of thinking about the world have moved from considering the planet as a source of resources for humanity[17] to a world in which a human self-organising system works in concert with physical and biological self-organising systems.[18] The present generation is slowly realising that while humans can choose to change in a way that will influence the rest of the system, they can never be independent of the other two dimensions of reality.

There will always be uncertainty generated from the dynamic interconnections among the three dimensions of change, the living, the non-living and the human mind. The human mind is not merely a particularly clever machine, programmed to think in a certain way. The mind is itself a self-organising system, one that determines the ways in which reality is perceived and is able to recognise the possibilities of human influence on that reality.[19] One extreme of this capacity comes from those seeking to geo-engineer entire landscapes and oceans;[20] another is the many global networks leading local transformational change. The issue for the current generation is to recognise that humanity can choose how to change in collaboration, rather than competition, with the other dimensions of the earth's systems.

Moving to a collective understanding of mind has its problems. The assumption that a mind is merely an inert product of its physical brain led to the same sort of error as assuming that mobility is located solely in the legs and sight in the eyes. In sight and hearing, as in thinking, the activity involves the whole person under the influence of their social and physical environments. Every fourth year the Paralympic Games proves that losing legs or eyes, or even parts of the brain, does not prevent people from choosing their own future and meeting the challenge of getting there.[21] The challenge is also to the society they live in, to enable all members of that society to have the full capacity to make that choice about their future and find support for their choice.

A collective mind is radically different from a mass mind. The mass minds that drove the Jonestown mass suicide[22] in 1979 and the Nazi movement of the mid-twentieth century started with the idea that there was one definitive recipe that would achieve a predictable type of society. All other principles were treated as secondary. In a mass mind many minds are thinking as one and joining in believing in a single solution, and so are easily swayed in a single direction. Collective thinking, on the other hand, calls on both the open versatile mind of the human individual and the diversity of the minds concerned with the selected issue.

The changeover from one way of thinking to another is never smooth. The conservative old guard, with their investment in how things are now, cling to their belief about how the world is, even in the face of new evidence and in spite of their own direct experience. The Inquisition refused to look through Galileo's telescope, despite his pleas. Classical ways of blocking the new include denial, ridicule, distortion and the moral righteousness of those who own the truth. Responses to the predictions of global climate are examples of all of these. People deny that the changes exist at all, ridicule anyone who thinks they exist, and distort the evidence so that it appears to prove the opposite of the research.

Moral righteousness is a very effective way of blocking the new, by claiming that the new ideas are undermining the 'true' version of 'the truth'. The new way of thinking can be undermined by natural caution, dislike of change, selfishness and desire for power and resources, and the economic-growth paradigm. Long after the publication of Darwin's *On the Origin of Species* and *The Descent of Man,* social Darwinism is still used to justify the existing hierarchy of rich and poor. Even the hymns of the time reinforced a 'natural order' of rank and privilege that hangs on in justifying the existence of social inequities today.[23]

### Hymn: All things bright and beautiful

1.
All things bright and beautiful,
All creatures great and small,
All things wise and wonderful,
The Lord God made them all.

3.
The rich man in his castle,
The poor man at his gate,
God made them high and lowly,
And ordered their estate.

All things bright …
*William Henry Monk 1861*

## Follow on: searching for wise sorcerers

Social and environmental changes are often described by following a timeline or a sequence of political events. This does not apply to shifts in human thought. Ideas generated in one century can lie fallow until the times are ready for them to be heard. Immunisation against smallpox by using cowpox was practised for a millennium in China and a century in Europe before Pasteur's germinal theory of disease gave the foundation for its effect.[24] In discovering gravity, Newton did not imagine a sky filled with aircraft that seemingly defy that gravity, even though Leonardo da Vinci had foretold such a world a century before. Charles Darwin could write of the steps of evolutionary change without access to the mechanism of gene transmission that had already been identified by Gregor Mendel.[25] The list of this pattern of ideas waiting to connect is almost endless. One reason for the discontinuity is that the heroes of one era of change do not necessarily represent the ideal practices for the next.

The question arises, how to explore the ideas and practices that best represent the emergence of the collective era? The Enlightenment tradition is to establish a timeline according to which each thinker builds on the one before. This ladder-like advancement of science is an artefact of the rules of science. The same ladder does not apply to the evolution of a new thinking tradition, as Thomas Kuhn has well documented.[26] Collective thinking principles have frequently emerged after being ignored or even rejected by the dominant tradition for centuries.

Another approach is to identify successful collective thinkers from any time and place who can act as a guide towards collective thinking for a humanely sustainable future. Plato and Socrates are frequently exhumed from another era to support the Enlightenment. In a new tradition, how do we decide what is successful? Emblems of success such as winning the Nobel Prize, becoming a best-selling author, and rising to seniority in a profession are all rewards from a previous tradition. Icons such as Albert Einstein, William Shakespeare, Abraham Lincoln and Leonardo da Vinci were collective thinkers embedded in their own life and times. What are needed are ideal prototypes for now, the outstanding collective thinkers who have catalysed the change from the Enlightenment to the Anthropocene. Criteria for selection are, first, that their transformative ideas contribute to a new understanding of how the world works; second, that the development of their ideas includes the full range of questions that shape the human mind; and third, that their ideas lead to a fresh tradition and a shift to an era of collective thinking.

The search for those who meet these criteria found three sorcerers of the mind. They are Charles Darwin[27] 1809–82, James Lovelock[28] 1919– and Norbert Wiener[29] 1894–1964. While they were not connected in time, Darwin's insights into continual evolutionary change led to Lovelock's idea of a self-organising dynamic world, a world now re-fashioned through Wiener's mental space of the World Wide Web. Each of these masters achieved their insights through combining multiple ways of interpreting reality and answering the full range of questions that arose in their minds.

Darwin's ideas on human evolution, Lovelock's on the planet Gaia and Wiener's on the power of cybernetics led eventually to dramatic changes in the human construction of reality. However, they did not do this unchallenged. Each of the three master thinkers was in their own time regarded as a heretic. Darwin's heresy was that humans are subject to evolutionary change driven by environmental pressure, like all other living things. Lovelock's was that the planet was alive, with all its life forms contributing collectively to its self-regulation and self-organisation. Wiener's heresy was to predict that a space created by human minds could provide the next environmental setting for human evolution. Eventually these heresies overcame the opposition to become the emergent realities of the twenty-first century. In all three of the present transformational changes there have been apprentices who carried the new thinking forward and visionaries who went beyond them (Table 1.1). The challenge of bridging this break in the framework of society was encapsulated in a hit song by Bob Dylan, 'The times they are a-changing'.

*Table 1.1* Evolution of the collective mind

| State of the world | Transformational change | Follow on | Where to next? |
|---|---|---|---|
| a physical planet | from a god given world to a fixed physical world: René Descartes 1569–1650 | Newton, Wilson, Dawkins | Popper, Ravetz |
| an evolving world | from a fixed physical world to a dynamic living world: Charles Darwin 1809–82 | Gould, Watson, McClintock | Teilhard de Chardin |
| a self-organising world | from a dynamic living world to a self-organising world: James Lovelock 1919– | Margulis, Odum, Roszak | Gregory Bateson |
| a networked world | from a self-organising world to a world shaped by the human mind: Norbert Wiener 1894–1964 | McLuhan, Page and Brin, Zuckerberg | Christopher Alexander |
| a synergistic world | from the idea of a dominating human mind to a synergy among the non-living and living systems, and the human mind | The collective mind | A collective society |

The tale of the sorcerer's apprentice[30] helps us to realise the nature of the challenge posed by moving from the Enlightenment to the collective thinking era. Told in many versions since it was first written by Wolfgang Goethe in 1797, the story goes like this. A master sorcerer has learnt to prepare magic potions that lead to transformational change. He can turn lead into gold, a weak human into a strong one and a hovel into a castle. His foolish apprentice steals the magic mixture and tries to apply it. In inexpert hands the transformation becomes uncontrolled and then uncontrollable. The wise master or mistress struggles to halt the wild chain reaction. They finally succeed. The superior mind is again in control and the over-ambitious apprentice is punished to make sure he never does it again. All is well.

## Next

This old story has a new twist. In the twenty-first century all is not well. The master sorcerers of the technological era have lost control of their own inventions. The capacity to release energy that had been stored for millennia, coupled with their own inventiveness has brought ways for humans to escape epidemic diseases, build great cities and live anywhere on the planet. Yet the same magical recipes have led to urban violence, disruption of the Earth's atmosphere, a flood of disinformation, and a willingness to wage genocidal wars.[31] In a reversal of the original story, it is the past master sorcerers' technical inventions that are running wild. Those technological skills are tipping the world into dangerous climate change, global food insecurity and cities too dangerous to live in. It is up to the apprentices, the following generation, to find a fresh source of inspiration, rather than simply follow in their masters' footsteps.

The apprentices, who include everyone who grew up in the previous era as well as everyone in this one, are faced with developing ideas that help to interpret the times as well as the task of controlling their previous masters' inventions. In this book we embark on a treasure hunt for those who were especially influential in making these changes. The treasure consists of three fresh master sorcerers, their apprentices and the visionaries who are looking beyond the present (Table 1.1). After exploring the lives of the three wise sorcerers responsible for the transformational changes that have moved the twenty-first century from the fading Enlightenment to the collective mind (Darwin, Lovelock and Wiener), come those who built on their work. Next come the visionaries who had the ability and the courage to forecast where those changes might lead. The result is a pattern of ideas rather than a timescale or a single piece of history.

Like all treasure hunts, the search follows an erratic path. Sometimes there is a direct link between ideas. In other cases, the thinker who takes an idea further has never even heard of, or in one case, had rejected the thinker they were following. In addition to those who have built the ideas of the world as it is now, Pierre Teilhard de Chardin,[32] Gregory Bateson[33] and Christopher Alexander,[34] are visionaries who offer changes of mind that could help to work with, rather than against, transformational change. Table 1.1 and the following outline sketch the key results of the treasure hunt. The contributions of the lead players are described in more detail in the chapters that follow.

In the mid-1800s Charles Darwin and Alfred Wallace discovered (separately) that the world is in a state of continual evolutionary change and that this includes the human mind. Contrary to conventional thinking, Darwin focused as much on collaboration as on competition as the guiding principle of evolutionary change. Following Darwin's ideas, Margulis[35] and Gould[36] described how collaborative systems add rapid evolutionary change to the slow pace of genetic mutation. In the 1930s, the mammalian archaeologist Teilhard de Chardin predicted that the next state of human evolution[37] would be the emergence of a collective mind, a state of mind in which all humans could share their ideas and achieve a collective wisdom. This was over half a century before a vehicle to carry that mind, the web of personal computers first imagined by Norbert Wiener, was even envisaged, let alone possible.

In his 1900s study of the planet's chemistry, industrial chemist James Lovelock established that Darwin's continually changing planet is made up of a complex web of self-organising systems. In calling the system Gaia after the Greek goddess of the Earth, Lovelock connected the physical planet with the human social, ethical and aesthetic systems that determine the future of planet Earth. Philosopher-scientist Jerome Ravetz confirmed this new direction for science by developing a Post-Normal Science.[38] Polymath Gregory Bateson brought parts and wholes together and linked social, ethical and physical systems, mind and nature, in a double-loop feedback system.[39] He described this feedback system as the pattern that connects.

Mathematician and child prodigy Norbert Wiener used advanced mathematics to identify the patterns that connect to predict the World Wide Web as early as 1940.[40] He was the first to foresee the immense evolutionary potential of electronic signals as extensions of the human mind. Wiener also foresaw the ethical dilemmas that may arise when minds evolve under the influence of other minds in addition to the biophysical selection pressures. At the same time Christopher Alexander developed a pattern language[41] that laid the foundation for the software designs that blossomed into the social media of Facebook[42] and Twitter.[43]

The three wise masters who had correctly predicted a world influenced by human thought were each trained as scientists, understandably since that was the dominant way of thinking of their time. They were each equally at home discussing the social and ethical consequences of their work, appreciating the aesthetics of their discoveries and in sympathetic collaboration with like-minded thinkers. Each had asked all the full set of questions whose answers led to a transformational change. They each had brought all the answers together in a leap forward which eventually influenced all human thought. The rest of this book relates to the practical implications of their collective thinking. The treasure hunt continues in the rest of the book, looking for evidence of social change influenced by their thinking.

## Future: the collective mind

The inheritance of the master sorcerers continues. Transformational movements like Transition Towns[44] and Healthy Cities[45] at the local scale and institutions such as the United Nations and the World Social Forum[46] at the global scale are seeking a world inspired by the rich contributions stemming from the differences that create a society. Each movement implicitly answers the full suite of seven questions in pursuing their own area of interest. Each group is committed to transformational change being open-ended, interconnected and collaborative, valuing uncertainty and diversity. This has proved difficult to achieve in a world still giving priority to the technological and the specialised and objective ways of thinking.

On the positive side, the key structures that go to make up a collective society are emerging in practice. They include an inclusive language, a Transformation Science, a direct democracy, reciprocal resource management, transformative learning and a collective identity. Each of these has a chapter to itself in Part II. Once these structures are established, a society will be a different place from its previous state as a site of conflict and competition. Inclusive language will include the adoption of 'and' instead of 'but', and 'both' instead of 'or'. Alexander's pattern language already offers a vehicle all can share. Transformation Science,[47] heralded by Post-Normal Science, will find evidence to answer each of the diverse questions.

Ailing democracy has a flood of defenders looking to reinstate deep democracy as the prevailing governance system. With content readily supplied by efficient search engines, educational initiatives based on teacher–learner dialogue generate fresh and original ideas. There have already been Nobel Prizes awarded for reciprocal resource management practices with micro loans and common pool resources that include forests, fisheries, cities and irrigation systems. Last, but certainly not least, is the change in identity that comes from imagining oneself as a competitive, neutral, independent individual to a person who is part of a collective identity, similar to the African *Ubuntu* 'I am I because of you; you are you because of me'.

Each of the new wise masters we have discovered, together with those that followed them, absorbed the full range of ways of experiencing the world into their thinking. Their courage and commitment carried them past self-doubt and negativity, and their times allowed them to experience the planet as a whole. Darwin was able to circumnavigate the world, Lovelock saw the first picture of Earth from space, and Wiener foresaw the technical capacity of cyberspace that set human minds free to work with each other. These thinkers lived in a world united by unprecedented global flows of people, information, resources and ideas – fertile ground for collective thinking and strong collaboration. They understood the relationship between the internal human mind and the external, world-accepted mind as an integral part of a global self-organising system. Their work laid the foundations for a transformational change from the Enlightenment to an era in which everyone can think with a collective mind.

The transformative thinkers were able to simultaneously draw knowledge from, and transcend the disconnected stores of knowledge that existed in their time. Combining multiple sources of evidence was common to the thinking of all three of the original thinkers of the new era,[48] of those followers who took their ideas further and of the visionaries who saw further again (Table 1.1). The task of the seven questions that make up collective thinking is to first establish the identity of the thinker: who am I? Then to bring the answers to the other five questions together, in order to answer a reflective question: what is the collective understanding of this? This power of collective reflection operates both within an individual and among a group. The first and last questions look inward for answers and look outward to the issue of concern.

The new generation of apprentices requires us all to be wise sorcerers in our own right. A capacity for collective learning along multiple ways of knowing is predicted to be the next step in the evolution of the human mind. Throughout the treasure hunt for collective minds that makes up this book, the collective mind has been treated as embracing the whole in several different ways. There is the whole that is the unity of the living, non-living and human mind that together make up the planet Earth.[49] Then there is the holistic thinking that is created when each individual reflects on their multiple ways of knowing the world. The social world in turn provides the context in which those individual reflections come together to form the spirit of a community.

The era of the collective mind is already underway in twenty-first century society. As the leading edge of thought, it is re-examining long-standing biological and social features of humanity and re-thinking the question of what it means to be human. There can be a new freedom and dignity in the future of the collective mind. New ways of experiencing, knowing, being and becoming that can put humanity in reach of new kinds of worlds through a collective and ethically-guided influence on inevitable transformational change.

## Notes

1  During the last two million years of life on Earth there have been five mass extinctions when 75 per cent of all species have died out. Today many scientists believe that there is another mass extinction occurring, this time human induced, which will dramatically change the Earth as we have come to know it.
2  Methuen, A. (1921) *An Anthology of Modern Verse*, London: Methuen and Company.
3  The Anthropocene refers to what many natural scientists call the human-generated age. It has not as yet been formally accepted into the Geological Time Scale at present. The Anthroposphere is the state of the Earth's resources generated during the Anthropocene.
4  Brown, V. A. (2008) *Leonardo's Vision: A Guide for Collective Thinking and Action*, Rotterdam: Sense.
5  Descartes, R. (1637/1946) *A discourse on the method of rightly conducting one's reason*, (tr. J. Veitch) London: Everyman's Library 570.
6  Doidge, N. (2007) *The Brain That Changes Itself: Stories of Personal Triumph from the Frontiers of Brain Science*, Melbourne: Scribe.
7  Lackoff, G. and Johnson, M. (1999) *Philosophy in the Flesh: The Embodied Mind and Its Challenge to Western Thought*, New York: Basic Books.
8  Howard Gardner's theory of multiple intelligences and its practice are covered in Gardner, H. (1983) *Frames of Mind: The Theory of Multiple intelligences*, New York: Basic Books and Gardner, H. (1993) *Multiple Intelligences: The Theory and Practice*, New York: Basic Books.
9  Lash, J. P. (1980) *Helen and Teacher: The Story of Helen Keller and Anne Sullivan Macy*, New York: Delacorte Press.
10  Newton's third law of motion.
11  Einstein, A. and Infeld, L. (1966) *The Evolution of Physics: From Early Concepts to Relativity and Quanta*, New York: Touchstone. See also, Hawking, S. W. (1988) *A Brief History of Time: From the Big Bang to Black Holes*, New York: Bantam Books.

12 Lovelock, J. (1979) *Gaia: A New Look at Life on Earth,* Oxford: Oxford University Press. Lovelock, J. (2009) *The Vanishing Face of Gaia: A Final Warning,* New York: Allen Lane.

13 Bateson, G. (1972) *Steps to an Ecology of Mind,* St Albans, UK: Paladin. Bateson, G. (1979) *Mind and Nature: A Necessary Unity,* London: Wildwood House. Bateson coined the phrase 'the pattern that connects', which refers to the way mind and nature form a unity.

14 Chapter 3.

15 Marden, O. S. (1908/2007) *He Can Who Thinks He Can,* Stilwell, Kansas, US: Digireads.com Book.

16 The sand-pile game and other experiments using rice grains and computer simulations are described in Buchanan, M. (2000) *Ubiquity,* New York: Crown.

17 O'Riorden, T. (1971) *Perspectives on Resource Management,* London: Pion.

18 Bateson, G. (1979) *Mind and Nature: A Necessary Unity,* London: Wildwood House. Capra, F. (1982) *The Turning Point: Science, Society and the Rising Culture,* New York: Simon & Schuster. Lewin, R. (1993) *Complexity: Life at the Edge of Chaos,* London: Orion Books. Goodwin, B. (1994) *How the Leopard Changed Its Spots: The Evolution of Complexity,* New York: Scribner's Sons.

19 Wiener, N. (1950) *The Human Use of Human Beings: Cybernetics and Society,* Massachusetts, US: Riverside Press (Houghton Mifflin).

20 Hamilton, C. (2013) *Earth Masters: Playing God with the Climate,* Sydney: Allen & Unwin.

21 The Paralympics is an international sporting event held every four years involving athletes with a wide range of physical and intellectual disabilities in the same sporting events as the standard Olympics.

22 See http://history1900s.about.com/od/1970s/p/jonestown.htm [accessed 3.6.13].

23 Monk, W. H. (1861) *Hymns Ancient and Modern,* London: Novello and Company.

24 Worboys, M. (2000) *Spreading Germs: Disease Theories and Medical Practice in Britain, 1865–1900,* Cambridge, UK: Cambridge University Press.

25 Mendel, Gregor Johann (1822–84) Austrian botanist who was ordained as a priest in 1847, he studied science at Vienna University (1851–53) and became an abbot in 1868. His research on the inheritance characteristics of plants was carried out from 1856–63. See http://www.biography.com/people/gregor-mendel-39282 [accessed 3.8.13].

26 Kuhn, T. (1962) *The Structure of Scientific Revolutions,* University of Chicago, US: Chicago Press.

27 Darwin C. (1859) *On the origin of species by means of natural selection or the preservation of favoured races in the struggle for life,* UK: John Murray. Darwin, C. (1871) *The descent of man,* UK: John Murray.

28 Lovelock, J. *Gaia: A New Look at Life on Earth,* Lovelock, J. (2000) *Homage to Gaia: The Life of an Independent Scientist,* New York: Oxford University Press.

29 Wiener, N. (1948) *Cybernetics: Or Control and Communication in the Animal and the Machine,* Massachusetts, US: MIT Press. Wiener, N. (1950) *The Human Use of Human Beings: Cybernetics and Society,* Massachusetts, US: Riverside Press (Houghton Mifflin).

30 The Sorcerer's Apprentice (*Der Zauberlehrling*) is a poem by Johann Wolfgang von Goethe (1749–1832).

31 Annual books published from 1984 on the State of the World by The Worldwatch Institute in Washington, DC, US document the effects of humanity on the planet. http://www.worldwatch.org/ [accessed 3.8.13].

32 See *The Phenomenon of Man* by Pierre Teilhard de Chardin (1955/1975) New York: Harper & Row in which Teilhard describes the evolution of the noosphere as a new sphere of human consciousness that is worldwide and is discussed in Chapter 2.

33 Bateson, G. (1972) *Steps to an Ecology of Mind,* St Albans, UK: Paladin. Bateson, G. (1979) *Mind and Nature: A Necessary Unity,* London: Wildwood House.See Chapter 3.

34 Alexander, C., Ishikawa, S., Silverstein, M., Jacobson, M., Fiksdahl-King, I. and Angel, S. (1977). *A Pattern Language: Towns, buildings and constructions,* New York: Oxford University Press. Pattern language is for anyone wishing to design and build at any scale, and also has been influential in software engineering. See Chapter 4.

35 Margulis, L. (1998) *The Symbiotic Planet: A New Look at Evolution,* New York: Basic Books.

36 Gould, S. J. (2002) *The Structure of Evolutionary Theory,* Cambridge: Belknap Press. Eldredge, N. and Gould, S. J. (1972) 'Punctuated equilibria: an alternative to phyletic gradualism' in Schopf, T. J. M. (ed.) *Models in Paleobiology,* San Francisco: Freeman, Cooper and Company, pp. 82–115. Gould, S. J. (1977) *Ever Since Darwin: Reflections in Natural History,* New York: Norton was the first book of Gould's popular essays on science.

37 Teilhard de Chardin, P. (1955/1975) *The Phenomenon of Man,* (tr. B. Wall) New York: Harper and Row. Teilhard de Chardin, P. (1966) *Man's Place in Nature,* (tr. R. Hague) St James's Place, London: Collins.

38 Ravetz, J. R. (1999) 'What is Post-Normal Science?' *Futures,* **31** (7): 647–53. See also Ravetz, J. R. (2005) *A No-Nonsense Guide to Science,* Oxford: New International.

39 Bateson, G. (1972) *Steps to an Ecology of Mind,* St Albans, UK: Paladin.

40 The World Wide Web was invented in 1989 by Tim Berners-Lee.

41 Alexander, C., Ishikawa, S., Silverstein, M., Jacobson, M., Fiksdahl-King I. and Angel, S. (1977) *A Pattern Language: Towns, buildings and constructions,* New York: Oxford University Press.

42 Facebook, the social networking service founded in 2004 by Mark Zuckerberg and fellow Harvard University students now has over one billion active users worldwide. http://en.wikipedia.org/wiki/Facebook [accessed 3.1.13].

43 Twitter, the online social networking platform and micro-blogging service enables its registered users to send up to 140 characters (tweets) at a time. Since it was set up in 2006 by Jack Dorsey and collaborators, over 500 million registered users generate some 340 million tweets and 1.6 billion search inquiries a day. http://en.wikipedia.org/wiki/Twitter [accessed 3.8.13].

44 Transition Towns is an international grass roots network of people working for positive social change. *The Transition Handbook: From oil dependence to local resilience* (2008) and *The Transition Companion: Making your community more resilient in uncertain times* (2012) provide the guidelines for social change. Both were written by Rob Hopkins, UK: Green Books.

45 Healthy Cities is a World Health Organisation (WHO) initiative to engage local governments in the development of better health through collaborative planning and capacity building in local communities. *Governance for health in the 21st century* by Ilona Kickbusch and David Gleicher is available through WHO's regional office in Europe.

46 The World Social Forum comprising civil society organisations is endeavouring to counter hegemonic globalisation while working towards a just democratic world of greater solidarity.

47 Chapter 8.

48 Darwin combined the fieldwork of a naturalist with the empirical observations of a scientist, called on experts from many fields and occupations and crossed the barriers of religious, scientific and political thought. Lovelock opened up the planet's place in the universe to both scientific and spiritual examination. In doing so, he challenged the internal hierarchies of the scientific and religious communities of his time. Wiener was a polymath, contributing major discoveries to the fields of mathematics, philosophy, psychology and statistics in his leap into an as yet unknown future in cyberspace.

49 Here the unconscious, conscious and human mind are both the parts of the collective mind and wholes in their own right.

# 2   The Darwinian mind

## The next step in human evolution

**Synopsis:** Charles Darwin's ideas on evolutionary change were a trigger for the major transformational changes in thinking of our time. Darwin's followers went on to discover the feedback loops and dynamic relationships through which the interconnected living and physical worlds continually reshape each other. Misconceptions have survived to this day that Darwin considered the evolution of species to be driven by competition, hierarchy and chance. To the contrary, Darwin described the planet's living systems and the human mind as having evolved through collective, collaborative relationships within the natural environment. Darwin's followers expanded on collaborative relationships while visionary, Pierre Teilhard de Chardin, proposed collective thinking as the next evolutionary step for humankind.

## Context of the change

Today it is difficult to imagine the outrage that met the release of Charles Darwin's *On the Origin of Species*.[1] The then fixed idea that the non-living and living parts of the planet had not changed since time began was stood on its head. Darwin established that the living world is in a state of constant change as a result of close and continuous interactions between the living and the physical environments. To the educated members of his society it must have seemed that the ground had shifted under their feet. Darwin went on to include human emotions among the changing life forms, shocking his readers even more.[2] The implication was that human evolution is not over; it is an ongoing process for both body and mind, and who knows where it might end?

The adoption of new thinking never follows an even course and evolutionary change was no exception. At the time, it was greeted by three quite different sets of responses: distortion, denial and disciples. The first major distortion of Darwin's work appeared in his own time. Darwin had referred to life forms changing in response to natural selection pressures from the physical environment, which of course included other life forms. The competitive spirit of the technological era was quick to translate that original thinking into a competitive struggle, as the 'survival of the fittest', a phrase not coined by Darwin himself.[3] Instead it is population limits, not innate competition that leads to natural selection. Species compete through inter-species aggression only in times of acute pressure for

*Figure 2.1* Charles Darwin at the age of 31 – portrait by George Richmond, 1840
(Wikimedia Commons)

resources. Even carnivores can share the one territory. In the African savannah the lion, leopard and cheetah all fill the meat-eating niche and avoid competition by dividing their hunting regime. The lion hunts at night in the grassland, the leopard by day from trees, and the cheetah in the savannah among the herds.

Darwin himself consistently emphasised that it was changes in the environment that created the selection pressure that favoured one species over another; not direct inter-species competition. The environment included both non-living and living dimensions. Other species would adapt as part of that environment, not as foreordained competitors. Given that all species are dependent in some way on others for food, living site and protection, the living world is more a system of collaboration than a system of competition. There is no doubt that Darwin himself recognised this, as can be seen in all his writing. The same bias towards competition was transferred to social fields such as economics and politics, leading to the false conclusion that the most socially powerful had an evolutionary advantage. This false conclusion was used to justify ruthless business competition and even civil war. At its extreme, this move led to pressures to remove the disabled and handicapped from the population, and even to the Nazi's program of ethnic extermination.

Like all original thinkers, Darwin's thinking came partly from the spirit of his times. He was not the first to note the difference in life forms being a result of their interaction with their environment. The idea had already been gestating in his grandfather's time.[4] Nor was he alone in describing the idea of evolutionary fitness as the match between life forms and their chance of survival in their environment. Biologist-explorer Alfred Wallace put forward the same argument and spurred Darwin to make his early work public.[5] Darwin in *The Descent of Man*[6] was, however, the first to recognise that, since all life forms are shaped by natural selection, this must include humans. The idea flew in the face of the religious beliefs of the time. He also drew attention to the close relationship between the physical body and the thinking mind. With his observations of facial expressions and body language in humans and in other animals, Darwin established that not only the physical human brain, but also its activity, the human mind, is a product of evolutionary change.

Before Darwin's time, humans were believed to have appeared about 2,000 years ago, and the world was due to end in 6,000 years. Interplanetary space was a mysterious place called heaven where no living human being could go. As in the Anglican hymn, the lord in his castle and the poor man at his gate were accepted as an unchangeable natural order of things. Human cultures were ranked according to their supposed advance towards civilisation, and the level of advance was judged by skin colour. Electric light was possible but rare – otherwise nights were dark and perilous. The hygiene revolution based on the germ theory of disease had not yet taken hold. Unhygienic hospitals were a source of disease rather than places for cure. Changes to all of this that we now take for granted were as disruptive then as social change is now. The current era of transformational change had begun.

By the time *Descent of Man* appeared in 1871 change was already in the air. An acceptance of a universal right to dignity and the basic resources for life was inconsistent with ideas of race, but consistent with Darwin's idea of constant human development. For instance, in Britain the British Education Act was passed in 1876 and the Slavery Abolition Act in 1833. Charles Dickens' story of *Oliver Twist*, who asked for more food from his orphanage, was an early warning signal of this change; the socially disadvantaged were starting to speak for themselves, as in the nineteenth century music hall song:

> They're digging up grandpa's grave to build a sewer.
> They're building it regardless of expense.
> They're disturbing his remains
> To make way for sanitary drains
> For some society dame's new residence.

Unions were on their way. Educators such as Maria Montessori and Rudolph Steiner were arguing for child-centred education,[7] a revolution in itself in an era where there was no concept of personal development, and children were to be seen but not heard. Darwin's message of continual evolutionary change was timely for a Britain that was widening its horizons as a result of Britons returning from India and Africa, and the higher level of education required to meet the needs of an industrial society.

## Peak of the change

The significant change in interpreting how the world works set off a positive chain reaction. Initiatives as diverse as the mapping of the human genome,[8] in vitro fertilisation (IVF)[9] and the productivity of the green revolution[10] that have reshaped the social and physical worlds are a direct result of Darwin's discoveries. In place of a belief in a ready-made planet, he left behind the realisation of how, over time, the pressures of natural selection shape all living things to best fit their environment. Darwin's trajectory continues into the future with the potential for a collective human future as the journey of this book.

The course of a transformational change cannot be predicted from its beginning, however hard people try. At the start of the nineteenth century, Darwin, the bearer of change, was an average performer in formal education, both at school and university, came from a conservative family and was an unlikely revolutionary. A closer look reveals Darwin's background was far from average, and his self-taught knowledge of life in the English countryside was part of his birthright. His family history combined the rural privileges of the so-called English gentry with the inventiveness of the potteries of the industrial era. The descendant of a string of marriages between industrialists and intellectuals, Darwin consistently escaped from unwelcome social pressures to the natural world that he observed in minute detail and made part of his inquiring mind.[11]

As a boy at an unsympathetic school, as a youth studying first medicine and then theology, and as an adult member of a conservative section of society, he maintained his passionate interest in the natural world. After roaming the fields as a boy and joining the round-the-world voyage of the *Beagle* as an adult, he constructed a miniature of the larger natural world for himself on his country estate. The sand walk that he walked every day when he was well enough was a stretch of his country estate at Downe, where he observed even the minutest changes from the day before.

The sand walk, Downe:

It is interesting to contemplate an entangled bank, clothed with many plants of many kinds, with birds singing in the bushes with various insects flitting about, and with worms crawling through the damp earth, and to reflect on these elaborately constructed forms, so different from each other, and dependent on each other in so complex a manner, have all been produced by laws acting around us …[12]

His great escape was, of course, the voyage of the survey sloop *Beagle*, on which he circumnavigated the world, a journey of more than five years. His key companions on that voyage were his sharply honed powers of observation and his reference library, of which the chief influences came from geologist Charles Lyell and traveller-philosopher Alexander von Humboldt. Lyell gave him insights into how the world was radically changed by natural events, and Humboldt the inspiration of the power of a human being to interpret the course of events. In addition, Darwin's imagination and inquiring mind induced him to make sense of his detailed observations of everything he experienced on the voyage. His *Journal of researches into the natural history and geology of the countries visited during the voyage of H.M.S. Beagle round the world* is an exciting adventure story in itself.[13]

It is interesting to wonder how we would understand the world if Darwin had not shipped on the *Beagle*. It was a close call: his father adamantly refused to pay for the journey. In a famous letter[14] that revealed the strength of Darwin's logical mind and determination, he put the case for travel one more time (Box 2.1). His father replied that he could go if he could find one man of good sense that supported the idea. Luckily, in such a diverse family he found the support of an uncle his father admired.

---

### *Box 2.1* **Charles Darwin's letter to his father**

I have given Uncle Jos what I fervently hope is a full list of your objections (to my going on the Beagle):
Disreputable to my character as a clergyman hereafter
A wild scheme
That they must have made the offer to many others before me
So there must be some serious objection to the vessel or expedition
That I should never settle down to a steady life hereafter
That my accommodation would be most uncomfortable
That you should consider it as again changing my profession
That it would be a useless undertaking.

Darwin's first inkling of his ability to deduce an original answer to a complex problem came not from his direct observations and his reference books. It came from a thought experiment.[15] While in South America he heard of the puzzle that, although coral reefs grow slowly upwards every year, they remain at exactly the same distance below the ocean surface. His solution was that the ocean floor must be sinking at exactly the same rate as the coral was growing upwards (the sea level was not yet rising). This was the first recorded instance of Darwin's delight in his capacity to bring together the intricate communication channels linking the biological, physical and mental worlds: to be expanded dramatically by our second transformative thinker, James Lovelock and even further by our third, Norbert Wiener.

Another insight that challenged Darwin's conservative upbringing was that humans themselves were shaped by their social and physical environments. In Tierra del Fuego, three indigenous people living a subsistence existence were taken on board the *Beagle* to be trained and returned as missionaries. This was in 1833. Five years later Darwin subsequently watched one of the men become an English citizen in language, dress and manner. On a return visit after the man had been returned to his birthplace, he saw that the man had reverted to his previous condition. This experience underpinned his later courage in extending his ideas of natural selection for environmental fitness from non-human life forms to humans, a dangerous heresy at that time.

Although Darwin is presented as a solitary giant figure, in practice he depended on three supportive environments: his family, his close friends and colleagues, and his collaborators. His extended family was unusually close and interdependent. His marriage to his cousin strengthened the link between the artistic Wedgewood pottery family and the landowning Darwins. In his own family, Darwin had the unwavering support of at least eight women: his loyal wife, four daughters, four sons and several female cousins. This was not only emotional support and admiration, but technical help as well. The well-to-do women with no formal occupations gave almost all their time to acting as his research assistants, editors and sounding boards.

The second source of support was a small group of fellow scientists who served as Darwin's defenders. Exhausted and ill from the mental and physical effort of producing *On the Origin of Species*, Darwin withdrew from any public part in the controversy that raged after its publication. He deputised the defence of his work to six scientists in particular: biologist John Henslow who had invited him onto the *Beagle*; biologist Thomas Huxley who became his advance publicist, known as 'Darwin's bulldog'; botanist William Hooker, director of Kew Gardens; and anthropologist John Lubbock and his parliamentarian son, a neighbour at Downe.

A famous argument between the Anglican Bishop Wilberforce and biologist Thomas Huxley has come to symbolise the introduction of the theory of evolution to English intellectual society. Regarded as a confrontation between religion and science, the exchange at a charged Oxford debate went like this. Bishop Wilberforce (angrily): 'I would be somewhat concerned if I was introduced to my ancestor as an ape at the zoo'. Huxley's recorded reply represents the tenor of the debate: '(If asked if) I would rather have a miserable ape for a grandfather or a man highly endowed by nature ... who employs those faculties for the mere purpose of introducing ridicule into a grave scientific discussion – I unhesitatingly affirm my preference for the ape.'[16] This reply has come into popular memory as 'I would rather have an ape for an ancestor than Bishop Wilberforce'.

The third group of Darwin's supporters he created for himself. A global network of correspondents became his informal research assistants. Darwin, while retiring in person, was a voluminous letter writer and had correspondents all over the world. Whether the subject was pigeons, orchids, barnacles, carnivorous plants or worms – the diverse themes of his own extremely careful and detailed observations – Darwin bombarded anyone interested in a particular field with requests for further observations that extended his own. Thus he effectively created a worldwide research collective, an early version of today's World Wide Web. Darwin's final piece of 'fieldwork turned experiment' on earthworms[17] was considered by his colleagues as a mere distraction for his old age. Nothing can have been further from the truth. He established that, over time, worm casts had raised the surface of Britain by some 50 mm.

This confirmed that the non-living environment is shaped by living things as well as vice versa. Moreover, Darwin established that worms could in some way think. In building burrows stopped with a curled leaf they selected a leaf of the right size and shape, fitting it to the burrow entrance with great precision.[18] This observation added to his conviction that mind was everywhere present in nature. This fresh understanding of the relationship between the animate and inanimate worlds was a forerunner to the description of a living planet that emerged from James Lovelock's work on Gaia.[19]

Darwin had a strong sense of identity that led him to follow his own path; a heightened sense of loyalty in his lifetime devotion to his estate, family and friends; devotion to the scientific method of making careful observations and detailed experimental records of physical events; social skills in recruiting powerful supporters who bore the brunt of disseminating his ideas; and an aesthetic sensitivity and delight in the natural world. Above all, he held a strong ethical position to the natural world as a world to be valued in its own right. Thus Charles Darwin posed the full set of introspective, physical, social, ethical, aesthetic, sympathetic and reflective questions that represent a collective mind at work.[20]

Darwin's funeral was a moment in time that illustrated the effect of his contribution to the long-settled, just-opening world of which he had been part. The eight pallbearers of his coffin were an unprecedented alliance of privilege. They included scientists, aristocrats, politicians and family, an unheard of collection in that time of fixed social hierarchies. His burial in Westminster Abbey established a new orthodoxy for his work, since he had earlier been vilified in churches across the country for denying God. The congregation represented an emergent Britain, socially and politically, accepting to various degrees the power of the idea of evolutionary change. A dramatic shift from the established order, the funeral was a sign that evolution by natural selection had been adopted by influential circles as a core part of establishment thinking.

## Follow on

Darwin's original thinking gave rise to fresh streams of specialised thought, following the intellectual fashion of the science of the day. This was in spite of his own insights being generated from a broad, systematic way of thought. The sciences of genetics and population ecology are often restricted by the tyranny of numbers.[21] Even ecology, as the study of the relationships of organisms in the living world, can become limited to individuals, populations and communities.[22] Within academic institutions it is only in the twenty-first century that broader approaches have resurfaced in transdisciplinary courses such as human ecology[23] and theme-based courses such as those covering cities and water.[24] James Lovelock continued in the broad thinking vein and pointed out that living organisms affect the non-living environment as much as the reverse; and Norbert Wiener carried the idea of self-organising systems into the open communication environment of cyberspace.[25]

Evolution deniers remain to this day. While no one today disputes that there is continual change, many religious positions still consider God to be responsible for species changing, not inheritance. Trained as a clergyman, Darwin in his early career had difficulty accepting any other reason; his wife never could. In Darwin's own time, a popular book, *The Divine Watchmaker*, by William Paley[26] argued that God created natural systems that then ran by themselves. In a rebuttal of this position by Richard Dawkins a hundred years later in his best-selling *The Blind Watchmaker*, he argues that there can be no such entity as God.[27] A position held by some of Darwin's home team was that the existence of evolutionary progression of species is established by biophysical evidence; the existence of God is established from an ethical argument, and both can stand side by side.

As well as the deniers and distorters, Darwin's apprentices included slavish followers who froze his ideas, and those who carried the ideas further. If a change has indeed been transformational, it will generate fresh physical, social and intellectual trajectories that will continue until it reaches a dead end, or else generate the next transformational change. Before the Darwinian era, the transformational change that was the scientific Enlightenment had developed rules that governed a predictable world subject to fixed physical laws.[28] As the idea of constant change was absorbed into the post-Darwinian mind, new lines of thought emerged.

Towards the end of the 300 years of the Enlightenment, the philosopher and chemist Karl Popper[29] argued that while the physical world exists in its own right, it can be interpreted only through the eye of the observer and in the context of the ideas of the time. Chapter 8 traces the twentieth century minds of the physicists Albert Einstein, Niels Bohr and Werner Heisenberg as they reshaped Newton's fixed version of physical laws. Bohr resolved the impasse between Newton's interpretation of light as a wave and Einstein's conclusion that light is carried by units of energy by arguing for complementarity.[30] If two different explanations of the same events could be established as being valid in their own right, they must be related rather than one being right and the other wrong. This proposition that different forms of observation construct different realities, all of them valid, also applies to the resolution of wicked problems, problems that require changes in the society that generated them.[31]

While Darwin had established the process of the evolution of species, he had not pursued the mechanism by which it occurred. He had, however, recognised that there must be a unit of inheritance that carried the potential for change. If the communications of the time had allowed Abbot Gregor Mendel's work on predictable patterns of inheritance in garden peas[32] to reach Darwin or his co-workers, they would surely have understood the significance. It was not until the 1900s that the units were labelled genes and the science of genetics was born. As an amusing aside, later statistical calculations revealed that Mendel did not bother to continue counting after he had established the pattern of dominant and recessive genes – he simply wrote in the numbers. Once he recognised the overall predictable pattern, he felt his work was done.

Two discoveries in particular were a direct challenge to the early post-Darwin belief that the primary evolutionary mechanism was always slow accidental genetic mutation. In 1951, Barbara McClintock was able to demonstrate how genetic information was either repressed or expressed from one generation of maize plants to the next as a result of changes in the environment. Changes could thus be instigated by the environment within a generation by a process that was neither slow nor accidental. Scepticism of her findings was at first so great she even stopped publishing her data. McClintock's method for discovering the pattern of movement of genes along their DNA[33] molecule (the double helix) was not usually acknowledged by science. She used her imagination to think of herself as a maize gene and mentally followed the erratic paths that she had identified experimentally, asking herself what a gene might do. Her findings were eventually confirmed and 'jumping genes' were accepted as the cause of some of the variation that allowed for natural selection. For this the then 81-year-old McClintock was eventually awarded the Nobel Prize for Physiology in 1983.[34]

Biologist Lynn Margulis' work also introduced other evolutionary pathways into the mix. Her study of symbiosis, mutual reliance among organisms, led her to recognise that their collaboration could give rise to new composite life forms. She argued that the pressures of natural selection led mutually beneficial organisms to become one organism, which then reproduced itself as a whole. This finding supported the idea that an evolutionary change could begin at the level of combined microorganisms long before it would be visible at the level of species. Thus the basic living cell that is the unit that makes up all plants and animals is partly the result of a symbiotic collaborative relationship among bacteria.[35]

It took some time before Margulis's transformative thinking on the extent of collaboration in creating a cell was accepted. As the idea slowly seeped into scientific thinking, it opened up a wide array of possibilities. Aggregations of cells were long known to form colonies and Margulis established that colonies could evolve into new species.[36] This led in turn to a re-thinking of the so-called ladder of life in which every organism was supposed to have built neatly on the one before. Other researchers started re-evaluating the evidence for an orderly evolution and realised that there was more missing evidence than there were actual fossils. Often there is simply no evidence at all of how lines connected. This re-examination leads in turn to the possibility that Neanderthal humans with their larger brain cases may have been more, rather than less intelligent than modern humans, and not simply the victims of superior weapons.[37]

Discovering another avenue for rapid and coordinated evolutionary changes, James Watson and Francis Crick identified the basis of inheritance, the chemical structure of DNA, in 1952. Watson's own account of the discovery reveals the effect of a complex mixture of personalities. Watson's autobiographical account of the discovery in *The Double Helix*[38] documents the drive of ambition, the role of ethics, the delight in the 'aha' of discovery and the beauty of the double helix solution. It revealed the difficult relationships with co-researcher Rosalind Franklin who was initially denied recognition for her key role in the discovery. A close reading of Watson's autobiography reveals that during the process of the discovery of DNA, introspective, empirical, social, aesthetic, ethical, sympathetic and reflective questions emerged, answered by Wilkins and Franklin's empirical work,[39] Crick's strategic management and Watson's creativity. Human relationships were deeply involved. This same battery of questions will regularly resurface in other accounts of transformational change.

Following the discovery of the structure of DNA, Carl Linnaeus's 200-year-old classification of living forms by their reproductive parts was superseded by classification based on their genetic pattern. The next move was the triumph of the mapping of the whole of the message of the human genome. By this means humans and their closest living relation, the chimpanzee, were estimated to have ninety-eight per cent of their genes in common,[40] a finding that would have badly upset Bishop Wilberforce. A further surprise was the similarity of the genetic pattern that governed all living forms. Two multidisciplinary teams, one with public and one with private money took five years rather than the expected fifteen to complete the map.[41] From here developed the fields of genetic counselling, genetically modified organisms and in-vitro fertilisation. This led to the question of using stem cells, the uncommitted basic cells of bone marrow and of the human foetus, to replace damaged tissue, another hotly debated ethical issue. Competition between the two teams also raised issues of the ownership of intellectual property, which became a dominant issue on the Internet.

Free-thinking palaeontologist and popular science writer, Stephen Jay Gould, brought another wave of fresh thinking into the post-Darwinian world.[42] His documentation of the evolutionary timescale led him to join the geneticists in questioning the then dominant model of a slow linear progression from the earliest to the latest forms of a species. Evidence of many unrealised lines of development led to him arguing successfully that there was no such linear progression. There are long evolutionary straight lines such as the modern racehorse and the mouse, and there are ragged lines of punctuated equilibrium[43] in which new species appear apparently out of the blue. For humans, Gould pointed out that social behaviours and ways of thinking have their own well-documented evolutionary trails. Cultural transmission, social learning and the person-to-person transfer of ideas are only a few of the pathways of social evolution, each with their own guiding principles very different from the discrete genetic units and mathematical rules.

One of Gould's important insights was that different metaphors support different explanations of the same phenomena, all of them equally valid. The same evolutionary patterns can be represented in the shape of a ladder, a tree and a bush. Here is Bohr's complementarity in practice.[44] One explanation of how there can be different interpretations of the same reality goes back to the Greek poet Archilocus and forward to a contemporary philosopher of ideas, Isaiah Berlin.[45] Berlin followed Archilocus in describing two dominant modes of thinking: the fox and the hedgehog. The fox runs hither and thither collecting the evidence but not necessarily connecting the pieces. The hedgehog collects the evidence in a search for the shape of the one big thing.[46]

The two types of mind construct different explanations for the same set of phenomena. One mind is interested in the parts, the other in the whole. Einstein's work on relativity brings with it the third idea that the relationship between the two is equally important. Each of these three forms of inquiry will collect different forms of evidence. As Bohrs predicted in his proposition of complementarity, all three will be valid explanations of the same phenomenon. A collective mind, of course, would include them all. Just as for Darwin, the inquirer has the option to use all three types of thinking: the careful, painstaking collection of data; resolving the puzzle of the meaning of it all; and the creative logic that connects the two. However, the long dominance of the scientific Enlightenment has privileged the specialised tradition of the fox. There were some interludes where the hedgehog broke through, notably in the cluster of poets of the Romantic Era, Shelley, Keats and Coleridge. As Berlin observed, there are also striking individual differences in how the three are combined, as for example in the work of the transformative thinkers we are describing here.

## Next

Palaeontologist, priest and visionary Pierre Teilhard de Chardin started out as an apprentice to the ideas of Charles Darwin, fascinated by the shaping of all living things by the constant pressures of natural selection. Born in 1881 on a family estate in the French countryside he, like Darwin, spent his early years in beautiful natural surroundings, making acute observations of the world around him. Like Darwin he came from a privileged intellectual family; his ancestors included the essayist and social reformer, Voltaire. Like Darwin he was fascinated by the time story embedded in the rocks. He became a noted palaeontologist and discovered an early mammalian tooth in an English fossil bed.[47]

As did Darwin, he had the opportunity to pursue his mission in all parts of the world, making significant discoveries on human evolution in caves in China. When his later ideas were hotly contested, he too became the nucleus of a diverse group of strong supporters.[48] Both thinkers were supported by a Huxley of high scientific repute: Darwin by Thomas Huxley (known as Darwin's bulldog) and Teilhard de Chardin a generation later by Thomas's grandson, Julian. Unlike Darwin, whose insights came in later middle life, Teilhard de Chardin's ideas turned his personal world upside down early in life. He recorded his intense concern for the future of humankind as a child, a concern that led him to enter into the strict training of a Jesuit priest at the age of 18.

*Figure 2.2* Pierre Teilhard de Chardin (1881–1955) French priest, theologian, scientist
(© photo by Apic/Getty Images)

In his late middle age, Darwin felt forced to abandon ideas of God and religion as the creators of all living things in the light of his insights into the evolutionary process. Teilhard de Chardin continued to see God as the focus of the human future. At the same time, he stressed that his original interpretations of the human evolutionary path were made from reflection and observation, not theology. This did not save him from the stern disapproval of his church in Rome. Far from Darwin's eminence at the end of his life, Teilhard de Chardin had to live with the knowledge that his superiors had determined that nothing he wrote would be published in his lifetime.

The church's life sentence did not prevent Teilhard de Chardin from continuing his palaeontological searches amid postings to Egypt, China, Africa and Britain. As part of his work as a specialist, he discovered a previously unknown fossil shark, *Tielhardia*. More importantly, in his time in China he was part of a team that worked on a rich fossil site of *Homo erectus pekinensis*. Dating the finds as three-quarters of a million years ago placed modern humans in a sequence from the two-million-year-old African finds to today. This explicitly contradicted the church teachings that humans were created at one moment about 5,000 years ago. This did not seem to bother Teilhard de Chardin, but it led to him being forbidden to teach. Nevertheless a committed following has persisted to this day. His major work *The Phenomenon of Man*,[49] duly published in the year of his death, 1955, is still in print.

During the 1914 war, Teilhard de Chardin found his peaceful role as stretcher-bearer among the fallen a shattering experience. Soon after, he read Henri Bergson's Nobel Prize-winning *Creative Evolution*[50] and, as he wrote, this gave him a radical vision of continuing human evolution. Sometimes described as anti-Darwinian, neither Teilhard de Chardin nor Bergson regarded their work as other than building on Darwin's propositions. Teilhard de Chardin connected the very sound of the word evolution, as he said:

> with the extraordinary density and intensity with which the English landscape then appeared to me – especially at sunset – when the Sussex woods seemed to be laden with all the fossil life that I was exploring, from one quarry to another, in the soil of the Weald.[51]

For both the French philosopher Bergson and palaeontologist Teilhard de Chardin, evolution through natural selection was a continuing open-ended process with a spiritual element that Bergson called 'The tide of life'.

Points where Bergson and Teilhard de Chardin differed from Darwin were: one, accepting a much greater speed of genetic change in the evolutionary process; two, questioning Darwin's separation of the non-living and living worlds; and three, considering a role for the spiritual and the emotional in the interpretation of the evidence. For the first, the post-Darwin discoveries by Margulis, McClintock and Watson of symbiosis, 'jumping genes' and altered DNA pairs supported this greater speed of evolutionary change. For the second, Darwin was working in the days of the Enlightenment's strict separation of objective and subjective, although he did consider the influence of human actions on the material world. On the third point Darwin never seems to have resolved his struggle with the religious biases of his time, and of his wife. Bergson, Teilhard de Chardin and many others considered that a spiritual element influenced human evolution through the human capacity for reflection and learning.

Pierre Teilhard de Chardin broke new ground in his conclusion that biological and social evolution generated a third consideration with the arrival of the human capacity for reflection on their own thinking. Teilhard de Chardin's proposition was that all human beings have a purpose and an ideal. They have the ability to reflect on and change that purpose and that ideal as a result of their reflections. Therefore the process driving changes in human behaviour and human physiology is very different from any other species. The human capacity for transformational change includes the interactions among the physical changes driving biological selection on the one hand, and the thinking processes driving social change on the other. Teilhard de Chardin called the sphere where the different ways of thinking came together the *noosphere,* the way in which they interacted *collective thinking* and he postulated a synthesis, *point Omega*, where the collective minds could think as one.[52] Being a Jesuit priest, Teilhard de Chardin believed that at point Omega the thinking becomes one with God, a belief not unlike the Buddhist enlightenment and most unlike the scientific Enlightenment.

One example of collective social evolution is the long pursuit of democracy in the Western nations, spreading to the Eastern worlds. The underlying capacities to collaborate as a social animal and to differentiate self from others are biologically determined, although expressed in almost infinite ways through language and thought. The ability to direct collaboration towards democratic principles and to accept responsibility for others is socially determined. Teilhard de Chardin argued that a new direction for the human mind is already emerging in practice, arising at the interface between biological evolution and social change. This emergence involves minds communicating directly with minds through shared reflection; this is what he called collective thinking. There are many similarities between Teilhard de Chardin's noosphere and Wiener's cybersphere, even though it is almost certain that neither knew the other existed.

The World Wide Web and the Internet in cyberspace are in a zone not even imagined when Teilhard de Chardin was writing. There was no such thing as a personal computer and early computers that filled a large room acted merely as giant calculators. Teilhard de Chardin was forbidden to publish at the time Wiener was working on information feedback loops. The situation with the parallel ideas developed by Teilhard de Chardin and Norbert Wiener can be compared to that between Darwin and Mendel. Darwin took on faith that there was a practical method for transmitting the pattern of change he had discovered. Mendel was concerned with discovering the practical mechanism for the changes he literally took on faith. Each presumed the evidence held by the other. The two sets of ideas eventually came together in the explosion of knowledge led by the double helix and genetic mapping.

The focus of the collective mind as projected by Teilhard de Chardin and demonstrated by Darwin and his supportive circles is not group think. It is a synergy developed from independent diverse human beings sharing their different interpretations on a shared issue. An example of a synergy is the medical success in halting the AIDS virus. A range of drugs reduced the symptoms slightly but given individually they did not prolong life. A cocktail of the same drugs given together extended the AIDS sufferer's life almost to the average life term. Another example from a different field was the post-Second World War Marshall plan.[53] This called for the combatant countries from all sides to collaborate on a recovery plan for the defeated; a plan designed to welcome them back to the company of nations. The plan led eventually to a thriving Europe and worldwide trade, a strong contrast to the divisive post-First World War punitive treaties that perpetuated the divide between winner and loser.

## The future

Teilhard de Chardin's vision of a collective mind is that it works through a three-dimensional synergy. There is synergy among the understandings held within the individual, synergy among the individual interests in the common issue, and synergy generated between the parts and the whole of the issue itself. Again this matches Bohr's ideas on complementarity. William Blake captured the image of the whole in the parts and the parts in the whole in his famous verse.[54]

> To see a world in a grain of sand
> And a heaven in a wild flower,
> Hold infinity in the palm of your hand,
> And eternity in an hour.
> *William Blake 1803*

One of the linking ideas that turns a synthesis into a synergy with its own driving force is Teilhard de Chardin's idea of complementary energies. Important in the process of natural selection is Newton's physical energy flow through a system. In the process of social evolution, energy emerges from the human sense of inquiry and discovery, and from commitment to the task. Interestingly, contrary to currently accepted wisdom, Teilhard de Chardin proposed that the more people on Earth the better, since that would increase the critical mass of mind. His emphasis was on the convergence rather than divergence of ideas, shared stories of change rather than measures of stability, and the value of diversity in collaboration rather than its reduction.

Teilhard de Chardin's prediction was that an increase in the number of human minds would open up the potential for convergence within the noosphere, permit a higher level of critical mass in human communication and generate a more intense and complex mental activity. Another of our wise masters, James Lovelock, whose story is in Chapter 3, would heartily disagree, predicting the consumption patterns of the human population would break down the self-regenerating systems of Gaia. On the other hand, Wiener and his successors described in Chapter 4 have been justified in their forecast that the ever-increasing use of digital feedback systems of social media would provide technically unlimited new mechanisms for social evolution.

The next two chapters follow the steps of two further dimensions of this era's transformational change, a world shaped by self-organising systems and by cyberspace. The story of the context, the lead-up to the peak and the follow-on to transformational change, is told through the lives and times of the leading players. This is once again not a time sequence; it is the treasure hunt we predicted in Chapter 1. Human learning is cumulative, but not always directly connected in time or in person. In the next chapter we return to the waning of the reductionist position of the scientific Enlightenment and the rise in the willingness to explore interconnections among diversity, with James Lovelock as the wise master. His apprentices take his fresh thinking into human ecology and the complex dynamics of systems theory. Teilhard de Chardin signalled the next transformational change as collective thinking in Chapter 2. In Chapter 3 we will look at how visionary Gregory Bateson suggests bringing together the human and the more-than-human world of all living things on the one hand, and the human conscious and more-than-conscious mind on the other: Bohr's complementarity in practice.

## Notes

1 Darwin, C. (1859) *On the origin of species by means of natural selection, or the preservation of favoured races in the struggle for life*, UK: John Murray.
2 Darwin, C. (1872) *The expression of the emotions in man and animals*, UK: John Murray.
3 The advocate of Social Darwinism, Herbert Spencer, coined the phrase 'survival of the fittest'.
4 Charles Darwin's grandfather, Erasmus, was not only a respected eighteenth century physician, but also poet, naturalist and philosopher who stimulated discussions on evolution, publishing his ideas in the two volume work *Zoonomia; or the Laws of Organic Life* (1794–96).
5 Darwin, C. and Wallace, A. R. (1858) 'On the Tendency of Species to Form Varieties; and On the Perpetuation of Varieties and Species by Natural Means of Selection'. *Proc. Linn Soc. Zool.*, **3** (9), 45–62.
6 *The Descent of Man*, published in 1871 comprises three parts: 'The Descent or Origin of Man', 'Sexual Selection and Sexual Selection in Relation to Man' and 'Conclusion'. Darwin followed up on his statement in *On the Origin of Species*: 'light will be thrown on the origin of man and his history'.
7 Chapter 11.
8 The Human Genome Project (HGP) is an international research project to determine the sequence of chemical base pairs that make up human DNA, and of identifying and mapping the approximately 20,000–25,000 genes of the human genome.
9 For definition see http://medical-dictionary.thefreedictionary.com/in+vitro+fertilization [accessed 4.8.13].
10 The green revolution refers to the post-war research, development and technology transfers to increase agricultural yields and alleviate hunger. See http://www.merriam-webster.com/dictionary/green%20revolution [accessed 4.8.13]. As with any wicked problem there were unintended consequences. Shiva, V. (1991) *The Violence of the Green Revolution: Third World Agriculture, Ecology and Politics,* London: Zed Books.
11 The zoologist and historian of science, Janet Browne, has written a comprehensive two volume biography: *Charles Darwin: Voyaging* (1995) Princeton, New Jersey, US: Princeton University Press, and *Charles Darwin: The Power of Place* (2002) London: Pimlico.

12  Charles Darwin, Collected letters 6:178.

13  Charles Darwin's journal was published in London in 1839. Its full title is *Journal of Researches into the Natural History and Geology of the Countries Visited during the Voyage of H.M.S. Beagle round the World, under the Command of Capt. Fitzroy, RN.*

14  See Browne, J. (1995) *Charles Darwin: Voyaging*, Princeton, New Jersey, US: Princeton University Press, pp. 154–55.

15  Ghiselin, M. T. (1972) *The Triumph of the Darwinian Method*, Berkeley and Los Angeles, US: University of California Press, p. 23.

16  Browne, J. (2002) *Charles Darwin: The Power of Place*, London: Pimlico, p. 122.

17  Darwin, C. (1881) *The Formation of Vegetable Mould, through the Actions of Worms, with Observations on Their Habits.* UK: John Murray. It was the most popular of all Darwin's 25 books, exciting many letters from the public.

18  Ibid.

19  Chapter 3.

20  Chapters 5 and 6.

21  Andrewartha, H. G. and Birch, L. C. (1954) *The Distribution and Abundance of Animals,* Chicago, US: University of Chicago Press.

22  Begon, M., Harper, J. L. and Townsend, C. R. (1986/1996) *Ecology: Individuals, Populations and Communities*, 3rd edn, London: Blackwell Science.

23  Human ecology grew from an early integration of biological and social sciences in the early twentieth century to a form of transdisciplinary inquiry and a university teaching program that spread from a narrow base in a few universities at the beginning of the 1970s to worldwide programs by 2009. Dyball, R. (2010) 'Human ecology and open transdisciplinary inquiry' in *Tackling Wicked Problems: Through the Transdisciplinary Imagination* (2010) Brown, V. A., Harris, J. A. and Russell, J. Y. (eds), London: Earthscan.

24  At Schumacher College (founded in 1990) there is an MSc in Holistic Science, an MSc in Sustainable Horticulture and Food Production and an MA in Economics for Transition. http://www.schumachercollege.org.uk/courses/short-courses [accessed 5.8.13].

25  Chapter 4.

26  William Paley's 1802 book uses the watchmaker analogy as support for the existence of a divine creator. The complex mechanisms of a watch are the work of an intelligent designer and, similarly, complex natural systems are the products of a designer.

27  Dawkins, R. (1986) *The Blind Watchmaker*, UK: Longman.

28  See http://en.wikipedia.org/wiki/Age_of_Enlightenment [accessed 4.8.13].

29  Popper, K. (1963) *Conjectures and Refutations: The Growth of Scientific Knowledge,* London: Harper and Row; Popper, K. 1972. *Objective Knowledge: An Evolutionary Approach,* Oxford, UK: Oxford University Press.

30  Bohr, N. (1955) *The Unity of Knowledge,* New York: Doubleday. Plotnitsky, A. (2013) *Niels Bohr and Complementarity: An Introduction,* New York: Springer, Springer Briefs in Physics.

31  Brown, V. A., Harris, J. A. and Russell, J. Y. (eds), (2010) *Tackling Wicked Problems: Through the Transdisciplinary Imagination*, London: Earthscan.

32  Chapter 1.

33  deoxyribonucleic acid.

34  *A Feeling for the Organism: The Life and Work of Barbara McClintock* (1983) by Evelyn Fox Keller, New York: Freeman. This popular biography was published a few months before the Nobel Prize for Medicine was awarded to McClintock.

35  Margulis, L. (1998) *The Symbiotic Planet: A New Look at Evolution,* New York: Basic Books.

36  Ibid.

37  Stringer, C. and Andrews, P. (2005) *The Complete World of Human Evolution*, London: Thames & Hudson.

38  James Watson's book *The Double Helix: A Personal Account of the Discovery of the Structure of DNA* was first published in 1968. There are numerous editions now available.

39 Maurice Wilkins, a physicist who worked on the Manhattan Project and Rosalind Franklin, an expert in X-ray diffraction did the empirical research that produced the key crystallography photographs that Watson and Crick used to determine the structure of DNA. The exciting story of the search for the molecule of life is told in Gribbin, J. (1985) *In Search of The Double Helix: Quantum Physics and Life*, New York: McGraw-Hill.

40 Diamond, J. (1991) *The Third Chimpanzee: The Evolution and Future of the Human Animal*, London: Hutchinson Radius.

41 The 2010 book by McElheny, V. K. *Drawing the Map of Life: Inside the Human Genome Project,* New York: Basic Books, documents the history and motivations for the Human Genome Project drawing on interviews with key researchers.

42 Gould, S. J. (2002) *The Structure of Evolutionary Theory,* Cambridge, US: Belknap Press.

43 Eldredge, N. and Gould, S. J. (1972) 'Punctuated equilibria: an alternative to phyletic gradualism'. In Schopf, T. J. M. (ed.) *Models in Paleobiology,* San Francisco, US: Freeman, Cooper and Co., pp. 82–115.

44 Bohr, N. (1955) *The Unity of Knowledge.* New York: Doubleday.

45 Sir Isaiah Berlin (1909–97) British philosopher and historian of ideas.

46 Berlin, I. (1998) *The Proper Study of Mankind: An Anthology of Essays*, London: Pimlico.

47 Speaight, R. (1967) *Teilhard de Chardin: A Biography*, London: Collins.

48 Teilhard de Chardin, Henri Bergson and Edouard Le Roy, the eminent professor at the College de France, became close friends and had many long conversations together on the nature of evolution. Ibid, p. 117.

49 Teilhard de Chardin (1955/1975) *The Phenomenon of Man* (tr. B. Wall), New York: Harper and Row.

50 Bergsen, H. (1907/2007) *The Creative Mind: An Introduction to Metaphysics* (tr. M. L. Andison), New York: Dover.

51 Speaight, R. (1967) *Teilhard de Chardin: A Biography*, London: Collins, p. 45.

52 Teilhard de Chardin (1966) *Man's Place in Nature*, St James Place, London: Collins.

53 See https://en.wikipedia.org/wiki/Marshall_Plan [accessed 4.8.13].

54 The first four lines of *Auguries of Innocence* in Blake, W. (1803/2004) *The Pickering Manuscript*, Whitefish, Montana, US: Kessinger Publishing. The poem is a long series of paradoxes.

# 3 The Gaian mind

## People and planet as a self-organising system

**Synopsis:** the first photograph of Earth from space revealed a living planet. The Darwinian idea of Earth was of a slowly evolving planet that shaped living things. Lovelock and his followers extended this to Earth as a rapidly changing self-organising system influenced by human ideas. Naming this system Gaia after the Greek goddess of the Earth helped unleash the counter-culture of the 1970s. The license it gave for social experimentation and technical innovation is still influencing the world more than 30 years later. Polymath Gregory Bateson proposed a three-dimensional world made up of the non-living and living systems and the human mind, a human mind that constructs a life-sustaining world through patterns that connect.

## Context of the change

By the time of Charles Darwin's death in 1882 it was generally accepted that, from the long neck of the giraffe to the colour of human skin, the physical form of all living organisms evolved in response to changes in their environment. Amazing as this seemed at the time, it was still only half the story. The other half sprang into the public mind with the first photograph of Earth taken from space in 1968.[1] As well as Earth shaping living things, living things also shaped Earth. The master sorcerer who understood the significance of this was an industrial chemist, James Lovelock (Figure 3.1). It was not new for Lovelock to break the bounds of the traditional practice of science. He wrote of starting out at age six with the ambition to become an independent, problem-solving scientist.[2] And that is exactly how he lived, in spite of the apparent impossibility of working outside the tight organisational base of how science was then practised. Lovelock managed to work as an independent scientist, self-funded from a base in a country village for most of his long life.

Unlike Darwin and Wiener, the other two architects of the present era of change, Lovelock was born into a low-income family with little education and badly needed the scholarships that took him to the University of Manchester. While a student he worked for an industrial chemist, unusual in research science where most employment was in government or research institutions. His first jobs were in medical research and then an agricultural institute met his life-long thirst for diverse problem solving. Lovelock described his vision of a scientist as one who, like an artist or a novelist, does his best creative work free from institutional

*Figure 3.1* Scientist and inventor James Lovelock, February 1997 (© photo by George W. Wright/CORBIS)

pressures. His capacity to take a lone stand served him well as a conscientious objector in the hard-hit London of the Second World War as well as in standing up for his commitment to the world as Gaia over a decade of attack from colleagues. Lovelock combined a strong sense of independence with a collective approach. His collective approach to his research emerged as he invented the diverse range of skilled instruments that would later give him his financial independence. In spite of his personal life as a lone scientist, all of his work involved close and friendly collaboration[3] with specialists in the particular field in which he was working at the time. Among his many discoveries were the microwave oven, developed as a sideline from reviving frozen animals; the ozone hole as a by-product of noticing the strange seasonal fog in his country retreat; and groundbreaking methods of detecting the makeup of atmospheric gases and of a method for freezing red blood cells.

Lovelock's freedom to work as he wished came from his reputation as an inventor. He was offered a NASA (National Aeronautic and Space Agency) grant to join the team exploring the moon. After the technical issues were resolved he became bored and moved on to the group working on exploring Mars. This seemed to Lovelock like heaven. The problems included how to power the instruments with only two watts available for each instrument; how to send radio messages that had never before been transmitted over such a long distance; and how to design equipment that had to stand the shock of entering and leaving space. He said of himself that successfully tackling such a variety of problems was a first step in recognising Gaia.[4]

As a research chemist he demonstrated that large masses of single-celled organisms in the oceans regulated the chemical mixture of the water in the oceans and the gases in the atmosphere.[5] When there was a change in the mixture, these organisms brought it back into balance. The planet was adjusting itself! This flash of insight came to Lovelock in the American space laboratories where he was working in September 1965.[6] He went on to discover the same effect of self-organisation throughout the living processes that made up the planet.

Close partnerships between living things and their habitats have been common knowledge for centuries. Lichens form fertile soil from granite rocks and forests hold mountainsides in place. Human societies change whole landscapes to supply their food and places to live. Lovelock's study of the Earth's feedback systems found that they encompassed the entire planet. He came to recognise that the planet's living and non-living systems make up a self-organising whole and, further, this is strongly influenced by the actions of one species: the human.[7]

As recognition of the complexity and dynamism of the world's feedback systems increased, so did interest in chaos theory. The original 1963 paper[8] on the butterfly wing flapping in Brazil causing a typhoon in Texas has become symbolic of all self-organising systems.[9] When the feedback system is large and complex enough, even a small shock is able to spin it out of control. Once out of control of their usual stabilising systems, the parts are free to reorganise into some entirely new shape.[10] The physicist's word for this is stochastic: a system composed of the interactions between random events and predetermined patterns, a feature of all transformational change.[11]

The nub of Lovelock's idea was that Gaia was formed through stochastic relationships between unpredictable human actions and the rule-bound life and physical forms of the planet. That this was central to the whole existence of the living planet was a shock to those who had only considered Earth through a single discipline or their own lived experience. When Lovelock called the whole system after Gaia, it was a challenge to the rules of the scientific community[12] to which he belonged. The immediate response to his well-founded interpretation of interconnectedness of Earth's systems was not praise. Instead he was ridiculed by scientists and trivialised by the popular press.

The rejection and distortion of such a transformational idea should not have been surprising. The same thing had happened to Darwin and many other ground-breakers before Lovelock. However, the idea of Gaia met a particularly unsympathetic mental environment. Darwin's legacy had opened up so much new ground that an avalanche of specialised inquiries had sprung up to cover the new field. Studies of the planet had become divided and sub-divided into different specialisations, losing the original breadth of Darwin's understanding of the world. The public mind had become unused to sweeping explanations.

This state of affairs did not go unchallenged. The host of critics who deplored the moves to specialisation included philosopher Stephen Toulmin and scientist Jerome Ravetz.[13] Their verdict was that the specialised disciplines had become self-referencing, answering questions raised in their particular field, rather than answering the larger questions about the state of society and the planet. Professions, libraries and educational curricula were so divided that they hindered, rather than supported studies of the interconnected way the world worked. Strong boundaries built around the specialised disciplines made it difficult to address twentieth century issues such as poverty, food security, global warming, drug use and pollution.[14] Meanwhile, a more holistic school of thought was developing in parallel to the specialisations.

The opening salvo on human-caused change to the physical environment was Rachel Carson's *Silent Spring* which was published in 1962.[15] The story of a sky empty of birds due to the widespread use of the insecticide DDT captured the public mind. The shock of *Silent Spring* was repeated with the publication of *Limits to Growth* a decade later.[16] Two American PhD scholars, Donella and Dennis Meadows, used forward projections of five variables, world population, industrialisation, pollution, food production and resource depletion, to demonstrate that the trends were unsustainable. The strength of the public concern in response to their simulation model stunned the young researchers.

Market economists, physical scientists and right-wing political figures alike attacked the methodology, the computer, the conclusions, the rhetoric and the people behind the project. On the other hand, biological and social scientists and left-wing political figures hailed it as a message for the future and pleaded for a transformational change in the current practice on all of the five variables. A 2010 study recalculation of the 1969 limits to growth scenarios 30 years later found them to be still largely accurate.[17] Donella Meadows, who continued her work in the field of systems analysis, became convinced of the need for collective thinking that employed two of the levers of change – multiple feedback loops and new mental models of what Earth is like.

In parallel with social and environmental disruption, ideas were emerging for a future that would be different from the past. As well as Cobb and Daly's economic strategy,[18] in the 1970s and 1980s, Barbara Ward and René Dubos[19] developed a social strategy, Paul and Anne Ehrlich[20] a population strategy, and Stephen Boyden[21] a public health strategy, all as part of a change strategy set in a collective understanding of the world. Each strategy included the recommendation to realign social structures towards smaller, more cooperative social and economic units and to ensure the cultural diversity of participants.[22] Each plan acknowledged the extent to which human beings' evolutionary direction now depended on ideas as well as biophysical feedback systems. The shift from the hierarchy and the specialist to the network and the collective mind was beginning.

## Peak

The risks from industrial pollution, including the level of carbon dioxide in the atmosphere, alerted the world's human population to major changes to the planet on which they lived. Then the first pictures of Earth from space sparked a transformational change that the risks potentially included everyone on the earth. Scientists had already developed an advanced knowledge of the geology and ecology of the planet and its political and social history was well documented. The connections between all these had not previously been understood or recognised by the research community or the world's industrialised countries. On the other hand, this unity had long been in the minds of citizens of pre-industrialised countries, many of whose cultures have parables of how the sky and the earth are one interconnected system.

When the first pictures of Earth arrived from space, James Lovelock had already laid the foundation for changing the prevailing reductionist mindset. He had discovered that the chemistry of the oceans and atmosphere was not only in a stable balance but was self-regulating through double loop feedback systems. In 1965, Lovelock's precise calculations on the exchange of chemical gases led to his 'awesome thought' that 'life on Earth not only made the atmosphere but also *regulated* it'.[23]

Gaia, as a name for the self-regulating planet, was the brainchild of William Golding, Nobel Prize-winning author of *Lord of the Flies*.[24] That combination of advanced science and ancient ritual produced a strong response from all directions. The acclamation from the counter-culture movement of the time was accompanied by outright rejection of the hypothesis by the scientific community. It seemed that the global system could not be considered as physical and social at the same time. The rejection extended to the scientists' behaviour at the inaugural scientific conference on Gaia. While the stated aim of the conference was to subject the new idea to an open debate, many of the speakers went to the extent of ridiculing Lovelock's scientific work.[25] This allowed the concept to be so devalued that it took nearly a decade to recover.

The idea that Earth is a unique planet whose life forms regulate its environment, as well as the reverse, began to spread to society as a whole. The Mars probe team from NASA asked Lovelock how to tell if there was life on Mars. His advice was to look for patterns anywhere, in the chemistry of the atmosphere or the minerals in the ground. If the patterns were uniform and unchanging, then there could have been no life. If there were signs of changing patterns, then life was operating on the physical processes. This is now the routine test for life applied to the planets in the solar system.

Eventually Lovelock achieved scientific recognition for his Gaia hypothesis with a mathematical model called *Daisyworld*,[26] which showed how, given the right circumstances, individual change events can translate into a self-regulated steady state planet. This acceptance brought a flood of discoveries about the interconnections that help the planet to support life. Scientists, politicians and local communities alike became conscious of the intricate connections between the physical world and the living world that make up the shape of both the locality and the planet.

Collective thinking had taken another giant leap with recognition of the self-regulatory capacity of Gaia. By the twenty-first century, recognition of the interconnected systems of the planet had become part of normal life. Much scientific research became based on this form of collective thinking. Flows of people, resources and information were recognised as global patterns of change. Google maps had the capacity to bring the patterns of population and resource movement to each household. Social media carried the passions for and against Gaia throughout cyberspace. Once Lovelock's vision of Gaia was shared, there was a surge of collective ideas around the planet, a social parallel to the adaptive radiation of life forms after physical environmental change.

Key scientific contributions to the idea of Gaia came from the microbiologist Lynn Margulis[27] and the ecologist Howard Odum.[28] Lynn Margulis compared the relationships that formed the living cell to the interconnections that created Gaia. The parts of a cell – the nucleus, the energy-generators, the bounding membrane and the chemical messengers – continue to perform their separate functions. However, their interdependence is so complete that no one part can do without the other and the cell can reproduce as a whole.[29] Margulis argued that all this is also true of Gaia, and so it can behave like a single cell, with the exception that it cannot reproduce itself – there is only one Earth. Margulis described Earth as the symbiotic planet.[30] The planet, like the cell, has built-in, self-adjusting processes that allow it to maintain its integrity to resist environmental change. So the largest unit of life and the smallest rest on the interdependence among their parts.

Working with biological scientists, brothers Eugene and Howard Odum developed Darwin's ideas into the then new discipline of ecology, the study of the living world as a dynamic interconnected system.[31] The Odums recognised the difficulty of establishing this all-embracing discipline in the compartmentalised thinking of the time. Howard set about developing a symbolic language that could indicate the interconnections in natural systems and bridge the ideas of the many contributing disciplines. His description stands as a suggestion for ways to develop a collective mind:

> when a group gathers around a table to talk about analyzing the main components of a new system or problem, one person can diagram for the group, enhancing the coherence of the discussion ... A group collective-thinking exercise stimulates memories and draws out qualitative and quantitative knowledge from combined experiences within the real-world system of concern.[32]

## Follow on

Darwin had identified the influence of the non-living environment in shaping the living. Lovelock broadened those relationships to include the influence of the living on the non-living, and the human mind on both. Radical changes in the human social system made themselves evident in the so-called counter-culture that erupted in the decades after the Second World War. This was not an uprising by the underprivileged of society. The 1960s movement was fuelled by a generation of well-educated, disaffected young people from the post-war baby boom.[33]

This cohort became sensitised to those who had missed out on the affluence of industrial development and to the continuing damage to the natural environment from humanity's industrial activities. There was a general recognition of the need for cooperative ways of living to remedy this injustice and to reduce the environmental impact. This break in the trajectory of Western society was encapsulated in a 1964 hit song by Bob Dylan "The Times They Are a-Changin": 'If your time to you is worth savin', then you better start swimmin', or you'll sink like a stone, for the times they are a-changin'.'

Spokesperson and guru for the counter-culture was Theodore Roszak, an American historian who had graduated from Princeton University in the US and then moved to the nursery of the counter-culture in London in the 1960s. Roszak's belief in the untapped potential of the human mind led him to apply the principles of Darwinian evolution to mind and society, and to characterise humans as an unfinished animal in evolutionary terms.[34] The counter-culture's interest in collaborative ways of living, sexual freedom, recreational drug use and the value of sympathetic communication spread into the thinking of the social mainstream. Roszak laid out the principles for the foundation of a counter-culture global village. These can be summarised as:

- Tapping the whole human potential, by including imagination, intuition, creativity, aesthetic appreciation, reflection, introspection and spiritual awareness. This deep subjectivity is a partner to the scientific objectivity that gives humans the capacity to grasp the existence of Gaia.
- Accessing lived experience, with sensitivity to embodied knowledge and to empathy. Reflection on lived experience no longer separates body and mind, but includes the evidence from all the senses: sight, hearing, smell, taste and touch, and the sixth sense of intuition, the heightened awareness of others.
- Exploring the sense of self, accessing the more-than-conscious understanding of the personal world created through the explicit and tacit dimensions of mind as exemplified by Polanyi.[35] This is the world created through the presence of archetypes and inherited cultural consciousness explored by Carl Jung.
- Accepting universality, with the core concept of convergence, in which everything can be connected in some way to everything else. This requires openness to the whole which transcends the parts, whatever the whole and the selected parts.
- Absorbing the central idea of wholeness, giving as much concern to the relationships between the parts as with the parts themselves. This requires going beyond the dichotomy which has ruled Western thinking for the past 300 years to explore the diversity of the parts of any given whole.
- Acknowledging the power of mysticism, the unknown, the irrational and the Buddhist 'thing without a name'. Much that humans share cannot be explained by any of the formal forms of language. Symbols, rites and icons have been powerful throughout the history of human thought.
- Valuing the commonplace, everyday ritual, body rhythms and responses to the seasons, the arts and crafts, all of which may seem to be part of an

unchanging way of life, and yet vary dramatically from place to place, culture to culture. What form would these take in a collective future?

- Envisioning a strong, connected community with collaborative roles for leaders, seekers, jesters, mystics and elders, and its coherence among Mumford's palace, granary and temples as universal spaces in cities.[36] Such a community has been the ambition of deliberate communities throughout human history.

Roszak's prediction of the future of the human mind matches that of Teilhard de Chardin. Both looked towards a shared consciousness that expands the human capacity for understanding each other and the world. Both writers emphasised the transformative nature of that understanding, while each emphasised a different element of the collective understanding they were predicting. Teilhard de Chardin wrote of the contributions of individuals to the noosphere, the realm in which the new consciousness resides. Roszak searched for the connections between fully conscious individuals and the unified world that they are capable of creating for themselves.[37]

The impact of human affairs on the living and the non-living dimensions of the planet has become great enough to emerge as an era with its own title: the era of the Anthropocene. Scientists have come to agree that knowledge cannot be purely objective, and that all knowledge of the world is necessarily anthropocentric, that is, constructed in the human head.[38] The advances in thinking that signalled the next phase of the evolution of the collective mind were made through two very different collectives of like-minded scholars over the course of the twentieth century. The second of these meetings of minds made great strides towards the global collective thinking forecast by Teilhard de Chardin.

In the 1920s a group of philosophers, mathematicians and physicists formed the Vienna Circle[39] with the aim of consolidating the thinking of the 300 years of the scientific era. Their aim was to produce a science of the sciences. The basis was to reject all evidence other than the observable and reduce complex issues to their parts. Despite the advances that this focus brought to disciplines such as mathematics and physics, this narrow reductionist perspective was beginning to generate considerable opposition. One of the original heroes of the Vienna Circle, the philosopher Wittgenstein, protested against their narrow outlook by reading poetry during their sessions.[40] The Vienna Circle argued that a collective world was impossible. They based their arguments on the law of entropy or the second law of thermodynamics,[41] that concentrations of energy in the universe are irreversibly being dissipated, that there is no such thing as purpose, and the complexity of Earth's stochastic system.

Two decades later, a series of meetings called the Macy Conferences[42] brought together a set of innovative scientists.[43] Each of the members had already established a new field of collective thought within their own specialisation (Box 3.1). The Macy Conference participants responded to these challenges. The first challenge was the second law of thermodynamics: given the fact of entropy, how can there ever be a collective increase in the world's stocks of energy and human resources? The counter argument was that the Earth is constantly increasing its stores of energy and knowledge through trapping the energy of the sun and maximising the capacity for human learning. Therefore the planet acts as an open cumulative system within the larger universe.

---

### *Box 3.1* Some of the participants in the seven Macy Conferences held between 1946 and 1953

- Ross Ashby, psychiatrist and pioneer of cybernetics
- Gregory Bateson, anthropologist, social scientist, linguist, visual anthropologist, semiotician and cyberneticist
- Julian Bigelow, pioneering computer engineer
- Ralph W. Gerard, neurophysiologist and forerunner of neuroscience
- Kurt Lewin, founder of social psychology
- Warren McCulloch, psychiatrist and neurophysiologist who connected brain and mind
- Margaret Mead, founder of social anthropology
- John von Neumann, one of the foremost mathematicians of the twentieth century
- Erik Erikson, psychoanalyst known for his theory of social development
- Norbert Wiener, mathematician, philosopher and the founder of the field of cybernetics and a leading figure at the conferences.

Source: American Society for Cybernetics

---

The second challenge lay in the scientific belief that it was impossible to identify purpose objectively and therefore impossible to establish that it existed. This would mean that human minds could not establish a shared purpose and work collectively. The response from the Macy group was that every living organism has its own governing program set in its genes. All organisms can be said to have as a guiding purpose the reproduction of their genetic program and an increase in complexity. Movement towards these aims can be identified in the organism's behaviour and its outcomes, from unicellular to complex organisms. For collective thinking there is a plentiful supply of evidence of intentional cooperation.

The third challenge faced by the Macy Conference participants was to establish that the direction of the self-organising systems of the planet was collective. During the conferences, the realisation emerged that self-organisation in the Gaian system depended on communication between the three dimensions of living and non-living systems and the influence of the human mind. This communication was in the form of double feedback loops which could influence each other, and hence were capable of collective learning (Figure 3.2). This conclusion, generated by the work of Gregory Bateson and continued by Norbert Wiener, led eventually to the design of the communication loops of the electronic world. It was Norbert Wiener who coined the word cybernetics[44] for the study of the operation of the feedback system.[45] Thus the need to respond to the challenges of established science brought a firmer foundation to the idea of a collective world.

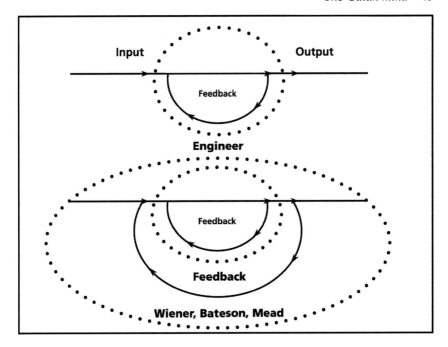

*Figure 3.2* Double feedback diagram from the Macy Conferences

## Next

One of the more prominent members of the Macy Conference was the polymath Gregory Bateson (Figure 3.3). His experience as an anthropologist, psychologist, social scientist and linguist led him to explore the links between living and non-living systems and the human mind. Although working at the same time as Lovelock, from the early twentieth to the early twenty-first centuries, Bateson did not come into contact with the concept of Gaia until the end of his life. He then rejected it as too embedded in the material world. It was Bateson who coined the phrases of the more-than-human world for the planet's total burden of living things, and the more-than-conscious mind to emphasise that conscious, rational thought occupied only a fraction of the human brain.

Gregory Bateson came from a similar background to Charles Darwin, from a well-to-do and intellectual English family. He also shared with Darwin the difficulty of taking some time to discover what he wanted to do in life. The deaths of two older brothers left him the sole hope of his father, William Bateson, an eminent biologist who rescued Mendel's work on genetics. Eventually Gregory escaped from biology into anthropology. Even then he had trouble establishing a satisfactory research site, since he wished to explore an intact culture; hard to find in a post-colonial era. The culture he found, the Iatmul of the Sepik region of New Guinea, led him to formulate a double-bind theory of the workings of the human mind.[46]

*Figure 3.3* Gregory Bateson, 1975 (photo by Barry Schwartz Photography)

This proposes that since thought determines behaviour (not the other way round) human existence is based in patterns of thought that mediate between opposites.

The Iatmul had very strict gender roles that considerably limited an individual's options. At regular intervals the tribe held a ceremony called *Naven* in which each gender dressed up and behaved like the other.[47] The ceremony generates considerable laughter and satire. Bateson suggested that the ceremony mediates between the polarised sexes so that they understand each other's point of view and are not in conflict with one another. In most societies, Bateson argues, there are ceremonial ways of establishing the positions that form the fabric of that society: old and young; rich and poor; male and female; sick and well; good and bad; strong and weak and divergent and convergent thinkers. As the seventeenth century satirist Jonathan Swift pointed out, it is a social decision whether to jail the criminals and treat the sick, or treat the criminals and jail the sick. Bateson considered that the more-than-conscious mind of intuition, imagination and cultural consciousness, as well as ethical and aesthetic considerations, plays a far greater role in the use of our minds than the logical and rational on which several generations have been taught to concentrate.

During the Macy Conferences, the participants arrived at the idea of mind as a communication hub for a complex system of feedback loops[48] (Figure 3.2). The communication system included the use of symbols, metaphors, poetry and icons to enable the full spectrum of the human capacity to communicate: the introspective, physical, social, aesthetic, ethical, sympathetic and reflective. The reach of the feedback system is very wide, describing the evolutionary process in terms of a metaphor:

a steam engine which checks and corrects any irregularities almost before they become evident; and in like manner (leaves) no unbalanced deficiency … because it would make itself felt at the very first step, by rendering existence difficult and extinction almost sure to follow.[49]

The label that was coined for the study of such self-governing systems was cybernetics.

The twenty-first century has begun with the consequences of the Macy Conference deliberations becoming evident. For the first time in human history, there is a general understanding of the double feedback loops between human ideas, human actions and human influence, and the future of the planet.[50] The understanding is subject to the usual pattern of responses to fresh interpretations of how the world works: distortion, denial and disciples. The distortion has been the continued separation of the social and physical worlds, barring the way to a collective understanding. Denial has been the response of the industries and political systems which most stand to lose by new understanding. Disciples and apprentices such as Norbert Wiener, Christopher Alexander, Microsoft's Bill Gates and Apple's Steve Jobs have transformed the human dimension of the planet into a collective communication web, filling the new world of cyberspace. A minimum definition of cybernetics by its creator Norbert Wiener is the science of the study of control and communication in the animal and the machine. As a master sorcerer, Norbert Wiener is the subject of the chapter which follows.

## Notes

1  The photograph of Earth was taken in December 1968, by the Apollo 8 crew during their voyage to the Moon. Subsequently, it became known as 'Earthrise' because it was an image of Earth rising in the dark vastness of space over a sunlit lunar landscape.

2  Lovelock, J. (2000) *Homage to Gaia: The Life of an Independent Scientist*, New York: Oxford University Press.

3  Lovelock wrote in his autobiography, 'I consider that the opportunity to mix freely, talk, and discuss problems with these competent engineers…was the greatest of my rewards for working there. I often felt like young apprenticed artists must have felt to be welcomed into the studios of a Leonardo or a Holbein'. (Lovelock, J. (2000) *Homage to Gaia: The Life of an Independent Scientist*, New York: Oxford University Press, p. 151).

4  Ibid, p. 152.

5  Lovelock recalled the first steps to his discovery that 'clouds, dimethyl sulphide from algae living in the oceans, and climate, are all intimately linked in a great ocean atmospheric cycle' in ibid. (p. 260).

6  Lovelock recalled the context and lead up to his 'awesome thought' in ibid. (pp. 252–54).

7  Lovelock, J. (1991) *Gaia: The Practical Guide of Planetary Medicine,* Sydney: Allen & Unwin.

8  Lorenz, E. N. (1963) 'Deterministic Nonperiodic Flow', *J. Atmospheric Sciences* **20** (2), 130–41.

9  This phenomenon that small effects lead to big changes is called the 'butterfly effect'. Edward Lorenz's publication in 1963 marked him as the father of chaos theory. He was awarded the 1991 Kyoto Prize for Basic Sciences for his discovery of deterministic chaos, a transformative change in the understanding of natural systems.

10 Buchanan, M. (2000) *Ubiquity: The Science of History … or Why the World is Simpler than We Think*, New York: Crown.

11  Gleick, J. (1987) *Chaos: Making a New Science,* UK: Penguin. Briggs, J. and Peat, F. David (1989) *Turbulent Mirror: An Illustrated Guide to Chaos Theory and the Science of Wholeness,* New York: Harper & Row. Lewin, R. (1993) *Complexity: Life on the Edge,* US: Macmillan. Capra, F. (1996) *The Web of Life: A New Synthesis of Mind and Matter,* UK: Harper Collins.

12  Lovelock, J. (2000) *Homage to Gaia: The Life of an Independent Scientist,* New York: Oxford University Press.

13  These critics also include Michael Polanyi whose book *Personal Knowledge: Towards a Post Critical Philosophy* was published in 1958 (London: Routledge) where he discussed how every creative act of discovery in science includes tacit forms of knowledge. Stephen Toulmin's book *Human Understanding: Vol.1: The Collective Use and Understanding of Concepts* published in 1972 (Princeton, US: Princeton University Press) developed the Toulmin model of argumentation. Stephen Rose's 1997 book *Lifelines: Life Beyond the Gene* (London: Oxford University Press) critiques the reductionist view of giving too much emphasis to the components of the integrated bodies and minds of humans. Ravetz, J. (1971) *Scientific Knowledge and its Social Problems* (London: Oxford University Press) coined the phrase Post-Normal Science. His 2005 book is *A No-Nonsense Guide to Science* (UK: New Internationalist).

14  This compartmentalisation is strongly reinforced in professional fields such as economics, medicine, health and education. In addition to specialist knowledge, complex issues require a whole systems approach such as advocated in the 2010 book *Tackling Wicked Problems Through the Transdisciplinary Imagination* (eds) Brown, V. A., Harris, J. A. and Russell, J. Y., London: Earthscan.

15  Carson, R. (1962*) Silent Spring,* Boston, US: Houghton Mifflin. It was also during the 1960s that 'ecology' and 'interdependence' became household words; Paul and Anne Ehrlich's 1968 book *The Population Bomb* (London: Ballantine) and Garrett Hardin's *Tragedy of the Commons* paper on the overexploitation of common resources such as the oceans was also published in the December 1968 issue of *Science,* **162**, 1243–48.

16  The Club of Rome, based at Bern, Switzerland, addressed 'the predicament of mankind': the environmental crisis generated by the demands placed on the Earth's carrying capacity (its renewable and non-renewable resources and associated environmental pollution). A world simulation model was made accessible to the general public in Donella and Dennis Meadows' 1972 *The Limits of Growth: A Report for the Club of Rome's Project on the Predicament of Mankind,* London: Potomac. In 1974, the second report of the Club of Rome entitled *Mankind at the Turning Point,* London: E. P. Dutton, by M. Mesarovic and E. Pestel was published. In between these two reports, in 1973, *Thinking About The Future: A Critique of "The Limits to Growth",* London: Sussex University Press, was edited by H. S. D. Cole, C. Freeman, M. Jahoda and K. L. R. Pavitt. As it turned out, while such 'hard' systems simulations are useful for engineering, they are not much use for decision making, especially for wicked problems.

17  Meadows, D. H., Meadows, D. L. and Randers, J. (1992) *Beyond the Limits: Global Collapse or a Sustainable Future,* London: Earthscan. The results of simulations in *Beyond the Limits* were consistent with those in *The Limits to Growth.* New data were added and counter-arguments to the criticisms directed at the two earlier publications.

18  Herman E. Daley is a co-founder of the field of Ecological Economics and with co-author John B. Cobb wrote *For the Common Good: Redirecting the Economy towards Community, the Environment, and a Sustainable Future* (1989/1994) Boston, US: Beacon Press.

19  Ward, B. and Dubos, R. (1972) *Only One Earth: The Care and Maintenance of a Small Planet,* UK: Penguin. The first Earth Summit (Conference on the Human Environment) was held the year before in Stockholm, Sweden. See also *Our Common Future* (1987) by the World Commission on Environment and Development (Chair: Gro Harlem Brundtland) New York: Oxford University Press.

20 The book *Ecoscience: Population, Resources and Environment* by Paul and Anne Ehrlich and John Holden was published in 1977 (San Francisco: W. H. Freeman).

21 Stephen Boyden is an Australian human ecologist who led a pioneering holistic and integrative study of the city of Hong Kong: Boyden, S., Millar, S., Newcombe, K. and O'Neill, B. (1981) *The ecology of a city and its people: The case of Hong Kong,* Canberra: ANU Press. See also, Boyden, S. (1987). *Western Civilization in Biological Perspective: Patterns in Biohistory,* London: Oxford University Press.

22 Schumacher, E. F. (1974) *Small is Beautiful: A Study of Economics as if People Mattered,* London: Abacus.

23 Lovelock, J. (1991) *Gaia: The Practical Science of Planetary Medicine*, Sydney: Allen and Unwin, p. 22.

24 Golding, W. (1954) *Lord of the Flies,* UK: Faber & Faber.

25 In Lovelock's *Homage to Gaia* (2000, New York: Oxford University Press) is his account of the first scientific conference on Gaia held in San Diego, 1988, and the subsequent ridicule and doubt hoisted on Gaia thereon, pp. 271–73.

26 A mathematical model of a world in orbit around a star, like the Sun, inhabited by two species of plants, dark- and light-coloured daisies. The model showed that natural selection led to the self-regulation of climate at a temperature near optimal for plant growth, despite large variations in incoming heat. When the star was young and cool, dark daisies covered the planet whereas as the star warmed, the lighter daisies began to grow and compete, and their reflection of sunlight cooled the planet keeping the temperature optimal as the star increased its output of heat. It is a synopsis of Gaia theory showing how organisms evolving under natural selection are part of a system that is self-regulating. See Lovelock's *Homage to Gaia* (2000, New York: Oxford University Press), pp. 264–67.

27 In his autobiography, Lovelock acknowledged Margulis as a friend 'who joined me in the development of Gaia in 1971'. He went on to tell how Lynn Margulis 'put biological flesh on the bare bones of my physical chemistry … [and] has courageously supported Gaia in spite of hostility from parts of the United States scientific community – that sometimes threatened her own standing as a biologist' (pp. x–xii).

28 Howard Odum completed his PhD in 1950 at Yale University under the supervision of G. Evelyn Hutchinson, a participant at the influential Macy Conferences (this chapter). Howard's thesis was on the biogeochemistry of strontium and its distribution in the biosphere and may have anticipated the view of the earth as one large interrelated ecosystem. He is an early systems thinking ecologist who wrote *Environment, Power and Society* (1971, New York: Wiley) and, together with his brother Eugene, was awarded the 1987 Crafoord Prize of the Royal Swedish Academy of Sciences for their pioneering field studies on energy and matter flows in aquatic and terrestrial ecosystems and for their contributions to systems ecology generally.

29 Margulis, L. and Sagan, D. (1995) *What is Life?,* New York: Simon & Schuster.

30 Margulis, L. (1998) *The Symbiotic Planet: A New Look at Evolution,* New York: Basic Books.

31 Eugene and Howard Odum's original textbook, *Fundamentals of Ecology,* was published in 1953. In approach, it gave emphasis to the dynamics of ecosystems, their structure and function and their worldwide interdependence. Two more editions followed with the third 1971 edition, 'greatly expanded and updated in light of the increasing importance of the subject in human affairs'. See Odum, E. P. (1971) *Fundamentals of Ecology*, Philadelphia, US: W. B. Saunders.

32 Odum, H. T. (1994) *Ecological and General Systems: An Introduction to Systems Ecology,* Colorado, US: Colorado University Press, p. 21.

33 Roszak, T. (1968/1995) *The Making of a Counterculture: Reflections on the Technocratic Society and Its Youthful Opposition,* Berkeley and Los Angeles, US: University of California Press.

34 Roszak, T. (1975) *Unfinished Animal: The Aquarian Frontier and the Evolution of Consciousness*, New York: Harper & Row. Roszak, T. (1992) *The Voice of the Earth: An Exploration of Ecopsychology*, New York: Simon & Schuster.

35 Polanyi, M. (1958) *Personal Knowledge: Towards a Post-Critical Philosophy*, Chicago, US: University of Chicago Press.

36 Mumford, L. (1961) *The City in History: Its Origins, its Transformations and its Prospects*, New York: Harcourt, Brace and World.

37 Roszak, T. (1979/1981) *Person/Planet: the Creative Disintegration of Industrial Society*, New York: Granada. Roszak, T. (1992) *The Voice of the Earth: An Exploration of Ecopsychology*, New York: Simon & Schuster.

38 Polanyi, M. (1958) *Personal Knowledge: Towards a Post-Critical Philosophy*, Chicago, US: University of Chicago Press. Berger, P. L. and Luckmann, T. (1971) *The Social Construction of Reality: a treatise in the sociology of knowledge*, Harmondsworth, UK: Penguin.

39 Baker, G. (ed.) (2003) *Ludwig Wittgenstein and Freidrich Waismann, The Voices of Wittgenstein: The Vienna Circle*, London and New York: Routledge. Honderich, T. (ed.) (1995) *The Oxford Companion to Philosophy*, New York: Oxford University Press.

40 Shorto, R. (2008) *Descartes' Bones: A Skeletal History of the Conflict between Faith and Reason*, New York: Doubleday.

41 See http://en.wikipedia.org/wiki/Second_law_of_thermodynamics [accessed 15.8.13].

42 The Macy Conferences were held from 1946 to 1953 to set the foundations for a general science of the workings of the human mind. They were organised by the Josiah Macy, Jr. Foundation. See Summary: The Macy Conferences at the American Society for Cybernetics (ASC) website: http://www.asc-cybernetics.org. [accessed 27.3.13].

43 The Macy Conferences attendees listed by the American Society for Cybernetics: http://www.asc–cybernetics.org [accessed 27.3.13].

44 The term 'cybernetic' (Greek, *kybernetes*: pilot, steersman) was coined by Wiener in 1948. See 'Defining Cybernetics, Summary: The Macy Conferences' at http://www.asc-cybernetics.org [accessed 27.3.13].

45 Chapter 4.

46 Bateson, G. (1973) *Steps to an Ecology of Mind: Collected Essays in Anthropology, Psychiatry, Evolution and Epistemology*, St Albans, UK: Paladin.

47 Bateson, G. (1958) *Naven: a Survey of the Problems Suggested by a Composite Picture of the Culture of a New Guinea Tribe Drawn from Three Points of View*, 2nd edn, Stanford, US: Stanford University Press.

48 Gregory Bateson and Margaret Mead contrasted first and second order feedback loops in this diagram during an interview with Stewart Brand in 1973, referring to cybernetics as 'the science of the whole circuit'. See 'For God's Sake Margaret: A Conversation with Gregory Bateson and Margaret Mead' in *Ten Years of CoEvolution Quarterly: News That Stayed News*, Kleiner, A. and Brand, S. (eds) (1986) San Francisco, US: North Point Press (pp. 26–46).

49 See Bateson, G. (1973) 'Conscious Purpose versus Nature' in *Steps to an Ecology of Mind*, p. 404, where he referred to this part of Wallace's description of the struggle for existence (natural selection) and reflected on its possible significance.

50 Flannery, T. (1994) *The Future Eaters: An ecological history of the Australasian lands and people*. Chatswood, Australia: Reed Books.

# 4  The cybernetic mind

## Human social networks in cyberspace

**Synopsis:** although the colonising of cyberspace is only 30 years old, Norbert Wiener foretold its existence and its future 70 years ago. Wiener saw the personal computer as an extension of the mind, not as a replacement for the brain, and predicted the vast reach of the electronic networks enabled by Facebook and Twitter. He foresaw that a new set of ethical principles would be needed to govern the human interactions in this new environment. Marshall McLuhan interpreted the new medium while Steve Jobs opened up an all-encompassing communication web which people instinctively knew how to colonise. Many of the program designs for this web were enabled by Christopher Alexander's pattern language, which also provides a pathway to collaborative design for future cities, landscapes and ways of living.

## Context of the change

The global war of 1939–45 was followed by two decades that have been described as the most socially turbulent in human history.[1] When the war started Great Britain was the world power, and when it finished it was the United States. The atomic bomb dropped on Hiroshima generated a new fear for the human future and a fresh concern about the products of science. The massive wartime allocation of resources had led to the development of amazing new technologies, of which electronic communication was only one. The skies filled with planes, and radio (then still called wireless) became an all-pervading global communication network. Newspapers were powerful organs of particular interests. When television went worldwide in the 1960s, the world became aware of the power of citizen opinion when coupled with the new electronics. The image of the planet in space reached an unprecedented number of households. A photograph of a burning child running down a Vietnam village street helped end the US-Vietnam war.[2]

Before the Second World War, the global social unit was a father in paid work or in the fields and a mother at home. Children surviving to adulthood had taken the global human population to unprecedented heights.[3] The pre-war Great Depression was only just ending and memories of its misery were still fresh. Post-war, the definition of the family unit entered a state of flux that has continued until today. Men returning from the war found their old jobs had vanished and new ones had taken their place. Women who had unwillingly left their wartime jobs to return to the household found that the hormonal contraceptives of the 1960s allowed them to reorganise their lives and move back into the workforce. The children of a newly affluent society and more relaxed parents sought more freedom for themselves and fomented the unrest so well described by Theodore Roszak.[4] The beat generation was well equipped and ready to take advantage of the electronic age that was just around the corner.

Richard Falk suggested that the restlessness of the post-war world was due to the interplay between the four global flows of finance, information, population and resources that had begun their sweep around the planet.[5] Developing separately from this globalisation-from-above was globalisation-from-below, in which the typical community was no longer localised, rural, authoritarian and closed. Communities have become globally connected, urban, torn by opposing interests and buffeted by the global flows of finance, information, people and resources. These conditions created the demand side of the electronic age, making the world ripe for communication networks that could link the complexities in a coherent World Wide Web.

The technical capacity to build this worldwide communication web emerged in the 1970s. The present era of transformational change in human communication had begun. Ever since that time, Darwin's ideas on the inevitability of change and Lovelock's on self-organising systems have been given maximum reach through the emergence of electronically-based information technology. In company with Darwin and Lovelock, Norbert Wiener was one of the master thinkers whose ideas have influenced the human thought of the twenty-first century. However, while Darwin's name is a household word and Lovelock's is widely recognised, the name of the visionary who foresaw the potential of the relationship between the human mind and the electronic medium has dropped out of sight. While the invasion of cyberspace by social media follows the path Norbert Wiener predicted, his ideas for the future of the impact on humanity are yet to be realised. His predictions include the introspective, physical, social, ethical, aesthetic and sympathetic consequences and the need to reflect on the human responsibility for those consequences.[6]

Norbert Wiener was very different from Darwin and Lovelock in personality and background. The others' transformational thinking appears to have emerged almost by accident. They were both members of dominant social establishments: Darwin was a member of the landed gentry and Lovelock of the scientific community. Wiener's family, on the other hand, were ambivalent about their Russian Jewish background. They had an unsettled life, moving from Russia to America looking for greater security. Wiener's father Leo eventually found recognition in the academic world as a genius in the study of languages. Leo deliberately reared Norbert to be a genius. Norbert Wiener was educated at home, graduated from school at 11 years old and university at 14, with a doctorate at 17. His doctorate from Harvard was on mathematical logic, while he also explored zoology and philosophy at a postgraduate level. Norbert turned out to be the genius his father wanted, although at a cost.[7]

*Figure 4.1* Professor Norbert Wiener, December 1948 (© photo by Al Fenn//Time Life Pictures/Getty Images)

Leo supervised Wiener's intellectual development to an extreme degree, always claiming that Norbert's many successes were the sole result of his upbringing. Even Norbert's wife was chosen for him by his parents. This led to suggestions from biographers that his upbringing was the reason that Norbert, while extremely clear-thinking as a scientist, became dogmatic and defensive in social relationships. As a result, Norbert's difficult personality has been blamed for his long wait for a permanent academic appointment. Nor was he invited to work on the Manhattan

Project[8] like other eminent thinkers of his time. He himself blamed this on anti-Semitism, although it may well have been simply that he was difficult to get along with and his thinking was ahead of his time.

In common with Darwin, Teilhard de Chardin, Lovelock and Bateson, Norbert Wiener's mind was not limited to any one way of thinking. While his strict upbringing led to an unreliable temper, this did not prevent him from forming close liaisons with mathematicians, physicists, philosophers, engineers and anthropologists until they broke down. He refused to accept any boundaries for a mind that ranged across all the issues of his time. Wiener consistently proposed solutions to problems that experts in the field did not even recognise as problems until decades later. Not surprisingly, this led to his work being sometimes seen as, and sometimes turning out to be, irrelevant and even wrong. He was the arch-example of the seeker in *The Hitch Hikers Guide to the Galaxy*.[9] While others knew that the answer was 42, Wiener kept asking 'What was the question?'

Wiener was more than successful enough to be recognised as a respected colleague by all the innovative minds of his time. Graduating from Harvard in 1912 he was immediately acclaimed as an outstanding mathematician and philosopher, and accepted as a peer by scholars such as Alfred North Whitehead[10] and Bertrand Russell.[11] He then turned to biology, philosophy, physics and journalism. His contempt for specialisation was clear:

> A man may be a topologist or an acoustician or a coleopterist. He will be filled with the jargon of his field, and will know all its literature and all its ramifications, but, more frequently than not, he will regard the next subject as something belonging to his colleague three doors down the corridor, and will consider any interest in it on his own part as an unwarrantable breach of privacy.[12]

Wiener focused his powerful intellect on the consistencies among the multiple fields he worked in, rather than on their differences. He identified one major consistency that now forms the foundation of all later work on communication systems, and on the Internet in particular. Wiener concluded that communication was the unifying and controlling force in all the non-living and living processes of the planet. He argued that messages necessarily convey orders or instructions that require decisions on action or inaction. Hence all communication is a form of control. All messages are anti-entropic, that is they work to organise the system, and so act against entropy, the ubiquitous disintegrating force of the universe first identified by Newton. Wiener concluded that the human species, having evolved the powerful communication system in cyberspace predicted by Bateson and Teilhard de Chardin, was so powerful that their thinking had become a third dimension to add to the non-living and living dimensions of the planet.

As early as 1940 Wiener set out the rules for the mind-changing personal computer (Box 4.1). He was able to write with considerable modesty of his early vision of the personal computer. Speaking of his foresight of the computer age:

At that stage of the preparations for war [writing in 1940], these ideas did not seem to have sufficiently high priority to make immediate work on them worthwhile … Nevertheless, they have proved useful, and it is my hope that my memorandum had some effect in popularizing them among engineers.[13]

---

### *Box 4.1* **Principles of electronic communication**

1. That the central adding and multiplying apparatus of the computing machine should be numerical, as in an ordinary adding machine, rather than on a basis of measurement, as in the Bush differential analyser.
2. That these mechanisms, which are essentially switching devices, should depend on electronic tubes rather than on gears or mechanical relays, in order to secure quicker action.
3. That, in accordance with the policy adopted in some existing apparatus of the Bell Telephone Laboratories, it would probably be more economical in apparatus to adopt the scale of two for addition and multiplication, rather than the scale of 10.
4. That the entire sequence of operations be laid out on the machine itself so that there should be no human intervention from the time the data were entered until the final results should be taken off, and that all logical decisions necessary for this should be built into the machine itself.
5. That the machine contain an apparatus for the storage of data which should record them quickly, hold them firmly until erasure, read them quickly, erase them quickly, and then be immediately available for the storage of new material.

Source: Norbert Wiener (1948)

---

## Peak

As a starting point for the new world of electronic communication, Wiener successfully transferred electronic signals through the thought processes of the human brain to a robotic artificial limb. Any such artificial extension of the human body is known medically as a prosthesis. Wiener foresaw that a personal computer could become a prosthesis that extends the capacity of the brain of every human being. This form of prosthesis extended the human capacity for thought rather than replacing it. This was at a time when the only computers in existence filled a large room and worked off punch cards.

Later this vision led to a spectacular split between Wiener and a formerly close colleague and equally great mathematician, von Neumann.[14] Von Neumann was pursuing the mathematics of a computer that acted *as* a human brain. He considered that the basic thought process must be step-by-step logic and the ultimate aim was for human control of events. Eventually he designed the first computer language. Wiener was pursuing the potential to expand the capacity of what he regarded as an irreplaceable and unique human brain. In other words, Wiener's idea of the personal computer did not include the computer mimicking the brain, but extending its capacity for creative leaps into new ideas and rich syntheses of diverse information. This far-reaching perspective allowed the creative development of the relational information systems of Google, Facebook and Twitter.

His vision of all communication – physical, social and mental – as double feedback control systems led to Wiener's initiation of the field of cybernetics. He defined cybernetics as the study of governing systems from the simple temperature control of an air-conditioning system to the command systems of a space vehicle. This vision led directly to the then new fields of robotics, neuroscience and the World Wide Web. While robotics has not yet fulfilled its early promise, leaps in understanding for the World Wide Web and the field of neuroscience have had major impacts on the non-living and living worlds. In the groundbreaking Macy Conferences of 1947–53 Wiener was a strong influence on the direction of their thinking about the future. He is on the record as influencing the principles of self-organising systems developed by William Ross Ashby,[15] the therapeutic psychology of Gregory Bateson and the social anthropology of Margaret Mead.[16]

The original principle of a self-organising chaotic system was formulated for cybernetics by Ross Ashby under the influence of Wiener in 1947. The principle holds that any complex system has evolved towards a stable state of equilibrium around some attractor. If destabilised by some external event, the system enters a chaotic state until it meets or creates a new attractor.[17] The system will then reform around that new attractor. This self-organisation applies to subsystems of a larger system as well as the larger system itself. In any complex system this process is going on in all the subsystems, so that the stability of each subsystem depends on the stability of all the others. The change from one system to another is the core of the transformational change. The familiar meteorology paper on the potential for a butterfly wing flapping in Brazil leading to a typhoon in Texas is one example of this self-organising process.[18]

Every complex system, taken as a whole, is made up of interacting subsystems. Taking any particular system as a whole, that system is the outcome of its subsystems having adapted to the environment formed by all the other subsystems. Each subsystem is at the same time a whole in itself. Subsystems are sometimes referred to as holons.[19] In this case all systems are embedded in other systems, and the master systems and the subsystems are all holons. This applies to the expanding universe as well as the smallest sub-atomic particle such as the Higgs-boson particle.[20] Each whole is not only more than the sum of its parts, the interactions between the parts create a whole that is different from the sum of the parts. Because those interactions can be unpredictable, any complex system has a dimension of uncertainty.

Consider, for instance, the role of food in the life of any group of human beings. Personal ideas of what is suitable for eating vary from oats to pig's eyes. The physical growing of the food, the social rituals for how it is eaten, the ethical principles for sharing the food, the aesthetic response to how it is served, the sympathetic feelings from breaking bread together are all equally important subsystems of the meaning of food for that group of people. Even without reflecting on all those subsystems, it is apparent that taken together they make a whole: a shared understanding of the life-support system that is called food. Mapping the feedback mechanisms between human beings, their food supply, cultural traditions, agricultural practices, soil physics and the planet is one example of cybernetics in practice.[21] Such mapping can now include fine details that were impossible before the computer era.

The idea that the dynamics of any subsystem can tend by itself to increase or disrupt the inherent order of the whole system has a long history; Descartes foresaw this characteristic of systems in the seventeenth century.[22] The relationship between any predetermined system and the inevitable occurrence of random events has its own term: a stochastic relationship. All cybernetic systems are stochastic, since all follow a pattern of rules that can never be guaranteed, since accidents will happen. The endless nature versus nurture debate is unnecessary when the relationship is accepted as being stochastic. The interaction that creates each individual is between a predetermined genetic code affected unpredictably by internal events in the DNA program, and unpredictably by external events in the social context. Transformational change is always stochastic: it is the outcome of established systems having been disturbed by an unpredictable change.

One far-reaching effect of Wiener's interest in double feedback loops was to bring to life Pierre Teilhard de Chardin's prediction of evolution through minds-on-minds. In a review of the immense potential of cybernetics for the future of communication in general, *The Human Use of Human Beings*,[23] Wiener yet again saw further into the future than people of his own or even our time. He wrote that since this would be the first time that human minds were evolving directly under the influence of other minds, separated from their physical environment, there would need to be a whole system of ethics to deal with the implications. Seventy years later a spate of court cases, including the WikiLeaks story and hacking by mass-media journalists, fully confirmed Wiener's prediction. In the WikiLeaks events, one individual was able to hack into the confidential diplomatic files of the United States and place them in the public domain. On the one hand, the worldwide reaction was that this was a case of treason and deserved the drastic penalties reserved for that crime. On the other hand, Julian Assange and Adrian Manning, who released the data, were hailed as heroes on a par with freedom fighters and patriots.[24] The debate over the public's right to know entered a new era. The final outcome was unknown at the time of writing.

Since Wiener became famous as a genius so young and in so many fields, there was the time and the interest to reflect on Wiener's own life. Of his many biographers, Pesi Masani[25] identified five elements of the way Wiener's mind worked, thus providing an insight into a collective mind in action. For each of those elements, Wiener demonstrated a different way of thinking about ideas usually treated as opposites. First came Wiener's capacity to absorb the ideas of other brilliant minds, coupled with his capacity to strike out on his own. Other minds can work well with others or develop their own ideas, usually not both together. The second element was his trust in his own deep intuition coupled with commitment to the strictest integrity in collecting objective evidence. Again, this is a marriage of opposites.

Third, he sought physical, social, ethical, aesthetic and sympathetic sources of evidence, while remaining acutely aware that reflection on these multiple aspects of reality was necessary to make up a whole. He considered the symbols of mathematics as aesthetic elements, using them as might an artist. The fourth element was his mental capacity to identify relationships between currently divided pairs, especially when linking social and physical environments. The fifth element of his collective thinking was his constant association of abstract ideas and practical actions, a matter that often seems confusing to other scholars. He claimed, as did Einstein and Leibnitz,[26] that the purest abstraction was the most powerful means of correctly interpreting facts.

Each of the five elements that distinguished Wiener's thinking involved joining together thought processes usually deemed incompatible. These elements are also present in the work of Darwin and Lovelock; very different personalities to Wiener. All three were involved in close knowledge-creating relationships with others, while being willing to think for themselves. Combining faith in their own intuition with a passion for accumulating detail seems to have been also part of their personalities. Going beyond the physical to include social, ethical, aesthetic and sympathetic implications of their ideas is characteristic of the work of all three sorcerers. All three recorded the delight they experienced in formulating new ideas about the structure of reality. The fifth element, recognition that ideas and practice are inseparable, that each has an echo in the other, is equally central in Darwin's, Lovelock's and Wiener's thinking. One is reminded of social psychologist Kurt Lewin's comment 'There is nothing so practical as a good theory'.[27] It seems that Masani's commentary has captured the essence of a collective mind.

## Follow on

Wiener's idea of a cybernetic world was of a world made up of a web of interconnected self-governing communication systems. The patterns of some of the most powerful webs, such as global energy flows, social networks and the spheres of influence of key individuals, were products of the human mind. The capacity of humans to generate ideas that become self-fulfilling prophecies means that there is a reciprocal influence between ideas and what happens in the material world. The inheritance of the Enlightenment gave humankind the physical and mental capacity to follow these webs in practice, and so to influence the non-living and the living dimensions of the planet. Thus, from the 1990s onwards, Wiener's projections on minds evolving under pressures from other minds and influencing, while not controlling, the earth was also being confirmed in practice.[28]

It took only one generation (30 years) to go from the use of the first personal computer as a typewriter and calculator in the 1980s to the social media of Second Life, Facebook and Twitter, facilitated by devices such as the iPad. As usual, at the beginning the old thinking dominated. The new channels were used as information resources, in the same way as the print and radio communication media that preceded them. By the 1970s, Marshall McLuhan had torn down the screen between the old and new media, writing that the medium for a message is also the massage: shaping the meaning of the message itself.[29] He traced human communication through the physical, mental and emotional involvement of speech to the intellectual abstraction of the print and technological era; then came the re-involvement of the emotions through the media of television. He, like Wiener, foresaw the transformation of the human mind through the individual involvement with the personal computer. McLuhan coined the phrase 'the global village' for the worldwide social interconnections of the electronic age.[30]

While McLuhan observed the effect of the new communication media on the human mind, others were exploring the nature of the mind itself. Chilean biologists Humberto Maturana and Francisco Varela[31] developed Wiener's cybernetics into a theory of an embodied mind.[32] As for Darwin and Bateson, their perspective included the human mind in the context of all minds, the more-than-human minds of all living organisms. Maturana and Varela argued that cognition and consciousness need to be considered in relation to the individual's experience as their physical self in their physical environment.[33] They introduced into neuroscience the concepts of 'first person science', in which observers examine their own conscious experience using scientifically verifiable methods. This is the first step in Transformation Science.[34]

The potential for total involvement offered by electronic media has positive and negative effects. Fresh uses of the electronic extension of mind emerge almost daily. Second Life is a program that allows people to adopt a second identity, an avatar that lives a different life in a different setting. To some players their second life in cyberspace can become more real to them than their first life. More and more couples meet in cyberspace. The ability of the few words of a Twitter message to involve the entire world population like a pandemic is reflected in the phrase 'gone viral'. United States president Obama based his successful election campaigns on this capacity of the Web. On the other hand, the perpetrators of the early twenty-first century massacres of young people in Norway[35] and in the United States[36] were all addicted to electronic war games, which some blame for their mindless violence. Children are spending longer playing electronic games and watching TV than they are in school or with their parents.[37]

In 1996, students Larry Page and Sergey Brin invented the first relational database, Google, while working in a friend's garage. Steve Jobs of Apple added sophisticated organisational skills. It was then back to the garage with Mark Zuckerberg of Facebook. The motto of Google 'Don't be evil'[38] was a step towards Wiener's plea for an ethical system governing cyberspace. So was the more technical 'to organize the world's information and make it more universally accessible and useful'.[39] This potentially presumptuous claim has actually been realised. By 2011 there were one billion distinct visits a month to the Google site.

With the expansion of cyberspace voices to most of the world's population there is a counter pressure to return it to the controls of the past. Moves to introduce data streaming and data matching would re-impose boundaries to the increasing openness of access to all information. Such moves, claimed as innovations, could restrict bodies of information to lifestyle marketing or increased specialisation instead of its broad collective possibilities. So far, the efforts of governments and corporations to control the web continue to be resisted by the openness built into the original Internet by the combined universities who set it up.[40] Open source versions of technical programs and the expansion of crowd-sourcing ideas and practices are continuing to keep cyberspace open. However, lawsuits, special interest lobbying, privatisation and narrow technical devices chip away at freedom. The transfer of the search engine Google from its inventor to a commercial enterprise has already changed the opening search screen to a marketing device.

Meanwhile, the designers of software for the broadening Internet platforms Web 2, Web 3 and Web 4 continue to provide fresh potential for new ideas. Wikipedia, the open encyclopaedia, has been evaluated as equally reliable to the classic *Encyclopædia Britannica*, and remains self-funded and crowd-sourced. The networks that feed information into the social media platforms and Wikipedia are in the form of distributed networks, a robust form of networking.[41] Among the myriad examples of distributed systems are food webs, research citations, traffic movements, search engines and the pattern of responses to social media sites. The multiple feedback loops of distributed networks have neither a single centre nor a dominant authority. As part of their self-organisation these networks spontaneously develop between five and twelve nodes at points where systems congregate. Mathematicians who specialise in small worlds calculate that such a distributed system forms the most robust network in responding to external change and the most responsive to internal change (Figure 4.2).

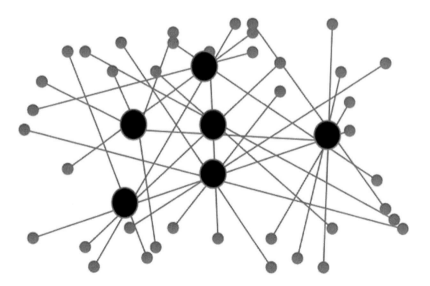

*Figure 4.2* Communication pattern found in computer searches and social media contacts (Adapted from Barabázi 2002)

The studies of networked systems have established that dynamic systems take certain predictable forms. These findings confirm Wiener's proposition that changing the contents of a system would have only a minor effect on its function. Changing the relationships that establish the system can have a major effect. Considering evolutionary change as competition between species creates a system that is starkly different to one based on evolution as collaboration. A collective system includes the dynamics of both competition and collaboration, a negotiated third system, as urged by Gregory Bateson. Transformational change can then be explored as involving all three possibilities, cooperation, competition and negotiation, rather than reduction to any one of these.

## Next

The visionary who brought together the promise of Wiener's prosthesis for the brain, the legacy of the scientific tradition, and the creativity inherent in human thinking is architect-philosopher Christopher Alexander.[42] Born in Austria in 1936, he was educated in England to escape the oppression of the Nazi regime. After earning the first doctorate in architecture ever awarded at Harvard, he went on to criticise other architects severely for failing to include the enriching role of diverse interests in any design for living. Not surprisingly, Alexander is seldom included in lists of eminent architects. He is, however, acknowledged as a founding father of collaborative design in many of the fields that make a difference to how people live. These include computer software programs, town planning, community development and collective social change.

*Figure 4.3* Architect Christopher Alexander in the living room of his Berkeley home, 2002
(© photo by Jerry Telfer/San Francisco Chronicle/Corbis)

Alexander made it his life's work to establish a design language that allowed all those for whom the design is intended to join in creating their own design for living. His aim was to generate synergistic patterns of interaction between humans and all aspects of their environment. His scope included cities, houses, rooms, services, nature parks; anywhere and any way that humans conduct their lives. To quote his own statement on his mission 'towns and buildings will not be able to come alive, unless they are made by all the people in society, and unless these people share a common pattern language, and unless this common pattern language is alive itself'.[43]

'Having life' to Alexander is a wholeness generated from compatibility between the parts of a design, achieved through a shared desire for harmonious order. For a transformational change to have life, it needs to develop a shared focus and strong centres that unfold smoothly into a dynamic design.[44] To achieve this Alexander developed the idea of a pattern language.[45] He and his followers believed that it is the process of creating a shared focus and finding a strong centre that determines the outcome. In other words, as Wiener predicted, the relationships that form a complex system are more influential than any particular content of the system. The principles of a pattern language provided the basis for the relational, open source software designs that became Google, Twitter and Facebook.[46]

A pattern language is not intended to be a recipe or a set of rules. It is a framework with a series of steps, which when taken collectively allows for maximum diversity and conviviality among the participants. A language can act as a medium for prose or for poetry. In prose, each word is expected to have one meaning, and each sentence one idea. In a poem and in a pattern language, each word carries several meanings. Thus each sentence or set of patterns in a pattern language holds an enormous density of interlocking meanings, which illuminate the whole. Patterns, in Alexander's thinking, offer a collage of a fully connected world. Examples are planning for a communal meal (Box 4.2) and for a neighbourhood (Box 4.3). One example is for the social and the other for the physical environment, while both need the answers to all the collective questions.

Including Alexander on the list of visionaries that built on the original work of Darwin, Lovelock and Wiener adds a collective communication tool capable of applying their insights to everyday life. A pattern language is a tool for the collective mind in the sense that it addresses the whole of an issue in a format that draws together the thinking of all those involved. While there is no evidence that Teilhard de Chardin, Bateson and Alexander even knew of each other's work, the three together offer a route into the future with a direction, a set of ideas and a tool capable of carrying those ideas.

From the work of these three master sorcerers and their visionaries, a pattern emerges that foreshadows a trajectory into the future. Applying the pattern language framework, the title of the pattern is 'Towards a collective mind'. The context is a world in a state of transformational change identified by Charles Darwin as evolutionary adaptive change. Pierre Teilhard de Chardin predicted that the next step in human evolution would be towards a collective mind. The evolutionary direction has been strongly influenced by the discoveries of the previous era of

## *Box 4.2* **Pattern language for communal eating**

**Context:** the importance of communal eating is clear in all human societies. Examples include wedding breakfasts, birthday parties, potlatches, Christmas and Thanksgiving dinners, wakes and family evening meals. Communal eating plays a vital part in binding people together, in making them feel part of a group, and giving opportunities to share experiences and resolve differences. In city-based societies it gives opportunities to broaden one's group to include the diversity of ideas, values and experiences.

**Issue:** without communal eating, a group may not stay together.

With the pressures of long working hours, commuting times, diverse activities with no common timetable, and the pull of electronic entertainment, family communal time is reduced. Organisations and interest groups have come to value efficiency over effectiveness and begrudge the time spent on social cohesion.

**Resolution:** make a common meal a regular pleasant event.

Mark off a pleasant place where people eat together. Make a common meal a regular event. Establish a routine where those eating share the preparation and clean up afterward. Make each meal a celebration of some kind. Invite guests and set up a reciprocal relationship.

**Examples:** a research group arranging a common lunchroom, with a common table to share lunch. Known as 'brown bag lunches' there is no compulsion to attend, and no work agenda. Conversation ranges freely outside the formal roles of those participating.

Source: Adapted from *A Pattern Language*. Pattern 147, pp. 696–700

## *Box 4.3* **Pattern language for a neighbourhood**

### A liveable neighbourhood

**Context**: a neighbourhood pattern sits within patterns formed by the mosaic of sub-cultures, the demands of scattered work, the magic of the city and the availability of local transport. People who identify with their neighbourhood have been shown to be healthier, safer, and happier than those who do not.

**Issue:** people need an identifiable spatial unit to belong to.
*Physical evidence:* neighbourhoods that people identify with prove to have small populations, to be small in area, and not crossed by major roads.
*Social evidence:* residents with light traffic: 'everybody knows each other; definitely a friendly street'; 'I feel my home extends to the whole block'.

**Resolution:** help people define and control the neighbourhood they live in.

The neighbourhood should be defined as not more than 300 metres across with no more than 400–500 inhabitants. Encourage local groups to support such neighbourhoods. Give each neighbourhood some degree of autonomy and responsibility. Keep major roads outside of the neighbourhood.

Identify gateways, centres and boundaries. Arrange housing clusters.

**Examples**: the Fuggerei in Augsburg, Germany; Freemantle, Australia.

Source: Adapted from *A Pattern Language*. Pattern 14, pp. 80–85

mind, the scientific Enlightenment. The very success of these discoveries has destabilised the dynamic interdependence between the non-living and living worlds and the human mind, an interdependence established by James Lovelock in the mid-twentieth century. In the last years of the twentieth century, the colonisation of cyberspace predicted by Norbert Wiener started to influence the evolution of the human mind, also affecting the interdependence of the three-dimensional world as described by Gregory Bateson.

At issue is the continuing emphasis on the physical components and the role of experts in the ongoing transformational change. This bias excludes the knowledge held by the community, organisations and key individuals on the options for responding to the change. It also diminishes the contribution of ways of knowing other than the physical, ways of knowing that are crucial for informed decisions on future directions.

The resolution is unclear at the time of writing. An emergent direction is the recognition of the need for a collective mind. This is the direction signalled by forward thinkers Jerome Ravetz as Post-Normal Science, Stephen J. Gould as punctuated equilibrium, Lynn Margulis as a symbiotic planet, and Theodore Roszak as a counter culture (Table 1.1). Following the advice and the examples of this long list of master thinkers, a suite of seven questions was found to access the key elements of the human mind. These seven questions, introspective, physical, social, ethical, aesthetic, sympathetic and reflective, are explored in the chapters that follow.

## Notes

1 Hobsbawm, E. (1994) *Age of Extremes: The Short Twentieth Century 1914-1991*, Michael Joseph, London: Penguin.
2 Kim Phuc, the little nine year old Vietnamese girl running naked from the napalm strike near Trang Bang on 8 June 1972, was shown a million times on American television.
3 It is estimated that the world population reached one billion for the first time in 1804; two billion in 1927 and three billion by 1960. Source: http://en.wikipedia.org/wiki/World_population [accessed 23.4.13].
4 Roszak, T. (1969) *The Making of a Counterculture: Reflections on the Technocratic Society and its Youthful Opposition,* California, US: University of California Press and Roszak, T. (1972) *Where the Wasteland Ends: Politics and Transcendence in Post Industrial Society*, New York: Doubleday.
5 Falk, R. (1999) *Predatory globalization: A critique*, Cambridge, UK: Polity Press.
6 Wiener, N. (1954/50) *The Human Use of Human Beings: Cybernetics and Society,* Boston, US: Da Capo Press. Also the biography: Masani, P. R. (1990) *Norbert Wiener 1894–1964*, Basel, Switzerland: Birkhauser.
7 Masani, P. R. (1990) *Norbert Wiener 1894–1964,* Basel, Switzerland: Birkhauser.
8 This collaborative Second World War research and development project from 1941–46 built and tested the first atomic bombs. It was led by the US with the support of the UK and Canada and administered by General L. R. Groves of the Army Corps of Engineers. The American physicist J. Robert Oppenheimer directed the scientific research. The Manhattan Project changed the course of human history as it led to the dropping of the first atomic bomb on Hiroshima, Japan. *Brighter than a Thousand Suns: A Personal History of the Atomic Scientists* (1958) by Robert Jungk (Boston, US: Houghton Mifflin Harcourt) tells the story of this collaboration.

9 Adams, D. (1979/2005) *The Hitchhiker's Guide to the Galaxy,* London: Picador. It is the film tie-in edition.

10 Alfred North Whitehead (1861–1947) an English mathematician and philosopher. Professor of Applied Mathematics at Imperial College, London (1914–24) and Professor of Philosophy at Harvard University (1924–37).

11 Bertrand Arthur William Russell, 3rd Earl (1872–1970) English philosopher, mathematician, writer and Nobel Prize winner. He wrote *Principia Mathematica* with Alfred North Whitehead (1910–13) that stands as a landmark in the history of logic and mathematics.

12 Wiener, N. (1948) *Cybernetics: Or Control and Communication in the Animal and the Machine*, Massachusetts, US: MIT Press.

13 Ibid.

14 John von Neumann (1903–57) was a Hungarian born American mathematician and polymath. http://www.britannica.com/EBchecked/topic/632750/John-von-Neumann [accessed 9.8.13]. Von Neumann architecture refers to a 1945 computer architecture description by the mathematician and others. See http://en.wikipedia.org/wiki/Von_Neumann_architecture [accessed 9.8.13].

15 W. Ross Ashby (1903–72) was an English psychiatrist, neuroscientist and pioneer of cybernetics. Ashby, W. R. (1954) *Design for a Brain: The Origin of Adaptive Behaviour*, New York: Wiley. He also wrote *Introduction to Cybernetics* (1956) London: Chapman Hall. See http://en.wikipedia.org/wiki/William_Ross_Ashby [accessed 8.8.13].

16 Summary: The Macy Conferences at http://www.asc-cybernetics.org/foundations/history/MacySummary.htm [accessed 25.4.13].

17 In complexity theory an attractor refers to the ability of complex systems to attract a trajectory. A point attractor occurs in systems tending towards a stable equilibrium and a strange attractor for corresponding chaotic systems. There are other attractors as well. See Capra, F. (1996) *The Web of Life: A New Scientific Understanding of Living Systems*, UK: HarperCollins, pp. 131–35 for a concise explanation of attractors and the 'Butterfly Effect'.

18 This 'Butterfly Effect' is introduced in Chapter 3.

19 The writer and philosopher, Arthur Koestler, coined the words holarchy and holon in *The Ghost in the Machine* (1967) London: Arkana. See also Koestler, A. (1978) *Janus: A Summing Up,* Victoria, Australia: Hutchinson of Australia.

20 The Higgs-boson particle (also 'God particle') is thought to be crucial to building the universe.

21 See http://www.globalhealthknowledge.org/content/km4dev-2013-taking-stock-knowledge-management-development [accessed 10.8.13], which is a website of continual discussion on such physical and social interaction in developing countries worldwide.

22 As in Capra, F. (1996) *The Web of Life: A New scientific Understanding of Living Systems*, UK: Harper Collins.

23 Wiener, N. (1950/54) *The Human Use of Human Beings: Cybernetics and Society,* Boston, US: Da Capo Press.

24 See http://en.wikipedia.org/wiki/Bradley_Manning [accessed 9.8.13].

25 Masani, P. R. (1990) *Norbert Wiener 1894–1964*, Basel, Switzerland: Birkhauser.

26 Leibniz, Gottfried Wilhelm (1646–1716) German philosopher and mathematician.

27 Lewin, K. (1951) *Field Theory in Social Science: Selected theoretical papers*, D. Cartwright (ed.), New York: Harper and Row.

28 Tim Berners-Lee had invented the World Wide Web in 1989.

29 McLuhan, M. and Fiore, Q. (1967) *The Medium is the Massage: An Inventory of Effects*, UK: Penguin.

30 McLuhan, M. (1962) *The Gutenberg Galaxy: The Making of Typographic Man*, Canada: University of Toronto Press.

31 Maturana, H. and Varela, F. (1987) *The Tree of Knowledge*, Shambhala, Boston. Maturana, H. and Varela, F. (1980) *Autopoiesis and Cognition*, Dordrecht, Holland:

D. Reidel. Maturana and Varela asked themselves two fundamental questions: 'What is the organisation of the living?' and 'What takes place in the phenomenon of perception?'.

32  Varela, F. J., Thomson, E. and Rosch, E. (1991) *The Embodied Mind: Cognitive Science and Human Experience*, Cambridge, US: MIT Press.

33  A comparison of the theory of cognition by Maturana and Varela with Bateson's criteria of mental process is in Capra, F. (1996) *The Web of Life: A New Scientific Understanding of Living Systems*, UK: HarperCollins, pp. 305–8.

34  Chapter 8.

35  See www.nytimes.com/2011/07/25/world/europe/25oslo.html [accessed 27.4.13].

36  The 14 December 2012 Sandy Hook Elementary School shooting, Newtown, Connecticut: http://en.wikipedia.org/wiki/Sandy_Hook_Elementary_School_shooting [accessed 27.4.13].

37  See, for example, http://www.thedailygreen.com/environmental-news/latest/kids-television-47102701 [accessed 9.8.13].

38  See https://en.wikipedia.org/wiki/Don't_be_evil [accessed 27.4.13].

39  Google's mission as stated on www.google.com.au/about/company/ [accessed 27.4.13].

40  This spirit of openness and collaboration was there at the beginning of the World Wide Web (WWW). Tim Berners-Lee conceived the idea of the WWW by which users could read and write via computers connected to the Internet in 1989. Subsequently, the WWW was established in collaboration with Robert Cailliau at the European Organization for Nuclear Research (CERN) and the decision was made to make Web 3, as it was called, freely available to other users. The first web page was created in 1993. See http://en.wikipedia.org/wiki/History_of_the_World_Wide_Web [accessed 27.4.13].

41  Barabási, A. L. (2002) *Linked: The New Science of Networks*, Cambridge, US: Perseus.

42  Alexander, C. (2002) *The Nature of Order. Book One: The Phenomenon of Life*, Berkeley, US: The Centre for Environmental Structure. Alexander, C. (2002) *The Nature of Order. Book Two: The Process of Creating Life*, Berkeley, US: The Centre for Environmental Structure. Alexander, C. (2003) *The Nature of Order. Book Three: A Vision of a Living World*, Berkeley, US: The Centre for Environmental Structure. Alexander, C. (2005) *The Nature of Order. Book Four: The Luminous Ground*, Berkeley, US: the Centre for Environmental Structure.

43  Alexander, C., Ishikawa, S., Silverstein, M., Jacobson, M., Fiksdahl-King, I. and Angel, S. (1977) *A Pattern Language: Towns, Buildings and Constructions*, New York: Oxford University Press, p. x.

44  Ways to find the focus and the strong centre of an enterprise are explored in Chapter 7.

45  Alexander, C., Ishikawa, S., Silverstein, M., Jacobson, M., Fiksdahl-King, I. and Angel, S. (1977) *A Pattern Language: Towns, Buildings and Constructions*, New York: Oxford University Press.

46  Schümmer, T. and Lukosch, S. (2007) *Patterns for Computer-Mediated Interaction*, Chichester, UK: Wiley & Sons. Kelly, A. (2008) *Changing Software Development: Learning to Become Agile*, Chichester, UK: Wiley & Sons.

# 5 The Herculean mind
## Seven challenging tasks

**Synopsis:** the architects of the current era of transformational change moved beyond the fragmentation of knowledge inherited from the previous era. Between them they pointed the way to repairing the separation of mind and body, parts and wholes, stability and change, individual and collective, rational and creative. A study of the architects of the changes has found that their collective thinking has led them to ask seven questions: introspective, physical, social, ethical, aesthetic, sympathetic and reflective. Answering those questions proves to be a Herculean task requiring a readjustment of the mind from divided to collective thinking.

## Context of the change: living in a three-dimensional world

The question 'What will the future bring?' looms large in times of transformational change. The dynamic changes in the Earth's interconnected physical and social environments make it impossible to predict just what the future will be. However, the thinkers whose ideas initiated the transformational changes in the first place have also given us some ideas about the future. The first step in answering that question is to look in the directions they are pointing. The second step is to learn to apply the transformative thinkers' collective patterns of thought to ourselves and so do our own forward thinking.

A snapshot of the contributions of the master thinkers Darwin, Lovelock and Wiener and visionaries Teilhard de Chardin, Bateson and Alexander offers a baseline from which to start. Darwin thought of the living and non-living dimensions of the planet as constantly shaping and re-shaping each other. The living dimension includes humans as social beings. Human physical and social evolution continues, now shaped by dramatic physical and biological changes wrought by the ideas of those humans. Visionary Teilhard de Chardin predicted that the next giant step in evolution would be the development of a human collective mind in which all human minds were in touch with each other.[1]

James Lovelock went on to identify the way the world works, not as a two-way, but as a three-way self-organising system. He observed the ways in which interconnected feedback loops link living and non-living systems and the human mind. All three of these systems are self-organising and part of an overarching self-organising system. Therefore, while the human mind has become so influential that it makes up a third dimension, it is not in control.[2] Gregory Bateson suggested that human societies survive the threats from changing social and physical environments by creating mediating social structures such as language, science, governance, economics and education. For the future, he suggested that the ability to create collective mediating structures will lead to healthy individuals and flourishing societies.[3]

Norbert Wiener considered that the world could be best understood as governed by a vast communication system of double feedback loops connecting the physical, social and mental worlds. This opened up the arena of cyberspace, the now rapidly expanding zone of connected human minds. In this arena minds interact with other minds independently of their interactions with their physical and social environments. Wiener identified the greatest risk to a human future as the lack of a mediating ethical system that could take into account the collective relationships generated in cyberspace.[4] Christopher Alexander developed guidelines and principles for a pattern language, a human communication system that could help to establish a collective future.[5]

Darwin, Lovelock and Wiener each wrote highly detailed reflective autobiographies that throw light on their thinking. Reading their reflections on their thinking uncovers a consistent pattern. They each organised their minds through seeing the answers to seven questions. Following their examples by learning to explicitly address all seven questions in a world long devoted to accepting only single answers and objective evidence could be considered a Herculean task. The many-skilled Greek hero was given twelve seemingly impossible tasks, while a prospective collective thinker needs to complete only seven. However, some of the tasks have much in common. During one of Hercules' tasks he took the world from Atlas' shoulders onto his own. Many of those facing the task of responding to transformational change also feel as if they carry the world on their shoulders (Figure 5.1).

Another of Hercules' tasks was to clean the Augean stables of huge quantities of waste accumulated over many years. A comparable task is to clear away the streams of misinformation and distortion that block the further development of the new ideas. There is still a tendency to replace the Darwinian web of living organisms with social Darwinism, as if it were a pyramid of competing life forms with humans at the top. There is still a likelihood that the self-organising systems of Gaia are dismissed as metaphysical, that is, as ideas only, when they have now been well documented in practice.[6] The World Wide Web risks being focused on the efficiency of the hardware and on commercial advantage, rather than on fulfilling its promise of connected minds.

Yet another hurdle is the inheritance from the scientific tradition of the organisation of ideas into a neat sequential order. Examples of this are the conventional ladder-like pattern attributed to evolutionary progress, and the organisation of new ideas into a neat historical series. As in the treasure hunt for the future of mind that makes up this book, the story of human evolution has gaps and dead ends. Human ideas can lie fallow and then leap across centuries, cultures and places. Taken together, distortions inherited from a previous transformational era do indeed make up the equivalent of an Augean stable that needs to be cleaned before we are able to interpret the next transformation.

*Figure 5.1* Hercules Farnesse (Wikimedia Commons/Paul Stevenson)

The challenge for those coming after Darwin, Lovelock and Wiener was to absorb the dramatic changes to existing ideas. Between them, the transformative thinkers had reoriented many of the paradoxes in common use. They accepted that body *and* mind are inseparable; everything is both a whole *and* a part; all complex systems are stable *and* dynamic; society is both individuals *and* the group; and human thought is both creative *and* rational. Treated as paradoxes, these were placed in opposition to one another.[7] Bateson's mediating social structures had therefore become adversarial. Specialised languages had divided potential collaborators; science had become the knowledge of the few; patriarchal governance had privileged the individual. The individual had withdrawn from the group.

In a collective society, the paradoxes dissolve. The social structures of language, science, democracy, finance and education are then built on connections not competition. Thus a system of governance can become a web of supporting relationships rather than a hierarchy of different layers of control. As discussed in Part II, collective social structures already in place include pattern languages, Transformation Science, direct democracy, common pool economics and open education. There is a choice. Relationships between parts and wholes, stability and change, the individual and the collective, and creativity and rationality can be either cooperative or competitive according to the ideas, behaviours and rituals that a society has laid down.

In trying to influence transformational change it is important to recognise that re-connecting the paradoxes and the next step, asking seven collective questions, are matters of common sense and everyday experience. The strength of the connections is demonstrated in everyday practice. It is the connections, not the oppositions, that form the basis for a creative mind and an adaptive society. Negotiations between opposites become one core concern in responding to the opportunities of transformational change. Reflecting on how to combine the answers to a collective set of questions is the other concern.

## Lead-up to the change: asking collective questions

The seven questions that need to be asked when taking account of transformational change fall into two groups. Five outward-directed questions are concerned with the issue or event under examination. Two of the questions are inwardly directed, questions the inquirer asks of themselves (Table 5.1). In the case of the master thinkers, the first of these inward-directed questions was introspective, that is, they questioned their assumptions on the issue and their reason for asking the questions in the first place. The second is the reflective question, the central question that calls on all the learning from the others, the question which takes account of their answers to all of the rest.

In between the introspective and the reflective questions come five questions that address the key elements that make up transformational change. They act as reality checks. Asking physical, social, ethical, aesthetic and sympathetic questions about an issue or event gives a basis for a collective understanding of the whole (Table 5.1). These ways of understanding have also been identified in other contexts as multiple intelligences, knowledge domains and knowledge cultures.[8]

*Table 5.1* Collective thinking: seven questions and seven sources of answers

| Type of question | Sources of answers |
|---|---|
| *Outward-looking questions (from the inside out)* | |
| physical: | observations, measurements and descriptions |
| social: | narratives, norms, rules, myths and symbols |
| ethical: | ideals, principles, aims, standards of good and evil |
| aesthetic: | designs, visions, standards of beauty and ugliness |
| sympathetic: | feelings, relationships, trust, sense of the other |
| *Inward-looking questions (from the outside in)* | |
| introspective: | personal assumptions, experience, identity |
| reflective: | creative leap, pattern language, distributed networks, dialogue |

Philosophers, psychologists, anthropologists and sociologists of knowledge have written extensively on the forms of knowledge that can answer each of the collective questions; each separately from within their own specialist silos. One task of a collective mind is to open up the silos in which the elements that make up collective knowledge have been stored. One way to begin is through the thinkers who have led the way in answering each of the five reality-check questions on various topics (Table 5.2). Another is by bringing together specialists in each of the five fields who are willing to listen to each other in a dialogue. The crucial step is to choose a key issue and apply the questions afresh (Box 5.2).

*Table 5.2* Specialists who are collective thinkers

| Specialised field | Commentators on the whole * | Core theme |
|---|---|---|
| *Outward-looking questions* | | |
| physical: | Stephen J. Gould, James Watson | evolutionary change |
| social: | Thomas Berry, Jane Jacobs | power of community |
| ethical: | Isaiah Berlin, Pierre Teilhard de Chardin | responsibility for others |
| aesthetic: | Arthur Koestler, Mary Midgley | human creativity |
| sympathetic: | Martin Buber, Howard Gardner | feelings for others |
| *Inward-looking questions* | | |
| introspective: | Paul Sartre, Michael Polanyi | the self |
| reflective: | Christopher Alexander, Gregory Bateson | collective mind |

*Web search engines have comprehensive accounts of each of these significant thinkers.

There is a risk that the treatment of the seven questions could be seen as a list or a grid, a hazard left over from the compartmentalised thinking inherited from the previous era. This is far from the case. Each question subsumes all the other questions in a seamless web. The need for the final inward reflection suggests that there is something in the structure of a human mind that requires identification of the parts as independent wholes as one step in understanding the collective. This is a mental device and not a reflection of how the real world actually exists.[9] Further, the questions are about how reality is constructed, not merely about perception or awareness. It is about how we believe things to be. We might ask where feelings fit? Feelings, thinking and actions are implicit in all of them: combining the head, the heart and the hand; remembering that everything is a part and a whole at the same time.

## Peak

Accepting the Herculean task, it is important to examine each of the suite of collective questions in their own light, before considering the most difficult task of all: ways to bring together the answers to reflective questions in a fragmented world. This challenging task is left to Chapter 6. In this chapter we explore introspective, physical, social, ethical, aesthetic and sympathetic questions. The collective understanding reached by answering the full set of questions applies to both the individual who asks them all for themselves, and a group that divides up the questions and connects them at the end. The result in either case resembles an artistic collage, not a jigsaw puzzle figure. As outlined in Table 5.1, outward-directed questions, physical, social, ethical, aesthetic and sympathetic can already refer to an expansive body of knowledge.

### Introspective questions

Before attempting to interpret transformational change, the inquirer needs to examine the foundations of their own thinking by asking introspective questions. They could ask themselves whether they are justifying their own conclusions, open to new ideas, or sitting on the fence. Adopting the reoriented paradoxes is a necessary position to take, since between them they sum up the core of the twenty-first century transformational change.[10]

The three transformative thinkers continually questioned their own position on the changes they initiated. Darwin refused to accept the limitations of a single course of study, a traditional profession or knowledge residing in formal institutions. His biggest challenge was whether natural selection was a part of an external reality, determined by God, or by chance? He settled for external reality. Lovelock as an industrial chemist had great respect for the practice of science, and at first would only consider physical evidence. Fellow scientists' early rejection of his findings on Gaia made him sensitive to the social and sympathetic dimensions of the practice of science. Wiener's solitary upbringing and mathematical genius isolated him from many social relationships. He foresaw a social environment that was purely mind on mind, to be made possible by a digital communication system that did not then exist.

Everyone begins a fresh enterprise from some established position. They will have predetermined experience and ideas arising from their gender, social role, cultural background and personality. They may be pessimistic or optimistic about the future. They may be trusting or suspicious of their fellow human beings. Together all these considerations make up the identity of the thinker. In addressing transformational change, all of these need to be suspended, at least temporarily, since they may all change with the changes. So whether the thinker perceives themselves primarily as separate individuals or primarily as part of humanity will be extremely influential in their approach to addressing transformation.

### Physical questions

Physical questions are questions asked about the material world, and answered from observations and direct experience. Evidence is gathered from what can be seen, heard, touched, smelled, tasted or felt; or by instruments that feed into those senses. Often this is called an empirical way of knowing, where 'empirical' means the answer is tested by one of the senses. Everyone's life is oriented by the answers to empirical questions: 'What happened?', 'Who are you?' or 'What is that?'. The answers are so absorbed into each person's thinking and so shaped by society, that it can be hard for people to realise that physical reality itself is negotiable.

In a Western culture, the reference point for 'Where am I?' is the compass: north, south, east and west. Personal physical orientation is determined from a street grid, the position of the sun, a compass and memory. In the growing number of large cities, a personal sense of position in the world can be referenced solely to the built environment, independently of the actual landscape. In Indonesian Bali, there are five reference points: north, south, east and west and a fifth, the sacred mountain at the centre of their island. All its inhabitants can visually and spiritually orientate themselves to the same point at all times.

Another example of a different physical reference point is the story of a Nepalese guide visiting a Western city. Except for a pagoda, he had never seen a building higher than two stories, much less a lift, a road wider than single track, or a shop of any kind. Asked how many new things he had seen, he replied 'Thirty'. On enquiry, his list was not made up of Western technical miracles; the items that had constructed his new world were unfamiliar animals and birds. These formed the basis of his physical world.

At the other extreme from the individual perception of physical reality is the highly skilled use of technical tools and devices. Images created by the electron microscope, ultrasound and Global Information Systems (GIS) are accepted as accurate representations of the real world. In a wide range of technical professions, these observations become the dominant reality, which leads to the need for a reality check on the ground; whole mountains have been found to be in the wrong place. A more humble and reliable approach to asking a question about a physical reality is to accept that the answer must always be incomplete, biased towards the observer, and temporary in a changing world.

### Social questions

Social questions involve asking of a society 'How do you manage your resources?', 'Establish your shared sense of being?', 'Design the mediating structures of law, medicine and education?'. When posed from outside the community as empirical questions, these questions can be answered by any of the social sciences: economics, sociology, anthropology and political science. However useful and reliable those answers may be, they remain restricted to answers based on observations from within an external framework. The expert answers then mask the lived experience of the community. Each human group has its own form of language made up of the words, images, metaphors, behaviours and beliefs that embody the communal image of reality and confirm their place in it. Answers to social questions will necessarily be in the language of that society, so that sensitivity to translation is also needed as in the case of Canberra[11] (Box 5.1).

### Ethical questions

Ethical questions take the form of 'How should we live with each other?', 'How should we share resources?' or 'Help others in need or live up to our own ideals?'. All human societies construct a complex network of rules for living together. All apply sanctions to those who transgress their ethical guidelines, whether explicit as laws or implicit as customs. These may or may not be incorporated into the fixed social rules. For instance adultery is generally regarded in Western societies as immoral, accepted as part of a wifely duty in parts of the South Pacific, while in Afghanistan law transgressors are stoned.

Ethical goals are ideals, derived from notions of honesty, justice, security, human dignity, independence and the right to spiritual fulfilment. They may be far removed from being realised, while keeping open the possibility that human lives can be better than they are. Abraham Lincoln called on 'the better angels of our nature'[12] to meet ethical goals. Liberty and equality are among the primary goals pursued by human beings over the centuries. Yet absolute liberty for the rich and powerful is not compatible with the rights to a decent existence of those with limited resources.[13]

One of the eternal visions for humanity as a whole is of arriving at a single ethical system to which everyone willingly subscribes. For centuries this vision has been common to the spiritual traditions of Buddhism, Islam, Hinduism and Christianity. Around the planet in recent centuries has been the promise of democracy.[14] Ethical principles for relationships between people require assent within the society in which they arise (a social question), realistic descriptions of the context in which they will be answered (a physical question), sensitivity to the feelings of the people involved (a sympathetic question), a hope for the answer to be inspiring and creative (an aesthetic question), and limited by the assumptions of the individuals charged with making the decision (an introspective question).

## Box 5.1  Answering social questions: stories of a city

Canberra, the capital city of Australia, is a planned city set down on a grassy limestone plain, deliberately separated from Australia's large commercial cities. To a visitor, a demographer and an urban planner this is a political, public service and university town, with the usual commercial centres of a large town and few commercial resources. The visitor may wonder at the lack of high-rise buildings and traffic jams, but would probably put that down to the small population of only 380,000 people.

The people who live there tell their own story. Internally, Canberra is thought of as a bush capital with a proud population protective of their ready access to public education and the surrounding natural bush. Planning laws forbid building profiles obscuring the surrounding hills. The abundance of national institutions, universities with extensive international expertise, organisational lobby groups and the public service executive makes Canberra a powerful knowledge-based city. The enveloping bush gives it its soul.

Lewis Mumford* used metaphors to suggest that all settlements from the simplest to the most complex are formed by establishing three features: somewhere to safeguard and store resources (a granary); a place of safety and protection for the citizens from local dangers (a palace); a gathering place that symbolises the most deeply valued beliefs (a temple). In a study of the citizens' understanding of Canberra, the granary was the public service departments, the research institutions and the Federal Treasury; the temple was the National Library, the Science and Technology Centre and the commercial centre; and the palace, Parliament House and the High Court.

Another initiative based on public dialogue produced the following results for the different ways of knowing Canberra:

- Physical: Canberra as a safe, healthy physical environment;
- Social: with many social rituals and celebrations and places of learning;
- Ethical: with ethical commitment to equity in housing, health services and peace;
- Aesthetic: its own music, dance, painting, sculpture, gardening, urban design;
- Sympathetic: small enough to share sympathy with neighbours, colleagues, family.

There are many Canberras.

*Mumford, L. (1961) *The City in History: its origins,
its transformations and its prospects*, New York: Harcourt, Brace & World.

### Aesthetic questions

Aesthetic questions may be dismissed as 'I know what I like' without any further thought. Yet the questions reach much deeper than that. The answers to 'Is this beautiful? Ugly? Inspiring? Disgusting?' are at once a biophysical sensation, a social construction, an ethical signal of what is valued and a deeply personal experience. Oscar Wilde,[15] for whom the generation of beauty for beauty's sake was the foundation of life itself, wrote 'Aesthetics is a search after the signs of the beautiful ... It is, to speak more exactly, the search after the secret of life'. His declared ambition was to live his life as a work of art.

A person, an action, a house, a symphony, a fragrance, a decision, a story, a painting, a piece of writing, an experiment and a mathematical proof can all be called beautiful. What characteristics do they share which give them that status? Arthur Koestler[16] suggested that an aesthetic question is inherently about the shock of the new, about the leap into the unknown. In transformational change, the stresses would become unbearable without the capacity to make that imaginative leap. Koestler provided a quick *aide-memoir* of the springboards for creativity, awe, discovery and humour: 'aaah, aha, and haha'. All three use the unfamiliar and the shock of surprise to produce an emotional release in the receiver. On the other hand, the intensely familiar also gives a strong emotional response, one that influences all human actions.

From the poets come the aesthetic senses of satisfaction from revealing the essence, the essentials of an idea. From Keats' '"Beauty is truth, truth beauty", – that is all Ye know on earth, and all ye need to know'.[17] And from Yeats: 'How can we tell the dancer from the dance?'.[18] Taken in all its forms, the aesthetic sense, the recognition of beauty and ugliness is part of the human condition and serves as an essential avenue for interpreting and facilitating transformational change.

### Sympathetic questions

A question often asked about sympathetic questions is how they differ from social questions. Social questions are asked about how people act in groups. Sympathetic questions explore the deep sense of understanding that develops within an individual, between individuals, between a human being and other living things, and between a human being and a special place. Jewish philosopher Martin Buber[19] explored the significance of the old English language distinction between 'you' and 'thou'. 'I and thou' refers to a deeper sympathy than 'You and I' or even 'We'. The feeling of sympathy may go even deeper and become empathy: that is, 'feeling as' the other. Sympathetic questions can only be answered through an emotional connection to the people involved.

A dimension shared by our collective thinkers is that they were each a notable loner and yet worked extremely closely with their colleagues and subjects. McClintock's Nobel Prize-winning genetic program was derived from her thinking like a gene.[20] Darwin's sand walk on his estate at Downe was the basis for his daily communion with nature. Aldo Leopold, in his *Sand Country Almanac*, entered into the spirit of the land through what he called 'Thinking like a mountain'.[21] Jane Jacobs as a sociologist,[22] and Wendell Berry as a countryman,[23] both identified closely with their communities.

A news story presents the strength of this human capacity for mutual understanding, even between strangers and even without words. In 2005, the *Daily Telegraph* reported on a fire on the fifteenth floor of a London apartment building. Desperate people could be seen clustered at the windows, hoping desperately for rescue. A watcher below saw the fire and smoke burst into the room, and people begin to jump – from such a height, to their certain deaths. A woman holding a baby came to the window, as if to jump. A man joined her and took the baby, obviously scanning the street below. His gaze locked into that of a bystander. Something invisible passed between them, and the man threw the child directly at this perfect stranger, whose upraised arms caught it safely as the flames engulfed its parents. For one minute, silently, two strangers had become one.

### Reflective questions

The ability to reflect on an event or issue, and then to reflect on one's own reflections, appears to be solely a human ability. Many mammals can do the first. It seems that only humans can then reflect on their reflections and so take part in a deeper learning in which they can change what they think. Such deeper learning is called by educators triple loop learning;[24] by sociologists and philosophers reflexive thinking;[25] and by Parker Palmer thinking with the heart.[26] The question here is 'What does this all mean?'.

Reflection on the answers to each of the five reality-check questions includes access to specialised information bases developed during the scientific era. Each of the ways of knowing, physical, social, ethical, aesthetic and sympathetic, has a classification in the library reference system, contributing disciplines and a community of practice. Access to rich information sources for answering the reality-check questions is not an issue. The problem for the would-be collective mind is that the specialised language and the closed specialists' doors for answering each form of question make the information effectively inaccessible. An antidote is to draw on the work of specialists who write from a holistic and collective perspective. There is a list of such resources in Table 5.2.

The greatest level of difficulty comes at the last step: bringing together all the answers to the questions on the selected issue. The difficulty in answering the reflective questions is that, after centuries of concentrating on analysis, the present era is only just beginning developing tools and structures for synthesis. A range of tools is presented in Chapter 6, and Chapters 7 to 12 examine societal structures.

## Follow on

Reflecting on the suite of collective questions opens our minds to fresh possibilities, extremely important for responding to transformational change. The constructive synergy from including all the answers is not created simply by reaching some agreement. Synergy is a fresh understanding generated by the interaction among the questions.

Each of the seven questions is both distinct in itself and a part of the collective understanding. The tension between these ideas is created by the web of feedback loops. Both the inwardly and outwardly directed questions may be initiated by an individual or by a group. However, the individual will need to take full account of the ideas of the community they belong to, and the group will equally need to take full account of the diverse ideas of the individuals that make up the community. Take an example that is concerning the world: human-created climate change (Box 5.2).

This Herculean task begins with considering the perspective you presently hold. This may be personal sympathy with the deniers, the distorters, the disciples, or another position altogether. The important thing is to ask inwardly directed questions that allow you to position yourself in the world of the time. In Box 5.2 a snapshot of the risks to humanity posed by climate change is coupled with the potential collective responses. The outline of the situation as of 2013 is that the modelling of physical risks is becoming more and more accurate and detailed. Social responses have become more sharply divided. Social risks arise from physical risks and hence where there is denial there is no political imperative to act.

---

### Box 5.2  Asking collective questions on an issue: climate change

**Focus question**: given the expected risks to human and the planet's health from climate change, what does it all mean for the future?

**Outward-directed questions**
*Biophysical:*
Risk: 20–50 years to severe heat stress, sea level rise.
Collective response: reduce $CO_2$ by putting a price on carbon, adaptation.
*Social:*
Risk: denial, hostility, fatalism.
Collective response: advocacy, education, policy, enforcement.
*Ethical:*
Risk: primary value: humanity and self, not nature.
Collective response: primary value: relationship between all three.
*Aesthetic:*
Risk: beauty in either humanity or self or nature.
Collective response: beauty in the synergy among all three.
*Sympathetic:*
Risks: identity restricted to own human groups.
Collective response: identity with nature.

**Inward-directed questions**
*Introspective:*
Risks: bias from one's own assumptions, values, experience and education.
Collective response: suspend judgment, open mind, listen to others.
*Reflective:*
Risks: failure to achieve collective interpretation among whole society.*
Collective response: develop connected personal and societal responses worldwide.

*This was ably expressed by Barack Obama in his second inaugural presidential address 'We cannot mistake absolutism for principle, or substitute spectacle for politics, or treat name-calling as reasoned debate. We must act. We must act, knowing that our work will be imperfect'.

Ethical risks include failing to accept responsibility for the environment as a principle of the human ethical system.[27] The aesthetic risk lies in the changing experience of generations that have lived urban lives without needing to consider natural systems. Sympathetic risks lie in humans identifying only with similar humans and being unable to identify with other humans and with other living things. A serious risk is that this excludes the synergistic three-dimensional world of the non-living, living and human mind adopted by Teilhard de Chardin, Bateson and Alexander. The reflective questions ensure that the inquirer and others involved are aware of each other's positions and the wide range of possibilities, rather than being locked into single prescriptive answers.

For each of the five questions that add up to the construction of reality, long-established answers can be found in any cultural tradition, including specialist traditions. Scientists answer scientific questions and ask questions with physical answers. Philosophers ask philosophical questions and answer them from their minds. Modes of reflection on all of them together have come and gone through the ages. Each of the religious traditions brings the answers together in their own way, forming their own collective thinking tradition. The ancient Greeks with Socratic dialogue, the Europeans with the Renaissance and Western thought with the Enlightenment were all centres of collective thought.

The present transformational era of the Anthropocene is the first in which the human mind itself is the lever for the transformation. It is the first in which the Earth has been recognised as Gaia, an independent self-organising entity. It is also the first in which the human mind has created a realm of its own, cyberspace.

## Next

What then of the future? Let's take the positive view. Teilhard de Chardin's vision of the next stage of human evolution is the power and wisdom of a collective mind. Gregory Bateson's vision is of humans able to access their more-than-conscious minds of imagination, intuition and empathy, as well as their conscious minds. Christopher Alexander's grand design is for a universal pattern language harnessing the full richness of the diversity of human thought. The next chapter explores how we can achieve these visions of collective thought against the background of the reconnected paradoxes: parts and wholes; stable and random systems; individuals and society; rational and creative minds.

## Notes

1 In *The Phenomenon of Man* Teilhard de Chardin (1975/1955, New York: Harper & Row) describes the evolution of the Noosphere as a new sphere of human consciousness that is worldwide.
2 Gregory Bateson coined the phrase 'the pattern that connects', which refers to the way mind and nature form a unity. Bateson, G. (1979) *Mind and Nature: A Necessary Unity,* London: Wildwood House.
3 Bateson, G. (1958) *Naven: a Survey of the Problems Suggested by a Composite Picture of the Culture of a New Guinea Tribe Drawn from Three Points of View,* 2nd edn, Stanford, US: Stanford University Press. Bateson, G. (1973) *Steps to an Ecology of*

*Mind: Collected Essays in Anthropology, Psychiatry, Evolution and Epistemology*, St Albans, UK: Paladin. (Part 11: Form and pathology in relationship).

4   Wiener, N. (1954/50) *The Human Use of Human Beings: Cybernetics and Society*, Boston, US: Da Capo Press.

5   Alexander, C., Ishikawa, S., Silverstein, M., Jacobson, M., Fiksdahl-King, I. and Angel, S. (1977) *A Pattern Language: Towns, Buildings and Constructions,* New York: Oxford University Press.

6   Schneider, S. H., Miller, J. R., Crist, E. and Boston, P. J. (2004) (eds) *Scientists Debate Gaia: The Next Century*, Cambridge, Massachusetts, US: MIT Press.

7   Discussed further in Chapter 6.

8   See Gardner, H. (1993) *Multiple Intelligences: The Theory in Practice*, New York: Basic Books. For knowledge domains and knowledge cultures see, respectively, Ison, R. L. and Russell, D. B. (2000) *Agricultural Extension and Rural Development: Breaking Out of Traditions*, Cambridge, UK: Cambridge University Press and Brown, V. A. (2008) *Leonardo's Vision: A Guide to Collective Thinking and Action*, Rotterdam, Netherlands: Sense.

9   The US psychologist, Jerome Bruner, discussed how our evolution as a species has specialised us into certain characteristics of knowing, thinking, feeling and perceiving in Bruner, J. (1996) *The Culture of Education*, Cambridge, Massachusetts, US: Harvard University Press, pp. 15–19.

10   Chapter 6.

11   Canberra is the National Capital of Australia and three and a half hours by road from Sydney. See http://en.wikipedia.org/wiki/Demographics_of_Canberra [accessed 13.8.13].

12   The last words of Abraham Lincoln's First Inaugural Address as American President, 4 March 1861. Bartleby.com, http://www.bartleby.com/124/pres31.html [accessed 9.3.13].

13   Mill, J. S. (2002/1859) *On Liberty*, New York: Dover Publications.

14   Chapter 9.

15   See article by Brown, S. (2000) 'Oscar Wilde's Rise to Fame', The British Library: http://www.mr-oscar-wilde.de/interactive/paper/rise_to_fame.html [accessed 9.5.13].

16   Koestler, A. (1964/1989) *The Act of Creation*, London: Arkana.

17   The final two lines to John Keats' poem, 'Ode on a Grecian Urn', published in 1820.

18   The last line of William Butler Yeats' poem, 'Among School Children' (from *The Tower*, 1928).

19   Buber, M. (1958) (2000) *I and Thou,* 2nd edn, (Tr. Ronald Gregor Smith), New York: Scribner Classics.

20   Keller, E. F. (1983) *A Feeling for the Organism: The Life and Work of Barbara McClintock,* New York: Freeman.

21   Leopold, A. (1949) (1981) *A Sand County Almanac and Sketches Here and There*, London: Oxford University Press, p. 129.

22   Jacobs, J. (1972) *The Death and Life of Great American Cities*, Harmondsworth: Penguin.

23   Wendell Berry is a US farmer, writer, activist and academic living on a farm in Kentucky where he devotes his attention to the wellbeing of his family, community and the Earth. Berry, W. (1977) *The Unsettling of America: Culture & Agriculture*, San Francisco, US: Sierra Club Books. See also http://en.wikipedia.org/wiki/Wendell_Berry [accessed 31.7.13].

24   Triple loop learning integrates the context of learning. See also http://infed.org/mobi/chris-argyris-theories-of-action-double-loop-learning-and-organizational-learning/ [accessed 12.8.13]. See also Schon, D. (1987) *Educating the Reflective Practitioner*, San Francisco, US: Jossey-Bass.

25   Pels, D. (2003) *Unhastening Science: Autonomy and Reflexivity in the Social Theory of Knowledge*, Liverpool, UK: Liverpool University Press.

26   Palmer, Parker J. and A. Zajonc with Megan Scribner (2010) *The Heart of Higher Education: A Call for Renewal*, San Francisco, US: Jossey-Bass.

27   The United Nations Earth Charter generated by global consensus declares the fundamental values and principles are to build a just, sustainable and peaceful world. http://www.earthcharterinaction.org/content/pages/read_the_charter.htm [accessed 9.5.13].

# 6  The collective mind

## Asking reflective questions

**Synopsis:** seven collective questions are needed to interpret transformational change. The process is begun by questioning existing assumptions and completed by asking reflective questions on the whole of the evidence. In between the inquirer asks five reality-check questions. This process requires the collective thinker to hold past, present and future constructions of knowledge in their mind. If the resultant synthesis is to influence the future, it needs to incorporate the changes introduced by leading transformative thinkers. These include changes in the relationships between parts and wholes, chaos and self-organising systems, individuals and society; and conscious and more-than-conscious minds. Reflection on these changes introduces a third space, a new knowledge landscape and sense of direction.

## The context of change: changing one's mind

In responding to transformational change, we find that we are dealing simultaneously with knowledge constructions of the past, the present and the future. In the past, knowledge has been divided into neat parcels called disciplines with their own language, frameworks and content.[1] Currently there is an increasingly broader acceptance of knowledge as constructed by other ways of knowing as well as the disciplines.[2] However, these ways of knowing are still compartmentalised into individual, community, specialised, strategic and creative contributions to knowledge and treated separately, as if they are independent of one another.[3]

A collective future requires that people find ways to work together if they are going to influence the ongoing transformational change. They will also need to reconsider the paradoxes of the past, reoriented from polarised to connected by the transformative thinkers discussed in Chapters 1–4. The long-established divisions between parts and wholes, stability and change, individuals and society, and creative and rational thinking have been reformulated as relationships. Each of these relationships has formed a third space and that space is one of the drivers for transformational change.

In the exploration of transformational change so far, we have found that whether we look to the past, the present or the future, there is a regular pattern underlying the construction of knowledge.[4] Underlying the individual's thinking in the past and the present and presumably into the future is the human capacity to ask the suite of seven questions, often only asked implicitly and automatically.

In the previous chapter we have suggested that these questions need to be asked explicitly if we are to influence transformational change. In exploring these questions in Chapter 5 it became clear that they are constantly in use. Their full use is often hidden because of the custom of only one type of question being brought into consciousness at a time, and the power hierarchy which privileges some questions over others. The first of the collective questions is about the assumptions of the inquiry. Our assumption in this chapter is that fresh thinking about the relationships between parts and wholes, stability and change, individuals and society, and creative and rational thinking is crucial in working with the current transformational change.

## The peak of the change

The reorientation of the paradoxes in the thinker's mind needs to be taken into account in the reality-check questions that follow, that is, questions on the physical, social, ethical, aesthetic and sympathetic elements of the issue. During the Enlightenment the paradoxes had been set up as opposite poles, as if it was parts *or* wholes, individuals *or* society. As in any paradox, the implication is that one can only consider one *or* the other of the pair. Thanks to the transformative thinkers, each of these relationships is now being considered as the interacting parts of a whole. Collective thinking provides a means of escape from the old dividing paradoxes, while still including the valuable understanding of each of the parts inherited from the Enlightenment. As Gregory Bateson predicted, treating the connections as relationships creates a third space; another dimension of reality, not a continuum between opposites. This third space cannot be negotiated by continuing in an oppositional mode.

It is the seventh, reflective question that provides the crucible in which the answers to personal reflections and the five reality-check questions come together in a constructive synergy. Before addressing reality-check questions on any issue, a collective thinker will have considered their own position on the chosen theme, be it climate change, nuclear power or population control. As inheritors of the Enlightenment era, the collective thinker needs to consider the bias imposed by previous specialist training and whether the single goal of objectivity has framed their expectation of the topic.

As a human being, everyone has access to a powerful rationality and a transcending creativity. Once they have responded to the reality-check questions that together convey the whole of the situation, that is the physical, social, ethical, aesthetic and sympathetic questions, they have a wide canvas on which to reflect. The reflective questions then assemble the diverse information available into a collage. This is an imaginative leap that releases the synergy created by connecting the diverse ideas.

There are many paths to the take-off point for that leap. An imaginative leap may come immediately or some years after a new experience. Darwin's connection between the shape of finch's beaks and their food sources in the Galapagos Islands was made many years after leaving the islands. The leap may follow unexpectedly from many careful observations, as in Lovelock's sudden recognition that the planet Earth is a self-organising system. It may be made through thought experiments, such as Wiener's prediction of a worldwide web linking electronic signals and human brains. It may be in dreams, as in Wallace's 'dream' of evolutionary processes through natural selection during a bout of malaria,[5] and Kekule's dream of the structure of the benzene molecule as a ring of carbon atoms looking like a snake with its tail in its mouth.[6]

It is worth repeating that putting together diverse ideas in order to answer a reflective question is often wrongly described as completing a jigsaw puzzle. Nothing could be further from the case. A jigsaw puzzle recreates an existing picture in which all the pieces are predetermined and fit neatly together. What is needed is a way of making sense of pieces that make up a fresh picture and do not fit some pre-existing pattern. Seeking a synergy from multiple answers is more like creating an artistic collage. In a collage the pieces are still recognisable as wholes, as they overlap and inform each other. The resultant synergy conveys a fresh imaginative interpretation of the whole. The metaphor of a collage lies behind the following explorations of each of the reformed paradoxes.

### Parts and wholes

Everything in a system is both a part and a whole. In the Enlightenment science tradition that concentrated on parts rather than wholes, anything that appeared in two forms was treated as two separate realities. In reality this is purely a device, since for pairs such as man/woman, old/young, past/future, east/west, knowledge/ ignorance, individual/group, plants/animals, night/day, sick/healthy, citizen/ outcast, mind/matter it is not possible to have the idea of one without implicitly invoking the other. There can be no old without young, north without south, or knowledge without ignorance.

In moving to collective thinking, the entire list of antonyms in the thesaurus can be re-read as a list of relationships rather than opposites. To paraphrase Bateson, reflection on the patterns that connect is more important than concentrating on the differences that divide. It is not enough simply to mark the importance of the separate poles. That would not advance collective thinking any further. Bateson suggested that without that mediated third space, neither individuals nor societies would be able to function at all, since life would be polarised into conflicting extremes. George Kelly in his Personal Construct Theory described how the relationship between two opposite poles is seldom a continuum, much less a negotiated compromise.[7] For instance the third space between old and young is life as a citizen. Negotiations between war and peace have generated the United Nations and the defence policies of all major nations. The third space between love and hate can be many things: apathy, contempt, denial.

The third space is an important negotiating device that links parts and wholes in general. General Systems Theory[8] holds that every part is a whole in itself with its own internal feedback loops, and at the same time is part of a whole created by another system of feedback loops. For instance, the living cell has been long regarded as the single unit of life. Thanks to the work on the cell by Lynn Margulis, it is now known that the parts have their own independent existence. The nucleus is the headquarters, the ribosomes are the energy factories, and the bounding membrane is a system of gates, and all are independent wholes in their own right, with their own internal feedback loops. The so-called unit of life would not exist without these self-organising parts, making the whole we call the cell.[9]

Moving in the other direction, as cells join together, say in the human embryo, each cell contains the full blueprint for a final whole, the human adult. As cells divide to form the whole, they remain in control of their own feedback systems *and* in contact with each other's. Thus the first two or three divisions can produce fully formed twins or triplets. As the cells divide they assign different tasks to each other so that cells become eyes and kidneys. The two organs are still tightly connected in the adult. The technical capability to be able to take one cell with its whole program and stimulate it chemically to turn into the whole is now routine laboratory procedure, except for ethically forbidden human cloning. Stem cells from the peripheral blood of a donor can wholly replace bone marrow cells in treating leukaemia;[10] tissue from an almost extinct pine tree can create a contemporary forest.[11] The shift to accepting that each living cell is a part and a whole at the same time has coupled collective thinking with scientific studies to enable these apparent miracles.

In changing from examining parts to reflecting on wholes, the changes in thinking are so distinctive that they need to be recognised in the use of language. The English language divides thinking by using the words 'either/or', but, and 'only/neither'. To move to collective thinking, the use of 'or' to establish a contrast can be converted to 'and' to establish a connection. Try reading the list of pairs mentioned earlier, replacing the dividing stroke with 'and'. The entire landscape of thought is changed. The same applies to changing the words 'either' to 'both' and 'only' to 'also'. Try 'In this particular group, only individuals matter' and 'In this particular group, individuals also matter'. This book has been written using collective language wherever possible and tries never to use 'but' and rarely 'or'.

The apparent independence of parts as wholes in themselves can lead to a shock of recognition and a creative leap once they are connected – and also to denial that they are connected at all. Consider the initial rejection of Lovelock's idea of Gaia and Margulis's of the symbiotic cell. Koestler's account of creative thought includes a joke, a discovery and awe.[12] Outstanding examples of these connections come from artists often neglected in the Enlightenment, the poets. William Blake's poem[13] on the relationships among parts and wholes is worth repeating here:

> To see a world in a grain of sand
> And a heaven in a wild flower,
> Hold infinity in the palm of your hand,
> And eternity in an hour.
> *William Blake 1803*

### Living systems can be both stable and chaotic

Thinking about a system as stable and dynamic at the same time is a difficult mental somersault. However, it is basic to collective thinking, and has to be taken into account in any reflection on change. Examples of such stochastic systems are everywhere. Evolution by natural selection is carried out in the interaction between predetermined mechanisms and unpredictable environmental events. Similarly, with the eruptions of the earth's volcanoes, human wars, a child's development and Western democratic elections. The tension between the fixed rules that govern each system and the system's capacity to self-organise under some complex circumstances is the driving force in all these cases.

In both living and non-living systems, a chaotic unregulated system can generate its own stability, and a shaken stability can collapse into chaos. Thus these systems are random and non-random at the same time. For instance, molten lava can escape the inner core of the planet and produce steady state volcanoes. Moving continents can release disruptive tsunamis. An apparently stable society can erupt into chaos from one apparently random event. The relationship between stability and chaos is stochastic; it is both predictable and unpredictable at the same time.

A popular metaphor mentioned earlier for a stochastic system is 'the butterfly effect'.[14] Another example might be that the picking of edelweiss in Switzerland can make a polar bear tremble in the Arctic. The first is set in a physical change and the second in a biological change, while they carry the same message of randomness and connectedness. Transformational changes can move a rule-bound system to a chaotic system and the reverse. Before the change happens, it is not possible to reliably predict whether responses will be resilient, that is, able to return to the previous stable system, or remain technically chaotic, with systems collapsing and reforming around a fresh strange attractor.[15] Lovelock demonstrated that the planet Earth itself is both a symbiotic and a stochastic system.

For students of systems, systems thinking is routinely divided into hard (quantitative) systems, soft (qualitative systems), imaginative (creative) and double feedback (self-organising) systems. The four are frequently treated as if they are competing with each other for recognition. The collective mind, as usual, considers the four as complete ideas in themselves, and also as parts of the understanding of a whole system. To a collective mind, nothing can be solely qualitative or quantitative since all human thought is built on evidence that is a mixture of objective and subjective. The Macy Conferences that brought so much change to Western thought included recognition of the all-pervading influence of systems throughout the living, non-living and mental worlds. Bateson, Wiener, Ashby and Mead were present at the conferences and explored the ways in which the very simplicity of the basic feedback loop enables the apparently limitless expansion of feedback webs.[16]

In the double feedback loops that link biophysical systems, social systems and the human mind in a self-organising world, each system was found to have multiple feedback loops with their own mechanisms, each with its own form of a signal.

For the five reality-check questions that explore transformational change in practice, the signals for biophysical answers are measurements, for social questions they are symbols and stories, for ethical questions they are ideals, for aesthetic questions it is feelings, and for sympathetic questions it is empathy. A reflective question seeks the overall answers through finding coherence among the answers.

Many systems that had been treated as simple endless loops are now being re-interpreted as part of self-organising systems subject to change.[17] Once a system becomes chaotic, that is, unregulated, there is the possibility that it will reorganise around an event, appropriately called a strange attractor. Examples of self-organisation from chaotic systems are everywhere: chemical crystallisation, financial markets, animals swarming, robots imitating life and neural networks that recognise complex patterns. All these self-organising systems can be said to learn, in that they incorporate responses to fresh stimuli into their feedback loops. They can also be said to have an internal purpose, in that the pattern of feedback loops has developed to keep the system on a particular path. Thus ant colony messages have the purpose of increasing the colony to preset limits; single cells have a random Brownian motion that can eventually lead to a food supply; and birds have a flocking feedback system that facilitates seasonal migration. A brain can learn to over-program genetically based feedback loops for a particular purpose, such as a bird species learning a song or an animal (including humans) showing displacement behaviour rather than their fight or flight reflex. The human brain, with its capacity for reflecting on its own reflections, is distinctive in that it can decide on a fresh guiding purpose rather than conform to a pre-programmed one.

### *Shared learning for individuals and society*

Personally and professionally, we are all by definition involved in collective learning in our families, communities, organisations and professions. It has made us who we are, and allows us to fit into the society in which we live. It is a form of learning that inevitably combines the reflections of each individual. The extent of a society's capacity to change is a synergy of individual and community mutual learning. Social change brings some participants to question existing rules and boundaries, and find new solutions and ways of living. The extent of the learning depends on the willingness of the members of a society to go beyond their traditional social practices. However, rather than being welcomed, change can be strongly resisted. The pull of the traditional ways of defining individual goals, professional practices and organisational cultures can be stronger than the push of the need to change.[18]

A first step in collective learning is to recognise the need for social learning that celebrates rather than impedes change. A second step is to recognise that major change necessarily generates complex social issues. These complex issues require a quite different approach to that of addressing the simple problems of maintaining business as usual. The American wit Mencken wrote 'For every complex question there is an answer that is simple, clean and wrong'. A simple problem can be solved through applying the simple logic of cause and effect; a complex problem asks for far more.

Socially, the pattern of interconnected feedback loops creating a whole can be identified in both individuals and communities. Each individual is a unique whole with their own capacity to function independently even under the most adverse conditions. The Paralympic athlete, the autistic artist, the blind judge are obvious examples. Each has their own feedback system that assures them they are wholes, even when their society says they are not complete. When any number of individuals meets, different feedback patterns of communication develop, from the sympathetic exchanges between two or more, to the complex communication systems that create communities.

The capacity for collective learning among all the interests in a society may well be the key to successful transformational change. It is not so easy to achieve, however, in a society with strong divisions between ways of thinking about the world.[19] The divisions between ages, gender, beliefs, places and income build strong walls of thought and language that routinely serve to reinforce the existing system. To bring them together to listen to each other means that they can each reflect on each other's propositions, so that each can learn for all the others. The entry of women into the workforce, increasing economic inequality and an extended life expectancy are but a few of the changes affecting Western social systems. Windows can be let into those walls, so that collective learners can judge their full effect on the whole of society.

A seminal writer on individual adult learning, David Kolb, offers a blueprint for individual learning that can be used across a whole society to guide harmonious transformational change. Kolb put forward the proposition that all individual learning is based in the learner's reflection on direct experience. His approach is therefore called experiential learning.[20] In its simplest form, experiential learning is a matter of completing the learning cycle of first feeling that something is important, then watching what is actually happening, thinking about the possible consequences and acting on those thoughts (Figure 6.1).

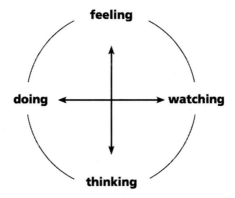

*Figure 6.1* Key elements of experiential learning (Kolb 1984)

The four forms of experience can be reflected as four questions:[21]

- Feeling: What are the ideals? What should be?
- Watching: What are the facts? What helps and what hinders the changes?
- Thinking: What are the ideas? What achieves the potential?
- Doing: What is the proper action? What is to be done?

### Human thinking is both objective and subjective, rational and creative

Throughout the 300 year period of the Enlightenment, the rational citizen and the creative individual were treated as if they were different varieties of human being.[22] In the sixteenth century the European Renaissance established that this division was false. This was done through the work of people like the painter, scientist and philosopher Leonardo da Vinci, and sculptor and writer Benvenuto Cellini. Descartes and Newton brought the division back.

The most effective, and at the same time, most limiting element of the Enlightenment was the response to Descartes' pronouncement on being a human being: 'I think therefore I am'. This powerful statement limited human thought to the purely rational, thereby establishing a taboo on the emotional, ethical and aesthetic components of thought. Howard Gardner recalled them under the headings of various types of intelligence[23] (musical, bodily-kinaesthetic, logical-mathematical, linguistic, spatial, interpersonal, intrapersonal). Even then they remained isolated as functions of the brain, ignoring the essential contributions of the emotions, the imagination and the intuition. American satirist Stephen Colbert quipped, 'We are a divided nation. Not between Democrats and Republicans, or rich and poor. We are divided between those who think with their head and those who know with their heart'. Put like that, it seems essential to acknowledge that every human being has access to both.

Even Descartes recognised that, although he was focused on one type of knowledge construction, there were many other forms of thought.[24]

> The diversity of our opinions does not arise from some being endowed with a greater share of reason than others, but solely from this, that we conduct our thoughts along different ways, and do not fix our attention on the same objects … To be possessed of a vigorous mind is not enough; the prime requisite is rightly to apply it.

A reflective question assumes that to rightly apply the mind is to include all the elements of human experience. These include the primitive brainstem, the reptilian brain, which can override the hemispheres in an emergency and in dreams. Major areas of the brain are devoted to hands and eyes, each with their own crossover connections that allow for unity in our perception of the world by touch and sight. It includes the *corpus callosum*, the tissue that coordinates signals between the left and right hemispheres and proved to be larger than usual in Einstein's brain.[25]

Reflection on reflections also includes the plasticity of the brain which modern neuroscience is finding to be significant. By the end of the twentieth century the tide had turned from a dominant concern for parts, to include a concern for wholes. A flood of books, films and organisations emerged to fill the long-neglected space: books on oceans, the planet, universal rights and the universe. In psychology, Oliver Sachs told stories of atypical people who lived full and satisfying lives, not in spite of, but because of impaired mental function.[26] These included a surgeon with a constant twitch, idiot savants with mathematical genius, and autistic artists producing best-selling paintings. His own patients gave Sachs the opportunity to point out the power of the human drive to a full identity, based on who they are in their minds, not on what they cannot do.

Educators began to argue for a collective approach. In the nineteenth century, Montessori developed education based on the whole child in the context of their environment, rather than particular skills.[27] While Montessori remained an isolated enthusiast, by the early 1900s Dewey had revolutionised primary schooling in the United States from the rote learning that was then in vogue.[28] Dewey saw the whole child as not fixed, but emergent, with their immense emotional, social, ethical and aesthetic potential still to be developed.[29]

Chemists and physicists, highly successful in their specialised fields, turned to exploring ways to understand the creative space between parts and wholes. In *The Turning Point*, physicist Fritjof Capra found that established practitioners had begun to move towards understanding the connections of their field in every discipline.[30] David Bohm was another physicist who turned to exploring the connections between the living and non-living worlds and human thought. He described the search for an understanding of reality as a search for an understanding of implicate order, of systems folding in upon themselves.[31] Bohm expanded on the essential role of dialogue in filling this space. Dialogue, whose Greek derivation 'suggests a stream of meaning flowing among and through us and between us',[32] is based on a strong discipline of thought. Each participant suspends disbelief in order to take seriously the diverse ideas of others. They also suspend judgment as to the validity of new ideas, asking for clarification rather than doubting them. As Bohm wrote, we learn from difference, not more of the same.

An approach that emerged from the same principles of supporting collective thinking as Bohmian dialogue was Christopher Alexander's invention of a pattern language.[33] His aim was to design an inclusive language that would allow innovation and creativity to emerge spontaneously in designs for living. Whether it was a village, a city, a house, a room or a type of service, Alexander was interested in producing designs created by the human beings who were going to live with their creation.

Alexander's approach eventually led to insights as diverse as a district's governance, innovative engineering projects, software designs such as Facebook and Twitter, professional training courses, and organisational change. His pattern language took the form of a title and a visual that convey the essence of the concern, an overview of the context of the selected issue, a description of a proposed mode of resolution and then examples of its successful application.[34] Using this *lingua franca*, people with widely different propositions could understand one another and work towards each other's goals.

**Next**

In Part I, we have presented an overview of the move towards a collective mind through accounts of three collective thinkers: Darwin, Lovelock and Wiener. Between them they reshaped the world as evolutionary, self-organising and cybernetic. Their story continued through three visionaries who predicted where the world might go from there. In 1930, Teilhard de Chardin foresaw the noosphere, a world of self-organising connected human thought, building on itself. In 1972, Bateson foresaw a three-dimensional Anthropocene, a human-dominated era made up of interactive non-living, living and human thinking systems. In 1977, Alexander foresaw life as best understood through a pattern language with strong centres in which everyone participated.

Collective thinkers are being asked to reposition themselves along the four shifts in thinking generated by the master thinkers and visionaries. These reorientations will of course change again in the course of time and in the light of collective learning. Meanwhile, each of the four reorientations is a change in the previous ways of interpreting the world. All parts are wholes and also part of other wholes. All complex systems can become self-organising systems. All communities are based on the diversity, not the sameness, of individuals. The human mind integrates the rational, creative, logical and imaginative as it thinks. Once one accepts one's own position in this changed world, the next step is to make the five reality checks on one's selected issue. Reflective questions will be needed to connect the reorientations and the reality checks as an encompassing whole. It is already apparent that it is not possible to explain any one reorientation without involving the others, thus together they form a seamless background to ongoing transformational change.

Once the new ideas generated by the reflective questions have been absorbed by the affected group, the unresolved question remains of how to act on this thinking. Radical action is likely needed, since the thinking has addressed potential transformational change. Radical action will need to include all the structures that make up the society undergoing change, its language, science, governance, economics, education and the self-images of its citizens. There has been a considerable reorientation in contemporary thinking towards a synergistic, stochastic, collective and creative world. Collective versions of each of these social structures are also needed and are beginning to emerge.

Taken together, these parts are beginning to add up to a restructure of the whole of human society in the next millennia. In Part II of this book we look at the emergence of the structures that make up a collective society. Master thinkers and their many apprentices are working together on these separate components of a collective society, drawing ever closer into a collective mind. Remembering the stochastic nature of the world, as both predictable and unpredictable, none of this development can be taken for granted. Nevertheless, there is enough of a movement towards Teilhard de Chardin's, Bateson's and Alexander's prediction of a collective mind to encourage its further development, if that is the choice.

In Part II we do make that choice and evaluate possible modes of advancement towards a globally interconnected mind. The changes occurring in each of the social structures are by no means uniform. A potential inclusive language is modified English, emerging already as we write, while needing a considerable expansion in representing creative and imaginative ideas. A transformational science is also already emerging, extending the evidence base of the Enlightenment era from more than the physical to include physical, social, ethical, aesthetic and sympathetic evidence. Government is now extending to governance and democracy to include deep, direct and deliberative democracies as different stages in the processing of the one ethic: negotiation between freedom and control. Thus governance would be through a collective democratic process that incorporated the several current democracies in their own right.

A collective economy is further away than a collective democracy, and faces more significant change. At present there are at least six economies in conflict, unable to arrive at common ethics or even shared goals. One pathway we explore here is the potential for a gift relationship to bring a common thread optimising human sharing of resources, be it through market, command, black, self-sustaining, reciprocal and free economies. Collective learning is open and engaged learning. Universal education has started in this direction, while radical educators such as Montessori, Freire and Steiner are showing the way. Individuals in Western society are just emerging from a long period of self-centredness, as the object of the distribution of goods in the economy; to find their connected self is often a new experience.

The future of the collective mind is still uncertain. However, the potential has been established and some practical pathways are emerging. In times of transformational change, there is the potential for creative leaps as well as the breakdown of existing systems. Reorienting towards the hope of the collective mind seems to hold the promise of an exciting and inspiring future. In Part III we will try to imagine the operation of a collected mind in a connected world, drawing on the most forward thinking ideas and activity of the current time.

We do know that humankind is starting out on a new journey. One aspect of that journey is adding the diverse thinking of the group and the crowd to the advance in individual thinking of the Enlightenment. One great advantage is the uniquely human capacity as a collective thinker to reflect on the whole journey, to take account of the many contributing events, and to look into the future.

## Notes

1  Toulmin, S. (1958) *The Uses of Argument*, Cambridge, UK: Cambridge University Press; and Toulmin, S. (1972) *Human Understanding Vol. 1: The Collective Use and Understanding of Concepts*, Princeton, US: Princeton University Press.
2  Brown, V. A., Harris, J. A. and Russell, J. Y. (2010) (eds) *Tackling Wicked Problems: Through the Transdisciplinary Imagination,* London: Earthscan.
3  Brown, V. A. and Lambert, J. L. (2013) *Collective Learning for Transformational Change: A Guide to Collaborative Action,* London and New York: Earthscan.

4  In Honderich, T. (1995) *The Oxford Companion to Philosophy,* New York: Oxford University Press, knowledge is discussed as justified true belief, p. 447.

5  Shermer, M. (2002) *In Darwin's Shadow: The Life and Science of Alfred Russel Wallace*, New York: Oxford University Press. Wallace's description of the malarial episode when 'there suddenly flashed upon me the idea of the survival of the fittest' is quoted on p. 113.

6  Roberts, R. M. (1989) *Serendipity: Accidental Discoveries in Science*, London: Wiley

7  Kelly, G. A. (1965) *Theory of Personality: The Psychology of Personal Constructs,* New York: Norton.

8  Von Bertalanffy, L. (1976) *General Systems Theory: Foundations, Development and Applications*, New York: George Braziller.

9  Margulis, L. and Sagan, D. (1995) *What is Life?* New York: Simon & Schuster.

10  http://www.cancer.org/cancer/leukemia-chronicmyeloidcml/detailedguide/leukemia-chronic-myeloid-myelogenous-treating-bone-marrow-stem-cell [accessed 16.5.13].

11  For example tissue culture was used to protect the relict population of the Wollemi Pine from trophy collectors. Woodford, J. (2000) *The Wollemi Pine: The incredible discovery of a living fossil from the age of the dinosaurs,* Melbourne: Text Publishing.

12  Koestler, A. (1964/1989) *The Act of Creation*, London: Arkana.

13  'Auguries of Innocence' by William Blake.

14  Chapter 3.

15  Chapter 4. An attractor in complex systems refers to its ability to attract a trajectory. A point attractor occurs in systems tending towards a stable equilibrium and a strange attractor for corresponding chaotic systems.

16  Chapters 3 and 4.

17  The first detailed description of self-organising systems was the theory of 'dissipative structures' by the Belgian Nobel Prize-winning physicist, Ilya Prigogine. Prigogine, I. (1967) 'Dissipative Structures in Chemical Systems' in Claesson, S. (ed.) *Fast Reactions and Primary Processes in Chemical Kinetics*, New York: Interscience; Prigogine, I and Stengers, I. (1984) *Order out of Chaos*, London: Fontana; and Capra, F. (1996) *The Web of Life: A New Synthesis of Mind and Matter,* UK: HarperCollins.

18  See Plimer, I. (2009) *Heaven and Earth – Global Warming: The Missing Science*, Ballan, Victoria, Australia: Connor Court.

19  Brown, V. A. (2008) *Leonardo's Vision: A Guide for Collective Thinking and Action.* Rotterdam, Netherlands: Sense; and Brown, V. A. (2010) 'Collective Inquiry and its Wicked Problems' in *Tackling Wicked Problems*, pp. 61–81.

20  Kolb, D. A. (1984) *Experiential Learning: Experience as the Source of Learning and Development*, New Jersey, US: Prentice Hall.

21  Brown, V. A. and Lambert, J. L. (2013) *Collective Learning for Transformational Change: A Guide to Collaborative Action*, (London and New York: Earthscan) presents comprehensive details of the practice of collective learning for transformational change covering contexts of individual change to whole cities and towns.

22  Berlin, I. (1998) *The Proper Study of Mankind: An Anthology of Essays,* Pimlico: London. Gould, S. J. (2004) *The Hedgehog, The Fox and the Magister's Pox: Mending and Minding the Misconceived Gap between Science and the Humanities*, London: Vintage.

23  Gardner, H. (1993) *Multiple Intelligences: The Theory in Practice*, New York: Basic Books.

24  Descartes, R. (1637/1946) *Discourse on the Method of Rightly Conducting the Reason* (Tr. J. Veitch) London: Everyman's Library 570, p. iv.

25  http://en.wikipedia.org/wiki/Albert_Einstein's_brain [accessed 10.5.13].

26  For example, Sacks, O. (1985) *The Man Who Mistook His Wife for a Hat,* New York: Summit Books.

27  Feez, S. (2010) *Montessori and Early Childhood: A Guide for Students*, London: Sage.

28 Dewey, J. (1916) *Democracy and Education: An Introduction to the Philosophy of Education*, New York: McMillan. The e-book is available from Project Gutenberg, http://www.gutenberg.org/files/852/852-h/852-h.htm [accessed 10.5.13].

29 See also Bruner, J. (1996) *The Culture of Education*, Cambridge, US: Harvard University Press.

30 Capra, F. (1982) *The Turning Point: Science, Society and the Rising Culture*, New York: Simon & Schuster.

31 Bohm, D. (1980) *Wholeness and Implicate Order*, London: Routledge.

32 Bohm, D. (1996) *On Dialogue*, New York: Routledge, p. 7.

33 Chapter 4.

34 This basic pattern language is used for chapters 7–12 in Part II.

# Part II
# Changing society

# 7   Inclusive language

## Hearing all the voices[1]

**Pattern:** collective communication.

**Context:** the far-reaching implications of transformational change make it crucial for all those involved to contribute to a shared understanding of the issues.

**Issue:** Ludwig Wittgenstein's edict 'The limits of my language mean the limits of my world' identifies a major barrier to reaching a shared understanding.

**Resolution:** it is possible for the many different interests in a complex issue to generate an inclusive language, and so reach a shared understanding that no one could achieve alone.

**Examples:** inclusive language tools include the use of collective questions, deep dialogue and the design of a pattern language.

## The context: a timeless dream

The dream of universal understanding among different peoples has surfaced and resurfaced throughout human history. The tradition of an overarching transcendent way of reaching that goal persists. The dream may be based in meditation, as in the Buddhist goal of enlightenment, and in citizen government, as in the Greek origins of democracy. It is played out in the dreamtime stories of the *Ubuntu* of Africa and the *Tjukurpa* of the Australian Aboriginal people. The building of the Tower of Babel was only made possible by all peoples being able to understand each other (Box 7.1). The dream in the present era is the World Wide Web and the United Nations, and in Teilhard de Chardin's predictions of a noosphere filled with the shared thinking of all humanity. The same dream is reflected in the framing of collective questions; a theme that runs throughout Part I of this book.

There are many ways that that dream can be translated into contemporary reality. During transformational changes new words and phrases come out of the woodwork to allow people to express the new ideas. Often the new terms are invented by one group and rejected as jargon by the rest. Suddenly a word, a phrase, a painting, a song, an action is picked up by all concerned and creates a shared understanding that leaps all barriers. The words of Martin Luther King's 'I have a dream' and Abraham Lincoln's Gettysburg Address have become

---

***Box 7.1*** **The Tower of Babel**

In the city of Babel, the peoples of the then world came together to build a tower. By speaking a language all could understand, they were able to cooperate in building the tower higher and higher. Finally it reached the heavens and their god became jealous of their power.

'Yahweh came down to see what they did and said: "They are one people and have one language, and nothing will be withholden from them which they purpose to do." So Yahweh said, "Come, let us go down and confound their speech". And so Yahweh scattered them upon the face of the Earth, and confused their languages, and they left off building the city.' Source: Genesis 11:5-8

---

universal for those promoting racial equality and peace. Communities adopt each other's rituals, as the festival of Christmas absorbed pagan, Christian and market economy traditions.

Experts are infamous for using technical terms that confuse outsiders quite unnecessarily since cardiac arrest means simply 'heart stopped', the precautionary principle is 'not fouling one's nest'. James Lovelock startled the world with the name Gaia for the living spirit of the planet. Organisations work hard to make their brand name part of everyday life, and often succeed; think of Coca Cola and Nestlé. Artists in all media have given the world access to new ideas, with Leonardo da Vinci painting saints as real people rather than as icons, and the soaring architecture of the peace memorial in war-damaged Hiroshima. There are many pathways to an inclusive language. However, there is often need for affirmative action to counteract the era of divided minds.

The primary language for a completely new vehicle of communication, the Internet, has been a language that some might not recognise as English at all. The hashtag[2] symbol of Twitter messages, or the in-your-face directness that has developed on Facebook, are new forms of inclusive communication; billions of people 'get it' at the same time. The emergence of Google as a database built on relationships rather than connections has enabled users to surf across disciplines, professions, nationalities and lifestyles, whatever they wish. Even the word 'surf' is part of the new language. Wikipedia, the online encyclopaedia, contains crowd-sourced knowledge that is self-organising and self-supervised. Volunteers act as critical reviewers for quality control. Informal videos filmed on an iPhone can go viral on the Internet via YouTube, reaching millions of viewers in an instant. One such video[3] influenced the course of an election in Iran; another aroused the world's concern for local violence in Africa.[4]

The new ideas that emerge during transformational change will need translation if they are to be shared. Without that shared understanding, the new ideas may go unrecognised, quite unnecessary conflicts develop and ways forward can be blocked by seemingly trivial misunderstandings. Even more seriously, conflicting ideas and serious misunderstandings may be covered over and left to fester. The necessary resolutions are not even attempted, or sometimes they are made only too late. The barrenness of the Sahara desert, the First World War trench warfare slaughter, and the Great Depression of the 1930s, are all examples of quite unnecessary senseless misery due to a regime change. So are many apparently simple neighbourhood disputes.

Issues arising from transformational change fall into the category of wicked problems, problems that involve changes in the society that produced them. Since there are so many interests involved, wicked problems cannot have a single definition, any more than they can have a single solution. The difficulty is not necessarily how to agree to respond to a concern; that comes after the shared understanding, not before. The reflective question is how to derive an inclusive language that respects the individual languages and thus the cultures of all the contributing interests, and yet is understood by all.

One school of thought considers that a language predetermines the thought patterns of its speakers, and so their thinking cannot be changed.[5] Philosopher Ludwig Wittgenstein put forward much the same proposition in 'The limits of my language mean the limits of my world'.[6] In practice these seem to be only temporary limits that will always be there although they can largely be overcome; human minds are extremely agile. Aboriginal Australian and Inuit peoples have no words for technology, yet members of these cultures can excel as mechanics. People change their countries and their professions, and can become competent speakers of new languages that they need to master.

The richness and comprehensiveness of a full language evolves in a stable group of people over hundreds, if not thousands, of years. In transformational change the need for a new phrase may arise at short notice and will need to override existing prejudices and misconceptions. As part of a transformational change, the new terms need to be able to satisfactorily answer the full reality-check set of questions: physical, social, ethical, aesthetic and sympathetic. The terms biodiversity (ecology), stem cells (medicine) and social media (computing) have passed this test and moved into everyday language. Climate change and the GFC (global financial crisis) are examples of phrases quickly accepted, although with mixed fortunes in finding generally acceptable responses.

## The issue: hearing many voices

For the 12 years 1992–2004, the Local Sustainability Project[7] worked with over 300 communities in four different countries (Australia, China (Hong Kong), Malaysia and Nepal) on resolving sustainability issues (Table 7.1). They found that members of five groups were needed for all lasting decisions: individuals, the community, the experts, organisation members and creative thinkers. The divisions between different interests were strong enough to lead to distinctive languages that differed in content, communication channels and carriers. Taken as a whole, each of the groups proved sufficiently distinct to be called a knowledge culture. Individuals' language reflected their own experience, the community their shared symbols and rituals, experts their technical languages, organisations their own agendas and creative thinkers had the artistic media of painting, sculpture and literature.

*Table 7.1* Language sources for collective thinking and six knowledge cultures

| Individual | Community | Specialised | Organi- sational | Holistic | Collective |
|---|---|---|---|---|---|
| personal lived experience (intro- spective) | stories, place-based symbols (sympathetic) | occupations, disciplines (physical) | reports, regulations, cost/benefit analysis (social) | symbols, metaphors, images (aesthetic) | all of these plus ethical (reflective) |

There is a risk of confusing the rule-bound languages of knowledge cultures with the simplicity and directness of asking collective questions. The introspective, physical, social, ethical, aesthetic, sympathetic and reflective questions explored in Part I of this book are derived directly from individual thinking and common sense. They have been identified in the thinking of individuals from the intellectual giants of Darwin, Lovelock and Wiener to creative writers and thinkers across time. Since those questions are to be asked of all the knowledge cultures, the posing of them will need to be in an inclusive language.

In every community studied, each member potentially held the roles of individual, citizen, specialist, a member of an organisation and a creative thinker.[8] Everyone therefore had the potential to ask all the collective questions. The action research project found that for each person the dominance of one of the subcultures led them to base their knowledge and so their language primarily on that one.[9] Thus people, thinking of themselves as individuals, reflected on their lived experience and often kept the rest of their ideas to themselves. Community members shared stories and symbols based on their common experience. Specialists talked in their own particular jargon to their fellow specialists. As members of an organisation, people adopted their organisation's agenda as their own and spoke in the language of that agenda, as in the use of acronyms by bureaucrats. Although communities differed in their degrees of cultivating and suppressing creative thinking, it is a medium available to all human beings. Imaginative contributions proved equally important in riding the ups and downs of transformational change and in achieving that inclusive language.

A major impediment to collective learning is the hierarchy of power among contributing knowledge cultures. Specialised knowledge has held the dominant position in the English-speaking world since the seventeenth century Enlightenment. In the twenty-first century this leadership is giving way to pressure from organisational agendas.[10] While the two forms of knowledge vie for prominence, they each carry more weight than the contributions from community, individual or holistic knowledge. In the developing worlds, this uneven power balance has been, and still is, part of colonisation by industrialised cultures.[11] Even in Western communities the way in which language is spoken reinforces existing social and economic inequities.

The obvious solution, a formal universal language with its own dictionary, has been tried and found wanting. Esperanto, a well-developed language, has never taken root. Where two cultures intertwine, a mixed language can develop, such as Creole in the Americas and Pidgin in the Pacific. While their speakers argue that these have developed into complete languages, they remain context specific rather than universal. Every culture has its identity embedded in its language. So meeting the need for everyone involved in transformational change to share an understanding of the change has to be two-fold. One, there is need for an inclusive language that grounds events in the cultural understanding of all the participants; two, there is a need to find existing words that cross the boundaries.

Thankfully, after an era of specialisation and fragmentation, in this new era of collective thinking there are growing signs that we are starting to rebuild that tower. Tools have been developed that help ensure all the contributing groups ask the full suite of collective questions; introspective, physical, social, ethical, aesthetic, sympathetic and the reflective question. Some inclusive tools that address the inevitable cultural bias (in a positive sense) and draw on the diverse ideas from among the diverse participants are the suite of collective questions,[12] a knowledge mandala,[13] Bohmian dialogue[14] and Alexander's pattern language.[15]

## Resolution: towards an inclusive language

By default, English is fast becoming a vehicle for collective thinking. It comes with its own strengths and weaknesses, the chief of which is the risk of reducing the richness of local languages. A comparison with other languages finds that English is more linear in its logic than Greek, more restricted in words connected with creativity than French, and less rich in its emotional language than most other languages. For instance, English has comparatively few words for colour and shape. It has only single words for key social concepts such as love and language, while French has two. English makes much use of single clauses, while Greek allows for nine.[16]

French, the diplomatic language of the nineteenth century, has given way to English. English carries the stigma of having been imposed on the peoples of the widespread British Empire, often with violence. Yet while colonised countries officially returned to their original language on gaining independence, English remains their language for education, science, commerce and international trade. Figure 7.1 offers an inclusive framework, presenting constructive relationships among the decision-making knowledges as a mandala of a non-hierarchical nested set.

The framework shown in Figure 7.1 represents a nested set of knowledge cultures and their languages. Each of the languages tends to privilege one of the reality-check questions above the others. A ring of dots forms the outer circle made up of the personal anecdotes of individual knowledge. These are largely based on introspective questions. Next there is community knowledge, constructed by the shared experiences of many individuals, communicated through stories and symbols: these to be derived from the answers to social and sympathetic questions. Hence they are shown with a wavy line, indicating the diversity of communities' experience.

## Combining knowledge cultures requires

- Individual knowledge
- **Local knowledge**
- Specialised knowledge
- **Organisational knowledge**
- Holistic knowledge

*Figure 7.1* Mandala for a collective language (from Brown 2013)

Specialised knowledge depends in its turn on observations supplied by individual communities of practice. Since each specialised community has its own language (Table 7.1), that layer is presented as a ring of separate boxes. The influence of the scientific era ensures that their questions have a physical bias. Organisations build on each of the foregoing knowledges to set and circulate their agendas as a guide to their strategies. The closed circle with unidirectional arrows symbolises the extent to which their members adopt the organisation's objectives. They therefore ask limited social questions. At the core of this nested set is the capacity for a creative synthesis, signalled in Figure 7.1 by a star. In times of transformational change this language emphasises ethical and aesthetic questions, and is the source of crucial new ideas.

In spite of and because of its limitations, the English language is adaptable. Changes are more readily accepted than in some other, more expressive languages, for example, French. Donella Meadows[17] has argued that to allow all possibilities to be included, the English language needs to replace 'but' with 'and', and 'also' with 'or'. Over the past few decades, the English language has changed to accept gender equity. 'Chair' has replaced 'chairman' as head of a committee. 'Man' and 'mankind' are now 'human' and 'humankind'. The standard use of 'he' has changed to 'he and she' and 'they'. Similarly, warlike language has changed to allow for non-violent courses of action, using goals rather than targets, resources rather than war chests, and programs rather than campaigns.

A dilemma for an inclusive language is when to retain the parallel languages of diverse interest groups. Consider the relationship between a community and its environment. In the language of sociology this is a matter of a community's bonding and bridging social capital.[18] In anthropology, the relationship is primarily endogenous (internally focused) or exogenous (externally focused). In ecology, it is a range of habitats making up an ecosystem. For an organisation the relationship is a matter of the potential risks and benefits to the organisation. These multiple perspectives are not mutually exclusive. Taken together they make up a collage that is able to bring a more complete understanding. Accepting the diversity of the contributing ideas is part of the process of collective thinking.

Each of the contributing languages will have tried and true expressions for their areas of interest and well-established communication channels for spreading their ideas. Taking the examples above, speaking an inclusive language will include making observations, telling stories, using dialogue and designing an inclusive framework. Since the result from different interest groups will be different versions from each of these, the reflective question, 'What does it all mean?' remains the crux of an inclusive language. This brings the need for a thesaurus of words for inclusive relationships, such as symbols, analogies, similes, symbiosis, parasite, narratives, parables and patterns. It is nothing new for English to adopt words from other languages for ideas foreign to English culture: *Zeitgeist* for the spirit of the times from the contemplative German. *Pro bono* for a voluntary contribution is lawyer's Latin. *Comme ci, comme ça,* like this or like that, from the open-minded French.

The need to name and to sort ideas seems to be inherent in the human development of language. For some reason, naming something new or mysterious seems to make it come to life, and may give a false sense of security. As well as revealing a truth, words can be used to hide an unacceptable truth. *Iatrogenic* is the word coined for medically caused disease, giving no clue as to the actual cause, which was the people in charge of the treatment. *Rendition* was invented to describe illegal transfer of prisoners to countries with laxer ethical rules. *Schizophrenia* was a word hailed with relief, until it became clear that it was being used to cover a miscellaneous group of mental dysfunctions and obscuring the origin.

So far in this book inclusive words have been imported from all manner of language traditions. A short list important to collective thinking would be as follows: Anthropocene, cyberspace, Gaia, noosphere, prosthesis, strange attractors, self-organising, stochastic and symbiotic. Each one would be strange to some readers from different traditions and well known to others. Each conveys ideas that other languages ignore. To make the terms inclusive, we have explained each word when it is first used and listed it in the index. In addition, they can be found online in the free Wikipedia. There has been a fashion for inventing words to make a collective noun, as in *glocalisation* combining local and global. This seems a backward step. They mask the issue they are designed to explain. Lewis Carroll wrote a whole poem, 'The Jabberwocky', in such portmanteau words: 'Twasbrillig and the slithytoves ...' can be translated into 'it was a brilliant evening and the silvery little turtledoves ...'.[19]

While naming is an important constituent of language, sorting is just as influential. Sorting words for ideas and for things fixes a word in a particular context, a context which may radically change the meaning. Sorting can be through classification, organisation, standardisation, coding, filing, stratification, systematics and collecting. Charles Darwin could not have made his discovery that Galapagos Island finches' beaks are adapted to their diet if his shooter[20] had not sorted them by their beaks to take back to England. In all cases, in all languages, there is a framework within which the words will be interpreted. One of the most well known and influential is the Linnaean classification of all living things according to their reproductive systems. Previously, Aristotle had sorted them by usefulness to humans. After the decoding of DNA, a whole new set of relationships emerged, requiring a new systematics based on inheritance patterns. This helped to uncover previously invisible patterns of evolution.[21]

The same variability applies to sorting people and their environments. People are sorted by DNA profile, religion, age, height, health, income, skills, appearance, personality, nationality, language, intelligence, empathy, skin colour, hair colour, weight, strength, sexual preferences and more. The categories are not trivial; they can position a person for life. An extreme example is South African apartheid in which, when once classified as black, coloured or white, people were allocated to different legal systems, occupations and districts. In South Africa this condemned some people to an intolerable life. In New Zealand the same classification opened up particular programs, rights and privileges and included special electoral representation for mixed culture groups.[22]

Stakeholder, scenario and jigsaw are all terms that need to be used with caution in an inclusive language. Stakeholder implies that the outcome of negotiation is production of goods and services of some kind. Its use limits the person or group to those with a recognised interest in the outcomes. This can exclude the contributions of marginalised and emergent interests. A rainforest may have a spiritual value and a public good interest simply because it is there. Its conservation may be of great importance to a future generation. Stakeholder negotiations rarely include spiritual values or the rights of the unborn. Interest groups would be a more inclusive phrase.

A scenario predicts a future on the basis of what is known. It can be based on a wish list, a projection and a prediction. A wicked problem (a complex problem with no obvious solution) requires creative thinking on what could be, rather than what is already known. In an inclusive process, all parties are free to use their imagination on all possible futures, sharing their creative ideas. Visioning would be a more accurate description of this process.

It is standard practice to refer to combining the elements of a complex issue as completing a jigsaw puzzle. Where the goal is collective learning, this is far from an accurate description. A jigsaw repeats a predetermined picture and the shape of the pieces is fixed. A better analogy would be an artistic collage. Here the pieces are brought together afresh to illuminate a central idea. The unique combination creates a fresh picture no one contributor has seen before.

Closer examination of existing practice offers ideas of how a collective language works. A collective language can be carried by multiple channels to reach its diverse audience: text, voice, music, actions, social media, stories, symbols, agendas and any of the arts. Any one channel may be the appropriate one for any one culture. However, for many cultures, their basic understanding of the world is already inclusive. *Ubuntu* is an African concept that rests on the twin principles 'a person is a person through others' and 'the left hand washes the right hand and the opposite is true'. No individual is seen as, or regards themselves as, separate from others.[23] The worldwide creative community was able to cover the planet in a single hour with Bob Geldof's Live Aid Concert.[24] Over US14 billion dollars were collected for the 2.4 million people directly affected by the 2004 Pacific Ocean Tsunami.[25]

Australian Aboriginal people also think collectively, although their languages express the spirit of their collective quite differently from Africa. The land itself is the speaker. Particular people responsible for listening to the land are recognised by everyone as having both the right and the duty to speak. Others will remain silent rather than intrude on those rights. Each community is bound together by their *Tjurkapa* or dreaming story, which establishes their relationships among each other and with the land. With no written language and as a migratory people, *Tjurkapa* is conveyed through dances, songs and body and rock painting.[26]

## Examples: dialogue and pattern language

The dream of a collective language able to maintain the richness of its contributing languages seems not so far away. Having reviewed the difficulties that face the development of an inclusive language, it is a relief to find that there are inclusive frameworks that are being successfully applied, some of them inspirational. Two communication strategies in particular offer pathways that can be followed to answer the reflective questions that arise from collective thinking. These are the use of dialogue and the design of pattern languages.

### *Dialogue*

Dialogue promises to be one of the most sensitive and rewarding ways of carrying multiple language cultures towards a collective understanding. However, the warning still applies that language is always spoken in the context of a cultural framework. Depending on the speaker, dialogue can be confused with three other ways of talking to each other on controversial issues: discussion, discourse and debate. Discussion is usually unstructured and often confirms existing positions. Debate is a form of discussion based on dichotomy and aimed at winning rather than resolution. Discourse takes place within a given culture, and will have established a fixed interpretation. Each of the knowledge cultures has its own discourse.

Dialogue on the other hand is ideally an open communication process that encourages a shared exploration of all aspects of human experience. The openness of the set of collective questions allows for mutual questioning of existing personal assumptions and social rules. This then allows for sharing the contributions of creative and rational, subjective and objective, personal and social ways of thinking in answering introspective questions then physical, social, ethical, aesthetic and sympathetic questions. For the concluding step of asking reflective questions on the full set of answers, an inclusive language is more important than ever. The Greek roots of *dia* and *logos* imply 'flow of meaning' through speaking, not the common interpretation of two speakers. A dialogue can involve many speakers or one person talking to themselves. The spread of the use of dialogue is a mark of a changing culture that is valuing collective understanding.

One of the seminal thinkers and practitioners of dialogue, David Bohm, a physicist turned philosopher, argued that dialogue is an essential basis for any collective discourse. Bohm had a larger idea of a collective mind than most writers, an idea that matches the noosphere of Teilhard de Chardin and the three-dimensional world of James Lovelock and Gregory Bateson. Bohm suggested that human communication takes place at three levels, originally all at the same time and then fragmented during the scientific era. He considered that a move to a collective mind was reuniting the three dimensions of individual, participatory and cosmic mind.[27]

One dimension of human thought is the thinking process of each human being. Individual collective thought is a matter of assimilation of all the experiences and expectations of a lifetime up until the moment of reflection. This dimension is explored in some detail in Chapter 12. For the second dimension of a collective mind, Bohm described the participating mind as a way of thought,[28] an idea expanded by Henryk Skolimowski in his *The Participatory Mind*.[29] Bohm explained that by this he means that all human minds are in touch with the almost limitless realm of the thought of other humans, accumulated through the lifetime of the species. This participatory thought includes the shared inheritance of the so-called reptilian brain, Jungian cultural consciousness, adaptation to the natural environment, and the thinking of all the humans that have ever existed. Bohm described his formless but all-pervading participatory mind as having been downplayed during the scientific era, which magnified individual conscious thought. One of the objectives of Bohmian dialogue is to put people back in touch with this second dimension of collective thought.

Bohm's third dimension is the realisation of being one with the natural world, with the rhythms of that world, the seasons, the days, the sun and the moon. He pointed out that the earliest signs of human existence are accompanied by evidence of a spiritual dimension, sacred objects and funeral rituals, almost always connected with natural systems. Animist religions are the oldest forms of belief in how the world works. Carolyn Merchant wrote of the consequences of exchanging this sensitive bond for an objective understanding of events as *The Death of Nature*.[30] Bohm called this broken link the cosmic mind. He described how the dialogue he espouses restores fragmented thinking to a wholeness that combines all three dimensions of mind: individual, participatory and cosmic.[31]

A cohort of dialogue practitioners have developed a set of guidelines derived from David Bohm's book *On Dialogue*. The guidelines in Box 7.2 differ markedly from the standard pattern of a conversation in which one puts one's own case. It is typical to reply to an opinion from others, with one of our own: 'my own opinion is …'. In contrast, the first step in dialogue is for each participant to put their own case aside and commit themselves to open-minded learning from others. The guidelines emphasise that this does not mean abandoning one's own position, rather accepting the positions of others as real for them, however alien to the others in the dialogue. The second step, listening and speaking without making a judgment, is more difficult than it may seem. It is almost automatic to reply

'I agree/disagree with you'. More can be learnt from listening to positions with which you disagree than from ones with which you agree. A dialogue-type response would be 'What can we learn from each other?'.

---

### *Box 7.2* **Guidelines for effective dialogue**

Throughout the dialogue:
1. Commit yourself to the process.
2. Listen and speak without judgment.
3. Identify your own and others' assumptions of reality.
4. Value other speakers and their opinions.
5. Balance inquiry and advocacy.
6. Relax your need for any particular outcome.
7. Listen to yourself and speak when moved to.
8. Take it easy – go with the flow – enjoy.

Source: Drawn from Bohm (1996) in: Gang, P. and Morgan, M. (2004)
'Rules of Dialogue', TIES Curriculum documents,
Massachusetts, US: Endicott College.

---

Critical questioning is common to Socratic dialogue, scientific method and Bohmian dialogue alike, but the purpose differs in each case. The Socratic approach maintains an atmosphere of critical doubt. Scientific method means abandoning one's own perspective in order to make objective observations. In dialogue, participants identify assumptions in a spirit of critical loyalty, able to criticise positively since they have the others' interests at heart.

The fourth step, respecting each other's ideas, does not mean either agreeing with or correcting them. It is about indicating mutual respect for what each of you are saying, and checking that you have heard them correctly: 'Tell me more about that idea'. Fifth, inquiry and advocacy are easily confused. Practice is needed here, to remove long-standing habits of arguing for one's own cause. Six, remaining free of a predetermined outcome leaves the conversation open to new and innovative ideas. This is difficult too. A whole era of task-oriented thinking has made thinkers feel inadequate if they do not commit to an outcome. The seventh and eighth steps refer to the experience of taking part in a dialogue. The differences in the interactions generate conviviality, not argument. Work in the field confirms that this brings the exhilaration of mutual problem solving.[32]

Another outcome of dialogue is mutual learning. Bohm pointed out that we learn from difference, not more of the same. This has wide ramifications for all responses to change. Table 7.2 gives traditional, radical and collective responses to change, leading to three quite distinct discourses that reflect three quite different ways of interpreting reality. Even here the use of language sets the context for the thinking. Writing 'construction of reality' implies that it is built deliberately from concrete materials; 'creation of reality' implies that ideas of the nature of reality emerge from human heads. Collective thinking assumes both are true.

*Table 7.2* Traditional, radical and collective communication

| Component | Traditional | Radical | Collective |
|---|---|---|---|
| introspective | expert | free spirit | networked |
| physical | concrete | relative to thinker | round tables |
| social discourse | tested frameworks | revolutionary agendas | multiple realities |
| ethical principles | objectivity | telling truth to power | mutual responsibility |
| aesthetic thrill | certainty | uncertainty | unity in diversity |
| sympathetic | colleagues | fellow spirits | critical loyalty |
| reflective | testing hypotheses | degree of change | achieving synergy |

### *Pattern language*

For an inclusive language it is important to remember that the message sent can never be the same as the message received. An essential element of any language is that words are interpreted within a given framework. Every individual brings a unique framework developed through their personality, their culture, their experience and their expectations to any exchange. An inclusive language is no exception. Architect Christopher Alexander developed an inclusive language that has spread from the design of built environments to all aspects of living. Alexander works from a belief that everyone who lives has influenced their environment through making a contribution to the design of that environment. He fervently believes that there is a central principle that every design (word or deed) should have 'life', whether it is an apple orchard, a family, a Turkish carpet or a fervent kiss. In every case, this 'life' quality arises from its wholeness.[33]

Alexander faced the paradox that every communication is unique to the sender and the receiver and, for a good life that communication needs to be collectively understood. To resolve this paradox he drew from his extensive experience of designing environments with individuals, communities, cities and governments. He also reflected deeply on the design elements of accidental, natural and cultural environments, starting with the design of Turkish carpets. As a result he developed what he called a pattern language.

Each pattern holds a rule for making centres, acting much like a strange attractor[34] in complexity theory as discussed in Chapter 4. Strong centres are holistic and have life, and so contribute to a good society. Weak centres result in patterns without life, which Alexander regards as socially destructive. The first thing to notice in Alexander's list of the characteristics that bring wholeness or life to centres is that they are not meant to be separated. Everyone is considered equally important and a defining quality. Life is derived from the mutual presence and the synergistic support for each other of all the qualities in Table 7.3.

*Table 7.3* Criteria for strong centres that give life to patterns

| Criteria | Examples |
| --- | --- |
| differing levels of scale | space, time, structures, people, fractals. |
| structure-preserving | centres of action, nodes, nuclei. |
| fluid boundaries | zones of interaction, webs, river banks, edges. |
| alternating repetition | poetry, writing style, lattice, orbits, forests, ripples. |
| positive space | the space within the lines, bubbles, glades. |
| good shape | centres within centres, e.g., leaves on a tree, shells on a beach. |
| local symmetries | volcanoes, human body, book outline, a fingernail, stars. |
| deep interlock | interacting surfaces, overlapping systems. |
| contrast (not dichotomies) | male–female, up–down, positive–negative, night–day. |
| gradients | regular variations of colour, pattern, strength. |
| roughness | irregularity, unevenness, dappled. |
| echoes | repetitions of key characteristics. |
| the void | gaps and spaces that define systems. |
| simplicity and inner calm | simplest form consistent with purpose. |
| non-separateness | recognition that every system is connected to each and every other system at some level. |

After Alexander, C. (2005) *The Nature of Order. Book 4: The Luminous Ground*, Berkeley: The Centre for Environmental Structure.

A second point is that each criterion for wholeness encourages maximum freedom, not a limitation. A third point is that the list itself is only sequential because of the demands of the print medium. Two parallel lists could be constructed, one from an objective scientist, and one from a creative artist. Alexander's list creates a third synergistic space with its own 'wholeness' and integrity, and helps ground Bateson's solution to the double bind[35] of the era of specialisation.

A pattern language is not intended to be a recipe or a set of rules. It is a series of steps which, when taken collectively, maximises diversity and conviviality among the participants. A language can be a medium for prose or for poetry. In prose, each word is expected to have one meaning, and each sentence one idea. In a poem and a pattern, each word carries several meanings. Each sentence or set of patterns in a pattern language holds an enormous density of interlocking meanings, which illuminate the whole. A set of patterns in Alexander's thinking is a collage of a fully connected world. Examples are planning for a communal meal (Box 4.2), an identifiable neighbourhood (Box 4.3) and a collective basis for mind in Table 7.3.

These examples are only the tip of the iceberg. Patterns have been developed for software designs that have influenced the development of Google, Twitter and Facebook. They have been widely used in engineering, administration and planning. One pattern language project, led by educator Doug Schuler, is *Liberating Voices! A Pattern Language for Communication Revolution* that has over 150 patterns and a book on patterns for community-driven transformational change.[36] The project is continuing as a class in Social Imagination and Civic Intelligence.[37] Examples of the patterns are Street Newspapers, Friends of the Earth, Citizens not Corporations, Respectful and Mindful of Age, and Street Music.

A related project has developed a set of anti-patterns, patterns that explain how some events bar the way to community-driven transformational change. Examples are celebrating seven billion people on the planet; obsession with economic growth; incomplete notion of sustainability, and not recognising that ultimately we are all one community.[38]

As an example of practising what one preaches, each of the transformative social structures in Part II of this book is presented in the form of a pattern language. The pattern of a pattern language is developed as follows. A title identifies the strong centre of the change and an illustration sums up the significance of the change. Then comes a detailed description of the larger context in which the change is set. Only then does the pattern describe the issue to be resolved. Describing the issue in its context avoids the common error of assuming that the issue is a cause of the change. It also avoids the risk of approaching the issue as fixed, whereas in a time of transformational change anything is possible. For instance, the cause of the transformational change of the present era is often presented as climate change. Climate change is a result of human activity, not the origin.

To achieve the wholeness desired by Alexander, the issue is described through introspective questions followed by questions on the physical, social, ethical, aesthetic and sympathetic elements, and summed up through the reflective question 'What does this all mean?'. The response to the reflective question is in terms of a strong centre. Finally, examples of the resolution in practice allow the reader to evaluate the usefulness of a pattern for themselves. The examples do not have to have been successful. They do need to illustrate the process of change and the collective learning from the outcome. Box 7.3 gives an example of a pattern that addresses the main aim of this book.

The tools of dialogue and pattern language are keys to the development of a collective mind. Together they form a foundation for an inclusive language and a language that is the glue that holds a collective culture together. These tools are applied in each of the chapters that follow. As a set these chapters offer a structure for a culture of a collective mind. In the next chapter a pattern language forms the basis for a whole-of-community Transformation Science. In the chapter on deep democracy, dialogue is the vehicle for citizens to establish constructive collective positions on strategic issues. Pattern languages allow those positions to be shared and included. In the education chapter, an open educational framework requires such tools to function at all. In a sharing economics, dialogue and patterns provide a basis for agreement to replace cost–benefit analysis and risk profiles. A pattern

---

### Box 7.3  A transformational change to a collective mind

**Context:** the context for this pattern is an all-pervading question 'In times of transformational change, how shall we live?'. The future is uncertain because human actions have brought new social and environmental changes to a planet that had been self-organising since its inception five billion years ago. There is a wide acceptance that the disruptions are unprecedented and risk leading to permanent changes that will risk the viability of the human species. There is also acceptance that any response needs to be collective. All ideas and skills need to be harnessed in a collective response that permits the self-organising systems of the planet to continue to support life in general and humanity in particular. To harness all human capacities requires the answers to seven questions: introspective, physical, social, ethical, aesthetic, sympathetic and reflective.

**Issue:** at present the dominance of physical and social questions is obscuring the crucial replies to the others. This dominance has not only led to the fragmentation of knowledge and adversarial decision making, but also to the denial of the existence of the other constructions as legitimate forms of knowledge. The result has been a skewed understanding of contemporary problems, and an inability to achieve collective solutions.

**Resolution:** seven questions, answered in concert by all the principle interest groups, will reorient the issue into a shared dilemma rather than a fragmented problem. These interest groups will include key individuals, affected communities, specialists, influential organisations and creative thinkers. Strategies that make it easier for these groups to understand each other's languages, aims, timescales and expectations include an inclusive language based on dialogue and pattern languages.

**Examples**: this book Brown, V. A. and Harris, J. A. (2014) *The Human Capacity for Transformational Change: Harnessing the Collective Mind* and the guidebook Brown, V. A. and Lambert, J. A. (2013) *Collective Learning for Transformational Change: A Guide to Collaborative Action.*

---

language allows all the interests involved in any transformational change to discover the relationships between their answers to the reflective question 'In times of transformational change, how shall we live?'. A pattern language example of how to achieve a collective neighbourhood with which the residents can identify is in Chapter 4 (Box 4.3).

## Notes

1 This Chapter has been developed from Brown, V. A. (2010) 'Multiple knowledges, multiple languages: Are the limits of my language the limits of my world?' *Knowledge Management for Development Journal* **6** (2), pp. 120–31.
2 The hashtag is the # symbol used to mark keywords or topics in a Tweet. It was created by Twitter users as a way to categorise messages.
3 This was a video of the death of Neda Agha-Soltan who was a protester during the 2009 Iranian elections. Her shooting was captured by bystanders and broadcast over the Internet, becoming a rallying point for the opposition.

4 In this case it is of a Congolese peacemaker, Henri BuraLadyi who frees boy soldiers from rebel forces. See http://www.independent.co.uk/news/world/independent-appeal-africas-schindler-1835510.html [accessed 2.6.13].

5 Whorf, B. L. and Carroll, J. B. (1956) (eds) *Language, Thought, and Reality: Selected Writings*, Massachusetts, US: MIT Press. Whorf was a pioneering linguist who advocated the idea that language shapes our inherent thoughts: the Sapir-Whorf hypothesis.

6 Malcolm, N. (1984) *Ludwig Wittgenstein: A Memoir*, New York: Oxford University Press. For the quotation, see http://www.iep.utm.edu/wittgens/ [accessed 2.6.13].

7 Brown, V. A. and Lambert, J. A. (2013) *Collective Learning for Transformational Change: A Guide to Collaborative Action*, London and New York: Routledge.

8 Polanyi, M. (1958) *Personal Knowledge: Towards a Post-Critical Philosophy,* Chicago, US: University of Chicago Press. Lakoff, G. (1994) *Don't Think of an Elephant! Know your Values and Frame the Debate*, Vermont, US: Chelsea Green.

9 See also Keen, M., Brown, V. A. and Dyball, R. (2005) (eds) *Social Learning in Environmental Management: Towards a Sustainable Future*, London: Routledge. Brown, V. A. (2010) 'Collective Inquiry and Its Wicked Problems' in Brown, V. A., Harris, J. A. and Russell, J. Y. (eds) *Tackling Wicked Problems: Through the Transdisciplinary Imagination*, London: Earthscan, pp. 61–81.

10 Ralston Saul, J. (1992) *Voltaire's Bastards: The Dictatorship of Reason in the West*, New York: Simon & Schuster.

11 See for example, van Kerkhoff, L. (2010) 'Global Inequalities in Research: A Transdisciplinary Exploration of Causes and Consequences' in Brown, V. A., Harris, J. A. and Russell, J. Y. (eds) *Tackling Wicked Problems: Through the Transdisciplinary Imagination*, London: Earthscan, pp. 130–38.

12 Chapters 5 and 6.

13 Brown, V. A. and Lambert, J. A. (2013) *Collective Learning for Transformational Change: A Guide to Collaborative Action*, London and New York: Routledge.

14 Bohm, D. (1996) (2004) *On Dialogue*, New York: Routledge Classics. Isaacs, W. (1999) *Dialogue and the Art of Thinking Together*, New York: Currency. See also Chapter 9 where the 'worldwork' of Amy and Arnold Mindell is discussed.

15 Chapter 4. Alexander, C., Ishikawa, S., Silverstein, M., Jacobson, M., Fiksdahl-King, I. and Angel, S. (1977) *A Pattern Language: Towns, Buildings and Constructions,* New York: Oxford University Press.

16 McMahon, A. M. S. (1994) *Understanding Language Change*, Cambridge, UK: Cambridge University Press.

17 Meadows, D. H., Meadows, D. L. and Randers, J. (1992) *Beyond the Limits: Global Collapse or a Sustainable Future*, London: Earthscan.

18 Putman, R. (2000) *Bowling Alone: The Collapse and Revival of American Community*, New York: Simon & Schuster.

19 See http://www.jabberwocky.com/carroll/jabber/jabberwocky.html [accessed 4.6.13].

20 MacDonald, R. (1998) *Mr. Darwin's Shooter: A Novel*, Sydney: Random House. The book covers the life of Syms Covington who was Charles Darwin's manservant on the voyage of the *Beagle*.

21 For example see Sykes, B. (2001) *The Seven Daughters of Eve: The Science that reveals our Genetic Ancestry*, New York: Norton. The previously hidden pattern revealed by Sykes is that all modern humans are genetically related. He tells the story of how by using mitochondrial DNA and analyses of ancient DNA all modern humans can be traced to a small suite of prehistoric ancestors. See also, Oppenheimer, S. (2003) *Out of Eden: The peopling of the world*, London: Robinson, where the common human journey of the whole of humanity is revealed.

22 The New Zealand Treaty of Waitangi. See http://www.waitangi-tribunal.govt.nz/treaty/ [accessed 5.6.13].

23  wa Goro, W. (2007) 'Translating Africa and Leadership: What Is Africa to Me?' in Wambu, O. (ed.) *Under The Tree of Talking: Leadership and Change in Africa*, London: Counterpoint.

24  The Live Aid Concert in 1985 was one of the largest satellite link-ups and television broadcasts ever attempted. It was organized by Bob Geldof and Midge Ure to raise funds for the Ethiopian famine. The concert reached an estimated audience of 1.9 billion across 150 nations. See http://en.wikipedia.org/wiki/Live_Aid [accessed 5.6.13].

25  The Pacific Ocean Tsunami occurred on 26 December 2004. The estimated US$14 billion donated was more than seven times the amount of emergency aid provided to all recorded natural disasters from 1992–2004 (US$1.91 billion). https://crawford.anu.edu.au/acde/publications/publish/papers/wp2012/wp_econ_2012_04.pdf [accessed 5.6.13].

26  Pers. com. Lynette Liddle, Indigenous PhD student, The Australian National University, 2010.

27  Bohm, D. (1980) *Wholeness and Implicate Order*, London: Routledge. Bohm, D. (1994) *Thought as a System*, London and New York: Routledge.

28  See 'Participatory Thought and the Unlimited' in Bohm, D. (1996/2010) *On Dialogue*, New York: Routledge, pp. 96–109.

29  Skolimowski, H. (1994) *The Participatory Mind: A New Theory of Knowledge and of the Universe*, London: Arkana.

30  Merchant, C. (1980) *The Death of Nature*, New York: Harper and Row. See also Sheldrake, R. (1990) *The Rebirth of Nature: The Greening of Science and God*, London: Century, Mathews, F. (1991) *The Ecological Self*, London: Routledge and Plumwood, V. (2002) *Environmental Culture: The Ecological Crisis of Reason*, London and New York: Routledge.

31  Bohm, D. (1980) *Wholeness and Implicate Order*, London: Routledge. Bohm, D. (1994) *Thought as a System*, London and New York: Routledge.

32  Brown, V. A. and Lambert, J. A. (2013) *Collective Learning for Transformational Change: A Guide to Collaborative Action*, London and New York: Routledge.

33  Alexander, C. (2002) *The Nature of Order. Book One: The Phenomenon of Life*, Berkeley, US: The Centre for Environmental Structure.

34  An attractor in complex systems refers to its ability to attract a trajectory. A point attractor occurs in systems tending towards a stable equilibrium and a strange attractor for corresponding chaotic systems.

35  Chapter 3.

36  Schuler, D. (2008) *Liberating Voices: A Pattern Language for Communication Revolution*, Massachusetts, US: MIT Press.

37  See http://www.publicsphereproject.org/patterns/lv [accessed 20.7.13].

38  Pers. com. Doug Schuler, Faculty member of Evergreen State College, Seattle, USA.

# 8 Transformation science

## A science of change

**Pattern:** a science of change.

**Context:** in a complex world of wicked problems that require changes in the society that produced them, the current era of the Anthropocene is realigning the relationships between the non-living, living and human mind dimensions of the planet, and so poses a challenge to traditional science.

**Issue:** the conduct of science has been increasingly compartmentalised over three centuries and now needs to draw on its considerable capacity for collective thought.

**Resolution:** practitioners of transformation science draw on introspective, physical, social, ethical, aesthetic, sympathetic and reflective sources of evidence, bringing in a new era of collective scientific thought.

**Examples:** transformation science is applied to a snapshot of the expanding city of Kunming, China, and the potential pandemic of Severe Acute Respiratory Syndrome (SARS).

## Context: a complex world of wicked problems

The pursuit of scientific inquiry has much to gain and much to lose as it responds to twenty-first century transformational change. On any complex issue, physical evidence alone is not enough. Other forms of questioning – introspective, social, ethical, aesthetic, sympathetic and reflective – are increasingly being added to the essential physical inquiries in reaching an understanding of how the world works.[1] For scientists to continue to act as if objective inquiry was the only source of legitimate knowledge on an issue reduces the credibility of their findings. On the positive side, the sophistication with which the tools of science can contribute to knowledge has increased several-fold.[2] Consider the role of science in space exploration, the eradication of poliomyelitis, renewable energy and the social communication of Facebook. Physical science remains an essential contributor to the resolution of complex issues even if it is no longer universally accepted as sufficient in itself.

The Latin origin of the word science is 'knowledge', thereby putting forward a claim to be the fount of all knowledge, and so the very foundation of what it is to be human. When, post-Darwin, human beings were accepted as a species among other living species, scientists labelled us *Homo sapiens sapiens*, the thinking species that thinks, making rational thought the mark of humanity. The results of a scientific investigation are regularly equated with the entire truth. The frequent use of phrases like 'the science establishes that', 'because science tells us' implies that it is the definitive word about the subject and nothing more needs to be said.

Science has made extensive claims for its signature goals of objectivity and reliability ever since its beginnings in the seventeenth century. Normal scientific practice involves reducing complex physical, social and ethical issues to a few key factors that can be readily observed. Consider trying to judge the effect of a tsunami on a community by the physical damage alone; evaluating the health of a river system by the number of human faecal bacteria;[3] and estimating the wealth of a nation by community spending patterns. In each case, one measurable factor has been taken for the whole. Significant influences are left unidentified, and there is insufficient evidence to support the decisions needed for action in the real world.

For a long time during the nineteenth and twentieth centuries, scientists appeared justified in making this claim. The transformational change to objective thinking came with René Descartes' proposition that the human mind could stand apart from the rest of the world: 'I think, therefore I am'. Descartes himself did not believe that this was more than an artificial device to explore one way of thinking among many. He had no problem in maintaining his faith in God and recognised that there were other ways of thinking.

Not only humans, but also the non-living and living worlds of the planet have had to respond to the after-effects of one species learning to reflect on its own reflections. Sociologists call reflections on reflections 'reflexivity'.[4] It is not surprising that this transformational change of the seventeenth century was called the Enlightenment. The whole world became reflected in this new light of objective inquiry. The outcome was a technological revolution that engulfed the planet.[5] The next transformational change was generated by human activities driven by human thought, and so has been labelled the human-dominated era, the Anthropocene.

The Enlightenment began with René Descartes' inspired ruling that the basis for the existence of human knowledge was that he could doubt everything except that he was, in fact, doubting.[6] Rather than look out the window at the way the world actually works, science learnt to abstract particular segments of reality to address that doubt.[7] Apprentices were trained in the same reductive mould.[8] During the 300 years of the Enlightenment, science sought to reassure the doubtful by reducing complexity and eliminating uncertainty by reliable observations of the biophysical world. Despite their dramatic successes, the methods of the Enlightenment have failed to resolve human-driven climate change, food insecurity and the decade-long difference in life expectancy between the majority poor and the minority rich. Something more is needed.

## Issue: compartments of knowledge

Over the years the Enlightenment gave rise to separate communities of practice with their own organisations, power hierarchies, questions to answer and entry boundaries to protect their resources. These communities grew into tightly held organisations that shaped the social world. They gave rise to the educational institutions, bureaucratic departments and service industries that form the structure of society. Compartments of knowledge such as medicine, sociology and psychology tried to explain the workings of the human body, the society and the mind through physical cause and effect relationships that matched Newton's laws of motion. This direction continued on through the nineteenth and twentieth centuries, even in the face of the work of Albert Einstein on the relativity of time and space, Charles Darwin's treatise on human emotions as a factor in evolutionary change, James Lovelock's recognition of the world as being created by interactive patterns of self-organising systems and Wiener's now fulfilled predictions of the creation of self-organising communication systems.

It is a hundred years since Albert Einstein moved to the idea of energy exchange as a fluid relationship[9] rather than Newton's action and reaction energy transfer. It is also a century since Nils Bohr recognised that an observer's framework determined their interpretation of reality, and that more than one understanding of the world can be valid at the same time.[10] It is 50 years since Prigogine and Stengers[11] identified the shortfall between the laws of thermodynamics, where physical science established the rule of a universe of continually dissipating energy (entropy), and biological science that established that the world harnessed and stored energy from the sun. Transformation science has replaced the steady state Newtonian world with constant evolutionary change, complementary realities[12] and dynamic self-organising systems. Yet much of mainstream science continues to restrict itself to Newtonian images of physical reality.

The forefront of science now concedes that human brains can never provide a precise match for reality.[13] Humans must always interpret the world through their biologically inherited organs of perception and interpretation. Three distinct and co-existing arrows of time are now recognised in which Bohr's complementarity comes into play. Time in the non-living systems of the universe has been found to be measurable and reversible. The time scale is infinite and the context is space-time.[14] In the living biological world, time is irreversible. Each shift in genetic inheritance, way of thinking and cultural learning introduces permanent and continuing change into a dynamic system. The third arrow of time is that of the human lifespan, both personally and in conjunction with the lives of other human beings.

Human time is necessarily collective. Individuals modify each other's construction of reality since they are social animals. In nature dominated societies time can be circular, an unending sequence of seasons. The timescale of an individual's life experience has been estimated by anthropologist Margaret Mead as five generations, from grandchild to grandparent.[15] The extension of life expectancy to 85 years extends this possibility to seven generations. For each individual their memory is stored permanently as a chemical record that is continually being added to by their inbuilt capacity to learn.[16] Although individuals may not necessarily learn what their society or their families want them to learn, collective learning itself is inevitable.

Not only are there three distinct arrows of time, belief in a single physical world has been replaced by acceptance of multiple interpretations of reality.[17] Social, ethical, aesthetic and sympathetic dimensions of human existence are as core to human understanding as is the physical evidence issued from science.[18] The science community can regain their claim to being indispensable by working in partnership with each of these rather than dismissing them. Scientists themselves construct their understanding through these diverse contributions to knowledge: social learning in their communities of practice, their ethical commitment to using scientific methods, the aesthetics of an elegant investigation design, and the sympathetic exchange of understanding among close peers. These contributions to knowledge each have their own criteria for validity, their own tests for truth and their own body of accepted knowledge.[19]

As the Enlightenment continued, other versions of reality exploded. The nineteenth century work of the Romantic poets became part of the everyday English language.[20] However, this new knowledge was relegated to the arts and humanities outside science, thus isolating the remit of science ever further.[21] The painter Picasso opened a door between intelligence and creativity when he painted the horror of the impact of technology on the human world. In *Guernica* Picasso documented his reaction to the first aerial bombing raid on civilians, in Guernica in Spain in 1937 (Figure 8.1). His ethical outrage, aesthetic expression and sympathetic identification with the victims are as evident in the painting as a historical record of a real-world event.

A future direction for transformation science is to accept the different contributions to human understanding made by the seven essential ways of knowing. These include the reality checks of asking physical, social, ethical, aesthetic and sympathetic questions, and two further questions that call on inward reflection. The first, an inwardly directed question, establishes the position of the scientist in relation to the problem. The second, and concluding, step is collective reflection on the answers to the questions (Figure 8.2).

*Figure 8.1* Bombing raid on Guernica: Pablo Picasso 1937 (Museo Nacional Centro de Arte Reina Sofia/Scala)

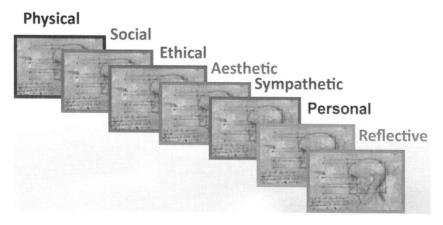

*Figure 8.2* Collective questions in Transformation Science

In their personal reflections, the would-be scientists will need to identify for themselves and their partners the role they intend to play: specialist, action researcher, advisor, learner or inquirer. They will need to clarify their ethical relationship to the inquiry: partner, independent observer, helper, teacher or fellow-learner; to consider the potential source of aesthetic satisfaction in the design of the inquiry, whether it will be tightly organised, have open-ended structures, practical implications and space to exercise the imagination; and to establish some means of sympathetic communication with their partners so that there is mutual understanding throughout the inquiry: dialogue, diary and conversation and discussion (not debate) occurs.

In Transformation Science the scientific community is returning to its central role in an inquiry, although it is now not alone. Scientists are instead working collectively with other ways of knowing, either personally or in groups. Having been taught to banish the self from their inquiry, sharing in collective thinking means that it is time for scientists to put themselves back in the picture. Anthropocentric thought, that is, putting the human position at the centre, is traditionally frowned on by science. Now it becomes a necessary step to recognising the full range of evidence relevant to any issue. Humans have no choice but to be anthropocentric, since their very capacity to reflect is a human characteristic. However, humility lies in realising that anthropocentrism is a limitation, as well as a human gift, since human understanding of the world is necessarily limited by the limits to their own thinking.[22]

The impact of a new way of thinking can be compared with Darwin's evidence for adaptive radiation in the environmental sphere. When a fresh context opens up, at first there is nothing there. Existing forms can move into the space without competition for resources with other forms. They are free to collaborate with one another, so new forms survive and flourish. A classic example is the story of the transformational changes in mammals after their warm-blooded, live-birth advantages had established their capacity to spread over the surface of the earth.

Their evolution from that point included re-invading the air (bats), the oceans (whales) and the trees (monkeys). They occupied the food niches of carnivores (lions), vegetarians (cows) and omnivores (humans).

The same can be said of the spread of ideas. When science adopted its straitjacket of pure objectivity it spread into all other forms of thought, the disciplines and professions. Once science accepts that this is a world that is increasingly being oriented collectively, bringing together multiple timescales, multiple realities and increasing complexity, it has an open environment in which to develop its skills. Science is free to work collectively with social, ethical, aesthetic and sympathetic ways of knowing an issue. However, as Thomas Kuhn predicted, much of its organisational structure, reward system and inquiry method continues to remain restricted to the physical world of normal science and so inhibits the ability to change.[23]

As well as accepting partnerships with other ways of knowing, the greatest step in a new direction is to answer the reflective question: what does it all mean? For science, defined by the chemist Medawar as 'the art of the soluble',[24] it is a challenge to reflect on diverse evidence with the recognition that certainty and a final solution are out of the question. For these questions, some form of synthesis is needed. From a scientist's perspective, one of the outstanding characteristics of the Anthropocene is the move to thinking of the world as a pattern of interconnected systems influenced by human ideas.

Evidence of a continually increasing complexity in both biophysical and social evolution has led to the study of chaos theory as a complex pattern of feedback systems.[25] When the diversity is great and the pressures for change extreme, there is coexistence of chance and necessity, of random events and predetermined rules, and chaos shapes itself into a self-organising system.[26] The classic descriptions of the beat of a butterfly wing in Brazil leading to a typhoon in Texas,[27] or the rich history of a city such as Paris generating its own capacity for survival,[28] are examples of the physical and social self-organising patterns generated within conditions of chaos.

Following the three arrows of time of the universe, social and personal worlds leads to space travel, social movement and a new discipline of cognitive science. The first arrow of physical time is still a primary concern of the scientist, although science is increasingly being joined with the other ways of knowing. The second arrow, of social time, has led to the social revolutions of direct democracy,[29] an exchange economy[30] and self-organising utopias.[31] The third arrow has led to a reconsideration of the individual as a collective learner.[32] Advanced technology applied to the study of the active brain has allowed cognitive science to establish the malleability, versatility and open-endedness of the capacity of the human brain.[33] This and the predictions of Teilhard de Chardin on the collective mind, and Wiener of the cybernetic mind, suggest that humanity is only at the beginning of the next transformational change to a collective mind.

Given these wholesale changes in understandings of time, diversity and complexity, science cannot avoid the need to change. If their physical and social environments are changing, so are scientists, personally and professionally, even if they do not realise it at first. Scientists are already bemoaning the fact that their findings and predictions are no longer automatically adopted as valid by the community or politicians. There has been a major shift toward accepting the complexities that accompany the transformational physical and social changes. Failure to take account of these interactions can lead to significant error or can make a whole study invalid.

## Resolution: science as a knowledge partner

In the mid-twentieth century the Macy Conferences initiated cross-disciplinary collaboration among leading thinkers of the time.[34] The now familiar frameworks of systems theory, cybernetics and cognitive science sprang from this collective interaction. By the 1970s, these ideas were mature enough to be making a difference to the practice of science, so that the reductionist strand epitomised by the Vienna Circle of specialist scientists,[35] and the Macy change-based transformational strand co-existed, as they do still. Institutions can still be torn apart by conflict between the two for dominance.[36] This polarisation seems unnecessary, since the ideas of adaptive radiation and complementarity allow both to survive in parallel.

In the early 1970s, planners Rittel and Webber wrote a paper[37] that faced up squarely to the complexity of the issues being faced by planners: the multiple interests, the local and global environmental changes, and the unknown future. They pointed out that, while planners had historically reduced complex problems to simple problems solvable by existing methods, the ground was increasingly moving under their feet. As it became accepted that human decisions were responsible for acute environmental and social changes, and new communication channels rapidly spread those changes within urban and rural lifestyles, they were being faced with a different task. Scientists were being asked to tackle the whole of complex problems, embrace change and uncertainty, and take account of the full context of an issue.

Rittel and Webber called these complex issues wicked problems, and characterised them as complex issues which are an integral part of the society that has generated them. Thus any resolution of a wicked problem necessarily changes the society that produced it. As well as different forms of governance and changes in ways of living, resolution of wicked problems requires a new approach to the conduct of an inquiry and so to science itself. A wicked problem can never be completely defined, given the many interests in its resolution. There can be no final solution, since any resolution will undoubtedly generate further problems. Solutions cannot be true or false, or good or bad, they are the best that can be done at the time. Such problems are not morally wicked, but diabolical in that they resist all the usual attempts to resolve them.

Rittel and Webber did make the statement, however, that they considered treating complex problems as if they were simple problems as morally indefensible.[38] The original paper on wicked problems has been followed by an unbroken stream applying these characteristics to problems in engineering, software design, education, policy, health and indeed all forms of human service. Together they make a foundation for a science that can respond to complex changes with options for response. Wicked problems cannot be simply solved, but they can be resolved, moving the issues in a fresh direction, ready for continuing resolution.

In the fast-changing world of the 1970s, Silvio Funtowicz and Jerome Ravetz developed a science to operate when, as they said, facts are uncertain, values in dispute, stakes high and decisions urgent – all typical of the conditions accompanying transformational change.[39] These authors called the new science Post-Normal Science, following Thomas Kuhn's work on the mechanical and repetitive nature of normal science. Post-Normal Science differs radically from traditional science in that, instead of simplifying, it embraces complexity by examining all the contributing factors in capturing the essence of an issue. These interests include the marginalised and vulnerable as well as the powerful, the old and the young, the North and the South. Most importantly, it includes the perspectives of the scientists themselves.

Kuhn had categorised original science as imaginative, creative and rule-breaking. Funtowicz and Ravetz proposed a Post-Normal Science that incorporated both normal and revolutionary science. They noted that science was already in pursuit of the complex problems of a changing world in the manner described by Gregory Bateson, who put forward a theory of mind as a negotiation for living sustainably within the living world, the non-living world and the world of human thought.[40] Post-Normal Science explains this negotiation as the integration of scientific and technical expertise with local knowledge and the legitimate interests, values and desires of all those affected by the change, including the scientists themselves.[41]

It takes a further step to complete the transition to Transformation Science. While Post-Normal Science included all the interests, it did not provide a bridging mechanism to bring together the essential reflective questions. In the post-Enlightenment's fragmented and compartmentalised world, different forms of thought did not readily come together, much less work collectively on the same issues. This has not proved impossible, however. The many examples of collective learning able to resolve seemingly unsolvable wicked problems include the post-war reunification of Germany, the eradication of SARS (Figure 8.5), the emergence of Myanmar-Burma elections and the global social movements of Amnesty,[42] Avaaz[43] and Transition Towns.[44]

Common sense and experience confirm that we all make use of the two inward-directed questions, introspective and reflective, and five outward-directed questions, physical, social, ethical, aesthetic and sympathetic, every time we make a significant decision that will affect our lives. We combine the physical evidence for our final choice with the social consequences, the ethical implications (for good or ill), the aesthetic sensation of something 'feeling right' and the sympathetic influence that comes from our role models. We mostly do this on the basis of our assumptions about the subject, making it hard for us to change. We may make our final reflective decision in the blink of an eye, or it may take us months of agonising. Since the Western cultural tradition privileges the physical and the social sources of information, and rarely reflects on the ethical, aesthetic and sympathetic, the first two may be the only sources reflected upon in even the most important decision.

In Transformation Science, however, since the context of the decision is part of the process of change, the concluding reflection will need to include the answers to all outwardly directed questions. The answers will each be tested for validity and truth. Transformation Science is principally responsible for exploring the observable, material dimension of the selected issue, and will contribute to the observable account of the other four questions. Having identified the responses to the five outwardly directed questions and confirming the assumptions of the inquirer themselves, Transformation Science needs to ask the concluding reflective questions: 'Taking all the answers together, what is the significance of it all?', 'What does it all mean?' or even, 'So what?'.

Retrospectively examining some collective enterprises gives an idea of how transformation science might collect its evidence. An example of Transformation Science perspectives on a city, Kunming, follows (Figure 8.3). The example of the city provides the evidence base for further inquiry into any special aspect of the city, such as its liveability, economy, public health and environment. The example of the disease SARS[45] (Figure 8.5) gives an insight into the collective thinking that underlies the collaboration involved in Transformation Science.

### Story of a city

#### Physical questions

Kunming is a once isolated Chinese city on a high plateau (1500 m) between Laos, Cambodia and Vietnam. This is the golden triangle for heroin drug production. Population growth was 6 million to 10.5 million in ten years, even with the one child policy, which is weaker in the country and often waived for rural people. The city covers 2000 km² and is still growing. There is a large gap between the urban rich and the rural poor who are flooding into the city. Industries are tourism, forestry, minerals, flowers and drugs. There is an equable mountain climate year round. Excellent transport routes and wide city roads are now clogged with traffic. Energy is cheap with local shale oil gas and solar panels – visible on all high-rise apartment roofs.

## Example: City of Kunming, Yunnan, China

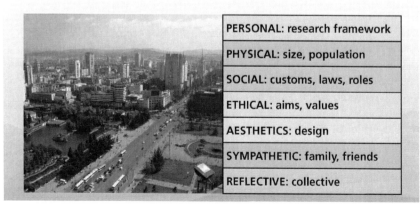

*Figure 8.3* Collective questions for the city of Kunming

*Social questions*

A trading post and cultural mix for centuries, Kunming has now embraced the Western technological world. A health transition is in progress, with both traditional and Western medicines being used. AIDS/HIV is present and drug (heroin and amphetamine) supplies come in from the golden triangle. Medical assistance is free, hospitals and clinics are available, but medical drugs have to be paid for somehow. Aged-care and education are universal and free, as are secondary schools, universities and trade schools. Women expect to be in the workforce. It is common to see grandfather, parents and one grandchild at lunch at one of the many local food stalls or cafes that everyone uses. This standard demographic profile is a remnant of the earlier deaths from childbearing and the shift to a high protein diet, now changing to the Western pattern.

*Ethical questions*

The formal ethical system is socialism (everyone shares equally in the national well-being) although free enterprise is increasingly coming into everyday practice. Buddhist and Moslem minorities coexist; although small in number they are still influential. There has been, and still seems to be, an age-old reverence for nature. Wealth inequality between senior party officials and the rest of the population draws criticism from the rest of the world, and is beginning to be voiced inside China. Formal communication (public speech, newspapers) is heavily controlled and criticism of the state is subject to heavy penalties.

*Aesthetic questions*

Traditional and modern buildings coexist; clothing is almost entirely Western. Food and food customs follow the local Chinese cuisine. Well-to-do weddings are photographed twice: in Western white bridal dress and then traditional Chinese dress. The Cultural Revolutionary phase of destroying Emperor Buildings for new structures and dressing in blue denim has passed. The old city wall was torn down by a youth brigade to build a road. The current problem is to carefully protect the old part of Kunming and take part in European high fashion design. Ballet, opera and theatre are a mixture of traditional and modern.

*Sympathetic questions*

People in the city have a strong sense of themselves as fellow residents of Kunming. As a place on the Old Silk Road, Kunming was a melting pot of travellers. Then, when it became a place of banishment and refuge during the Cultural Revolution, people stayed after it was over, preferring Kunming to wherever they had come from. At least to the outside observer, Kunming residents appear to be getting on with social and industrial development, and are not as vocal on human rights as other Chinese cities.

*Introspective questions*

The personal position of a Kunming dweller appears to be tending toward the centre. Male and female roles are becoming more alike in the workforce and at home. Men are freed from being the sole breadwinner, and women are freed from solely domestic duties. Males are still valued more than females. Live birth ratios in some provinces are 130 males to 100 females.

*Reflective questions*

To this outside observer, the strongest sense of the city of Kunming is self-sufficiency. People banished from Beijing to isolated Kunming chose to stay there. The local economy, energy supply and festivals are strong. Food and energy supplies are local. Kunming is a strong regional centre, people are there by choice and the future is open. Answers to questions from community members, civic leaders and creative thinkers, as well as scientists, are necessary before the overall synergy from the reflective answers can be complete.

Jane Jacobs was one of the most influential of the late twentieth century writers on cities.[46] She proposed that cities worked because they were self-organised by their citizens. She went beyond the built environment and social structures to an understanding of cities as organic systems – complex, evolving living things. For their inhabitants the city takes precedence over their nation, sets the local moral codes, and a city dies when the ethical principles stagnate. Jacobs saw patterns in the systems that make the city and that 'the list of patterns of ideas waiting to be connected is almost endless'.

Ways to describe a city in all its complexity and richness start to emerge from the example of Kunming. Whether the questioner answers all the questions themselves or recruits all available expertise depends on the occasion. Whether the answers are adequate is a measure of the inquiry, as in all cases of searching for the truth. To go into further detail there are two sets of questions that need to be asked: five plus two. Each makes use of a different source of evidence, a different dimension of the whole. The outer-directed five are asked by the investigator(s) exploring the chosen topic in its context. For the two inner-directed questions, the answers lie in the reflections of the investigator(s). For the five reality checks, much evidence will already be available. They can be answered from literature reviews, records, interviews and observations of behaviour and events.

The general principles that underlie the seven ways of understanding have been explored in some detail in Chapters 5 and 6. In this chapter they are applied to three examples: a city in China, a global network and a global epidemic.

The introduction of a collective creation of knowledge has been rapid and widespread. Since the 1990s, major investigations have been team affairs that included community representatives, and the results were issued in the forms of accessible syntheses compiled from thousands of pages of heavily referenced data. The synthesis papers of the Millennium Development Goals[47] and the International Panel on Climate Change[48] have had wider circulation among decision makers and were subjected to no greater dissent than the constituent specialist papers. The many documentaries such as Al Gore's *An Inconvenient Truth*[49] and Michael Moore's *Bowling for Columbine*[50] have been able to summarise wider swathes of information and quickly bring it to the attention of the whole population. Social media goes even further with a fresh piece of information 'going viral' and drawing reactions from all sources in a common format.

Also since the 1990s. formal organisations for arranging knowledge have moved to platforms for collective rather than specialist organisations. Centres for dialogue in Canada and Switzerland, think tanks drawing advice from different sides of political divides, peak forums for current issues such as the World Economic Forum and the World Social Forum, and the emergence of decision-making summits are all confirmation of a move to handling transformational change by collective learning where all sources of knowledge come together.

At a finer-grained level, the techniques for arriving at the collage constructed by multiple realities have multiplied. Systems diagrams, symbolic interpretations, narratives, modes of data visualisation, social media and crowd sourcing are all as much part of describing a collective society as the abacus was to finance in traditional Asian cities. Nevertheless, there are particular characteristics that distinguish them as collective rather than reductive and divisive. Systems diagrams place as much emphasis on the relationships between the parts as the parts themselves; on the arrows as well as the boxes. The systems are open-ended, making way for the transformational change, not endlessly recycling as in a steady state or resilient system. Using analogies, metaphors and symbols help greatly in describing a complex whole without reducing it to parts, although the hidden meaning needs to be carefully diagnosed beforehand.

The narrative mode, telling a story, allows for the insightful and highly relevant points to be made in context. Data visualisation takes advantages of the myriad ways in which computer graphics can convey a complex, many-faceted reality, from simple pie charts to animations. Social media can carry essential information and give a much-needed finding an airing just as well as they can carry social gossip and nonsense. Crowd sourcing is an interesting recent use of the potential of the all-pervading Internet. Effective for simple surveys on a yes/no basis, help forums, and for raising research funds for a neglected or controversial topic, crowd sourcing sends appeals for information and funds into the ether, attracting complete strangers with a common interest.

To ask and to answer reflective questions that combine other ways of knowing is the greatest challenge for Transformation Science. After so many generations of specialised thinking on the one issue, methods for collecting evidence, ways to bring it together and finally to convey the result to others are all so streamlined that it has become difficult for members of one specialisation to access the knowledge held by another. Transformation Science has to go back in history to before the Enlightenment and forward to the forefront of science to find a common language and first principles that the diverse contributors can share. Socrates, Plato, Aristotle and Pythagoras come to mind for the first, and in this book Darwin, Lovelock and Wiener represent the second.

No matter how many technical advances there are in methods for reaching a collective understanding, the heart of this understanding remains based in the familiar words of John Donne in 1624:[51]

> No man is an island,
> Entire of itself
>
> …
>
> Any man's death diminishes me,
> Because I am involved in mankind,
> And therefore never send to know for whom the bell tolls.
> It tolls for thee.
>
> *John Donne 1624*

## Examples: a global network and a global epidemic

### *The story of a global network: Transition Towns*

#### *Physical*

The basis for the Transition Towns movement is the prediction that severe climate change, a shortfall in global oil supplies and another global financial crisis will lead to transformational changes for the living planet. Over 400 centres in five of the seven continents have formed a global network of human settlements that embrace the goal of establishing physical and emotional resilience during the transition.

#### *Social*

The Transition Towns settlements are pursuing local self-organisation of ideas and actions that will allow them to maintain their identity and preferred way of life in the face of transformational change. Working together they hope to be able to mediate the impact of the changes on the planet itself. The springboards are the

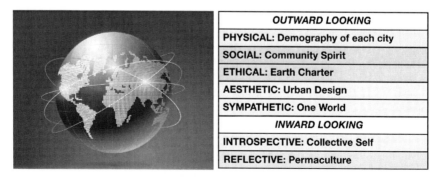

| OUTWARD LOOKING |
| --- |
| PHYSICAL: Demography of each city |
| SOCIAL: Community Spirit |
| ETHICAL: Earth Charter |
| AESTHETIC: Urban Design |
| SYMPATHETIC: One World |
| *INWARD LOOKING* |
| INTROSPECTIVE: Collective Self |
| REFLECTIVE: Permaculture |

*Figure 8.4* Totnes: a Transition Town

organic agricultural movement of Permaculture,[52] based on working in partnership with nature; and a local exchange trading system that creates a local economy with its own trading money, offering reciprocal social support such as cooking meals, child care or health care.

## Ethical

Transition Towns has a strong and well-articulated ethic: respect for the ability of people to generate a beneficial and resilient economic, cultural and spiritual existence as a community. Members provide support for any community that aims to fulfil that goal. Rules for project support are: the personal growth of all involved; to strengthen or build community; and work in the service of Earth. The project uses the Earth Charter[53] as a guide.

## Aesthetic

A key aspect of all the Transition Towns projects is the need for beauty and balance. The order in Permaculture plantations is always beautiful and productive; the trading schemes are emotionally rewarding and fun; and the organisation of successful change is a creative leap toward the community's goals.

## Sympathetic

The community spirit within Transition Towns is remarked on by all participants. This spirit is the driving force of the whole network.

## Reflective

The answers to all the external questions add up to a self-reliant, self-sufficient community, with its own self-sufficiency design, economy and agenda for action. The illustration is of the town of Totnes, which was the original launching site and which still acts as an example for all the others. Totnes has the Totnes Pound,[54] an internal economy.

Totnes Transition Town members work with members of local government and vice versa. The core (strong centre) of the Totnes program is derived from the 12 Permaculture principles, which can also be extended to collective democracy: 1) observe and interact with everything around you; 2) catch and store physical, social and mental energy; 3) obtain a result: any changes to any system should be productive; 4) apply self-regulation and accept feedback; 5) use and value renewable resources and services; 6) produce no waste; 7) design from patterns to details; 8) integrate rather than segregate; 9) use small and slow solutions, at the smallest possible scale; 10) use and value diversity; 11) use edges and value the marginal; and 12) creatively use and respond to change.

### The story of a global epidemic

In January 2003 a communicable disease with a mortality rate of 15 per cent, equal to medieval smallpox (physical), erupted into a world that thought it had the capacity to control such infectious diseases (social). SARS crossed species boundaries to human beings, causing a wicked problem locally and globally, socially, environmentally and professionally (reflective). Initially it could not be clearly defined from previous experiences of disease transmission. Its effects were immediate breathing difficulties (physical). Its onset was connected with the local Chinese diet of wild civet cats (social). It spread at an unprecedented rate (social and physical). The highest mortality rate was originally and surprisingly among the higher income residents and health workers, usually the lowest risks (sympathetic).

The high infection rate and mortality rates were of immense concern, both locally and as a precedent for the future (ethical). The existence of the public health threat was not apparent for three months, which allowed it time to reach 27 countries. SARS spread globally as rapidly as it did due to the disparity in public health resources, high urban density, and the ease with which humans have been able to move around the globe in recent decades (collective). Eventually it emerged that the origin of the virus was in local bats. Both bats and wild civet cats were slaughtered for food in the markets on the same chopping blocks, transferring the virus across species (physical and social). Only the wealthy could afford to eat civet cat (social). The early high frequency in health-care workers was explained by the aerosols used to administer the remedies spraying the virus into the air.

The World Health Organisation (WHO) coordinated a global surveillance and research information system in collaboration with national governments and affected communities to come up with a coordinated, holistic response that respected global integrity beyond any one way of knowing or any one jurisdiction. It sent teams to work in every stricken country and region and worked toward a shared understanding of the human condition in the new global context. WHO enlisted many experts and communities in working to build a nested understanding

| OUTWARD LOOKING |
| PHYSICAL: Epidemiology of SARS |
| SOCIAL: Cats and bats in the food market |
| ETHICAL: Medical whistleblowers |
| AESTHETIC: Respiratory vapour, masks |
| SYMPATHETIC: One species |
| INWARD LOOKING |
| INTROSPECTIVE: Collective risk |
| REFLECTIONS: Collective health |

*Figure 8.5* Severe Acute Respiratory Syndrome (SARS)

of those complex factors and how they related to each other (reflective). The global collaboration of networks of clinicians, of pathologists, of epidemiologists, of sociologists, of administrators, both in their own right and together was a notable outcome of SARS, one which remained as a shadow to move into the handling of bird flu seven years later.

With SARS the call to collaboration between public health, other occupations and affected communities was effective because of the significance of the problem. In asking reflective questions, it is possible to replace the crisis call by drawing on key informants, critical incidents, locally significant issues and sites of collective learning, to arrive at the answer. For instance, a Chinese medical practitioner from the infected area fled to Hong Kong to protect his family and in the hope of treatment, travelling up in a hotel lift with eight people from different floors. The consequent spread of the disease throughout the hotel without any apparent physical means badly confused the disease tracers until they had all the answers.

In the responses to SARS, as to any wicked problem, there were stories of prejudice and stories of heroism (introspective). Chinese authorities did not admit to a problem for three months after the first batch of sufferers were recognised. The world was alerted by a senior physician in a large central hospital who was promptly removed from his post. The first Vietnamese medical practitioner to treat the disease, on contracting it and realising that there was no known treatment, fled into the fields to die to avoid infecting his patients. Hospital nursing staff continued to treat SARS patients even as the deaths in the health sector rose.

In the case of SARS the clear information and the recognition of the collective responsibilities of individuals, communities, specialist practitioners and governments allowed transfer of information to catch up with the rapid spread of the disease (collective). Even the memorable label of SARS was a factor in the collective response and even the then-reclusive China opened up after three months. The eventually successful response to SARS among the threatened societies was for the diverse contributors being prepared to respond to all five reality-check questions. Individuals reconsidered personal hygiene, communities sought to safeguard their members through special SARS hospitals and a sanitised area replaced their rammed earth village walls. Scientists worked around the clock to identify the virus, the patterns of incidence and prevalence and response to an isolation and antibiotic regime. Private industry and governments not necessarily friendly to each other all collaborated freely. Strategists mounted policy and legislative campaigns to protect citizens (social); and citizen responsibility emerged even in closed societies (ethical). Collective learning was well in place.

## Notes

1 Chapters 5 and 6.
2 For example the Large Hadron Collider developed by the European Organisation for Nuclear Research (CERN) and used to discover the Higgs-boson particle. http://www.ask.com.wiki/Large_Hadron_Collider? [accessed 3.5.13].
3 *Escherichia coli.*

4  Pels, D. (2003) *Unhastening Science: Autonomy and Reflexivity in the Social Theory of Knowledge*, Liverpool, UK: Liverpool University Press.

5  'Planet' here and throughout the book refers to the site of the physical changes occurring and 'world' to the interaction between physical and social changes. Chapter 1, p. 4.

6  It is emphasised that this was the fundamental point that Descartes was making in 'The Light of Experience', Clark, K. (1971) *Civilization: A Personal View*, p. 209, London: BBC and John Murray.

7  Ronan, C. A. (1982) *Science: Its History and Development among the World's Cultures*, New York: Hamlyn.

8  See Carey, J. (1995) *The Faber Book of Science*, Boston, US: Faber and Faber, for an intriguing anthology and a celebration of the way that scientists as specialists think and conduct their research. And Rose, H. and Rose, S. (1970) *Science and Society*, Harmondsworth, UK: Pelican. The authors were founding members of the British Society for Social Responsibility in Science.

9  In 1905, Einstein proposed mass–energy equivalence which is summed up in the famous equation $E=mc^2$ where E is energy, m is mass and c the speed of light. The interchangeability of mass and energy may be likened to the way ice and water are interchangeable.

10 Bohr conceived the principle of complementarity in 1927. See http://en.wikipedia.org/wiki/Niels_Bohr [accessed 4.5.13].

11 Prigogine, I. and Stengers, I (1984) *Order out of Chaos*, London: Fontana.

12 'Complementary realities' refers to the way that all of the multiple realities interrelate.

13 The idea that there are gaps between reality and our knowledge of it is 'the problem of under-determination'. Russell, J. Y. (2010) 'A Philosophical Framework for an Open and Critical Transdisciplinary Inquiry' in *Tackling Wicked Problems: Through the Transdisciplinary Imagination*, (eds) Brown, V. A., Harris J. A. and Russell, J. Y., London: Earthscan, pp. 31–60. See also Capra, F. (2004) *Hidden Dimensions: A Science for Living Sustainably*, New York: Anchor Books. Also, von Bertalanffy, L. (1976) *General Systems Theory: Foundations, Development and Applications*, New York: George Braziller; and Bohr, N. (1955) *The Unity of Knowledge*, New York: Doubleday.

14 Einstein, A. and Infeld, L. (1966) *The Evolution of Physics: From Early Concepts to Relativity and Quanta*, New York: Touchstone.

15 Mead, M. (1978) *Culture and Commitment: The New Relationships between the Generations in the 1970s*, New York: Columbia University Press.

16 Doidge, N. (2007) *The Brain that Changes Itself: Stories of Personal Triumph from the Frontiers of Brain Science*, New York: Viking.

17 Smithson, M. (2010) 'Ignorance and Uncertainty' in *Tackling Wicked Problems*, pp. 84–97.

18 Brown, V. A. (2008) *Leonardo's Vision: A Guide for Collective Thinking and Action*, Rotterdam, Netherlands: Sense. Toulmin, S. (1972) *Human Understanding*, Vol. 1, Oxford, UK: Clarendon.

19 Chapter 5.

20 For example, Hill, J. S. (1972) *Imagination in Coleridge*, London: MacMillan.

21 Gould, S. J. (2004) *The Hedgehog, The Fox and the Magister's Pox: Mending and Minding the Misconceived Gap between Science and the Humanities*, London: Vintage.

22 Bohm, D. (1994) *Thought as a System*, London and New York: Routledge. Bruner, J. (1986) *Actual Minds, Possible Worlds*, Cambridge, US: Harvard University Press.

23 Kuhn, T. (1962) *The Structure of Scientific Revolutions*, Chicago, US: University Chicago Press.

24 Medawar, P. B. (1967/1915) *The Art of the Soluble*, London: Methuen.

25 Prigogine, I and Stengers, I. (1984) *Order out of Chaos*, London: Fontana; and Capra, F. (1996) *The Web of Life: A New Synthesis of Mind and Matter*, UK: HarperCollins.

26 The first detailed description of self-organising systems was the theory of 'dissipative structures' by the Nobel Laureate, Ilya Prigogine. See Prigogine, I. (1967) 'Dissipative Structures in Chemical Systems' in Claesson, S. (ed.) *Fast Reactions and Primary*

*Processes in Chemical Kinetics*, New York: Interscience. Fritjof Capra discussed models of self-organisation (Chapter 5) and dissipative structures (Chapter 8) in Capra, F. (1996) *The Web of Life: A New Synthesis of Mind and Matter,* UK: HarperCollins.

27  Chapter 3.

28  The phrase 'Paris is well worth a Mass' has come to mean doing the unexpected to gain the extraordinary. The phrase is attributed to the future king of France, Henry IV, who in 1593 renounced Protestantism for Roman Catholicism to secure the allegiance of French citizens so he could become their king.

29  Chapter 9.

30  Chapter 10.

31  Chapter 13.

32  Chapter 11.

33  Doidge, N. (2007) *The Brain that Changes Itself: Stories of Personal Triumph from the Frontiers of Brain Science*, New York: Viking.

34  Chapter 4.

35  Chapter 4.

36  Massy, C. (2011) *Breaking the Sheep's Back: The Shocking True Story of the Decline and Fall of the Australian Wool Industry*, St Lucia, Australia: Queensland University Press.

37  Rittel, H. and Webber, M. (1973) 'Dilemmas in a general theory of planning', *Policy Sciences*, **4**, pp. 155–69.

38  Ibid.

39  Funtowicz, S. O. and Ravetz, J. R. (1993) 'Science for the post-normal age', *Futures*, **25** (7), pp. 739–55.

40  Bateson, G. (1972) *Steps to an Ecology of Mind*, St Albans, UK: Paladin. Also Bateson, G. (1979) *Mind and Nature: A Necessary Unity,* London: Wildwood House.

41  Ravetz, J. R. (2005). *A No-Nonsense Guide to Science,* Oxford, UK: New International.

42  Amnesty International is a non-government organisation defending human rights around the world.

43  Avaaz refers to the 'voice' of people. Beginning in 2007, it is a global civic voice that promotes activism on issues such as climate change, human rights, animal rights and corruption. See http://www.en.wikipedia.org/wiki/Avaaz [accessed 7.5.13].

44  Transition Towns is an international grass roots network of people working for positive change. Hopkins, R. (2008) *The Transition Handbook: From Oil Dependence to Local Resilience,* UK: Green Books; and Hopkins, R. (2012) *The Transition Companion: Making your community more resilient in uncertain times,* UK: Green Books.

45  See the World Health Organisation website, http://www.who.int/csr/sars/en/ [accessed 17.8.13] and http://www.thelancet.com/journals/lancet/article/PIIS0140-6736(03)13077-2/fulltext#article_upsell [accessed 17.8.13].

46  Jacobs, J. (1972) *The Death and Life of Great American Cities*, Harmondsworth, UK: Penguin.

47  See http://www.undp.org/content/undp/en/home/librarypage/mdg/the-millennium-development-goals-report-2013/ [accessed 18.8.13].

48  See http://www.climatechange.gov.au/climate-change/climate-science/intergovernmental-panel-climate-change-ipcc [accessed 18.8.13].

49  Guggenheim, D. (2006) *An Inconvenient Truth*, Lawrence Bender Productions.

50  Moore, M. (2002) *Bowling for Columbine*, Dog Eat Dog Films.

51  Words from Meditation XVII, 1624.

52  Mollison, B. (1988) *Permaculture: A Designers' Manual*, Tyalgum, Australia: Tagari Publications.

53  See Chapter 9.

54  See Chapter 10.

# 9 Collective governance

## Democracy for the next millennium

**Pattern:** collective governance.

**Context:** democratic governance has become a worldwide social ideal although in practice it takes many forms and has many owners, many of whom are not at all democratic.

**Issue:** different forms of democracy compete with each other, rather than form collective governance capable of handling radical social and environmental change.

**Resolution:** a new version of democracy is emerging to suit the times, involving participatory systems of collective governance and making use of the tools of cyberspace.

**Examples:** collective democracies that work simultaneously across local, national and global scales include Switzerland and its local cantons, and the development of the moral principles of the global Earth Charter.

## Context: multiple democracies and collective governance

Currently, democracies have been shaped in the traditions of the northern developed world, Europe and North America. Many South American, African and Arab nations claim to have democratic governments, although there may be little evidence of democratic principles or even much change from a previous dictatorship or oligarchy. In the Asian world democracy is the design for government in Japan and Korea, and for one of the emerging giants, India, while it influences the other, China. Thus democracy has already emerged around the world as the almost universal vehicle for governance, although in many, often incompatible, forms.

As nations struggle to deal with transformational change, many incidents have been hailed as the death of democracy. English rotten boroughs, where members of parliament bought their seats; the Nixon Watergate scandal;[1] the unpopular Vietnamese war; and the mockery of democracy in Nigeria have all been used to justify that prediction. Democracy persists, although it remains a hard call. Dominance of the majority over the minority regularly replaces the democratic ideal of equal power for all. Representation by political parties is more frequent than direct voting by the individual. Well-intentioned autocratic leaders in Botswana have given their citizens more democratic rights than has the neighbouring democracy of Nigeria.

Yet the ideal of democracy never seems to die. It remains a vital negotiated system with many versions of individual rights and responsibilities that can be included in a collective whole. To an outside observer any democracy can appear as a chaotic canvas for religious, philosophical, political and intellectual convictions. From within, it is experienced as a working system with which everyone struggles as best they can. At its best being democratic rests on the uniquely human qualities of fellow sympathy, respect, adaptability, expectations and, in the words of Abraham Lincoln, 'the better angels of our nature'.[2]

In the world's first known example of practical democracy – the city of Athens in the sixth century BC – significant decisions were made directly in public by the citizens.[3] Minorities were guaranteed a voice and some leadership positions were decided by lot and people took their turn. It was after democracy was revived as a political system in the nineteenth century that it turned toward a representative democracy with a bias toward majority rule. Since then it has moved even further toward executive government by a selected few, in practice an oligarchy. It became routine for decisions to be made by representatives rather than directly by citizens and by formal governments rather than collective governance.[4] Yet the major reinvention of democracy was a collective enterprise. Democracy as a formal structure re-emerged simultaneously in Britain, the United States and Europe about 200 years ago. The leading protagonists from those countries, Edmund Burke,[5] Thomas Paine[6] and Voltaire[7] shared their ideas.

A quotation from the father of American democracy, Thomas Paine, acknowledges the harsh reality of introducing an ideal into the pragmatics of government:[8] 'Here then is the origin and rise of government; namely, a mode rendered necessary by the inability of moral virtue to govern the world; here too is the design and end of government, viz. freedom and security'. Paine did not regard the organisations of democratic government as being in control of society. He considered government to be the servant of society, acting as a safeguard against conflicts of interest between individuals, both within their communities and in the wider society. Paine's basis for the construction of a future democratic society is hardly starry-eyed, yet he set his mind on the potential for humans to be virtuous, and so to make the right decisions. In his classic treatise *Common Sense,*[9] he wrote: 'And however our eyes may be dazzled with snow, or our ears deceived by sound; however prejudice may warp our wills, or interest darken our understanding, the simple voice of nature and of reason will say, it is right'.

None of these writers could have foreseen the arrival of the powerful global organisations free from national affiliations. They were working before the convergence of corporate and governmental forms of organisation and the consequent blurring of democratic rights and responsibilities. They would not have predicted the giant global United Nations, World Health Organisation and International Labour Organisation. Even under these conditions, representative democracies managed to make some virtuous decisions. Some countries introduced a safety net for the socially disadvantaged. International sanctions on South Africa helped to end apartheid. On the other hand international sanctions on Iraq increased the rate of child starvation. In Australia 85 per cent of the people warned against Australia's involvement in military action against Iraq.[10] Overall, standard twentieth century democracy has a mixed record.

Gregory Bateson's double-bind theory holds that effective social rules are developed through negotiations between two incompatible extremes.[11] This theory offers an insight into how social structures are developed in the first place, shaping each of the building blocks of society. Democratic processes negotiate between freedom and control. The many varieties of formal government negotiate the space in between, each claiming the territory and often calling themselves democracies. A British local government, an Islamic Sharia court and the Fijian Council of Chiefs can all act on democratic principles; whether they do or not is a matter of cultural choice. As it adjudicates across the many cultures, the International Court of Justice[12] evaluates actions taken on the ground against core principles of human rights and natural justice, not alternative versions of democracy. In other words, a functioning democracy is as much the philosophy and assumptions behind it as the constitutions, laws and guiding principles that support it. Abraham Lincoln captured the underlying essentials in his Gettysburg address, praying:[13] 'that government of the people, by the people, for the people, shall not perish from the earth'.

The arrival of the Internet has now altered the way in which any form of democracy functions. In a connected cybernetic world, to link a billion people and any subset of those people with one communication system is technically possible. With Facebook and Twitter it happens every day. The technology is not the issue. The issue is the very immensity of the change, in which everyone in the world can be connected in a flash. All information, valid or not, can be made available to everyone. This changes the relationships at the heart of democracy: the relationships between freedom and control, privacy and transparency, independence and cooperation. The originator of cybernetics, Norbert Wiener, had warned that there would need to be a new system of ethics designed for human relationships forged on the web.[14] The ethical disasters of the hacking by journalists in the UK and the reaction to the WikiLeaks release of national security documents confirm that these ethics still need to be developed.

Julian Assange, the creator of WikiLeaks offers two possible principles. The first recognises that our civilisation is built on our intellectual record, so the record should always be as large and as public as possible. The second, because different interests will always try to alter the record, everyone has an interest in getting everything possible onto the record, as open and accessible as possible.[15] The appearance of independent vetting agencies such as Politifacts provides a way of evaluating what is suddenly being put on the record. Against this background, the several varieties of democracy need careful evaluation. The times ask for decisions on what needs to be treasured for collective governance, and what needs to be discarded as inhibiting it.

## Issue: too many democracies?

Democracies are variously described as instrumental, liberal, representative, parliamentary, participatory, deliberative, deep and direct. There is also e-democracy. Each has its own advocates as the 'real' democracy. It will be useful to go through them one by one to establish just how they fit together (or not); how they contribute to the negotiations between freedom and control, independence and cooperation; and how they would contribute to collective governance.

Taking each of the forms of democracy in turn, it is necessary to note that democracy can be adopted as a governance regime for reasons other than democratic principles. It may be that the goal is to access funding sources, to form alliances, to cover up unpopular regimes, to be in fashion or all of those reasons. While democracy can serve several purposes at once, no one of these would lead directly to a collective practice of democracy, so they need to be treated with caution. Liberal democracy is currently a fashionable approach, in which the agenda is representative government, multiparty elections and separation of the appointed law courts and the elected parliament. Since these are all mechanics of government, liberal democracy tends to be concerned with the structure of government rather than the extent of the participation of the governed. There are other, more collective options.

### Representative democracy

Representative democracy is so universal that it has become almost synonymous with democracy as a whole. Edmund Burke, Britain's architect of democracy, asked a great deal of a representative:

> it ought to be the happiness and glory of a representative to live in the strictest union, the closest correspondence, and the most unreserved communication with his constituents…It is his duty to sacrifice his repose, his pleasures, his satisfactions, to theirs; and above all, ever, and in all cases, to prefer their interest to his own.[16]

It is hard to recognise this ideal in twenty-first century parliaments, subject as they are to the influence of lobby groups, political factions and politicians' ambition for advancement. Burke made the responsibility even more challenging with 'Your representative owes you, not his industry only, but his judgment; and he betrays, instead of serving you, if he sacrifices it to your opinion'.[17]

In practice, the power of a representative is usually limited. It is usually limited through a constitution and by the separation of judicial and legislative powers. There is often an upper house with controlling powers, as with the United States Senate and the British House of Lords. Republic is a term often applied to a representative democracy, usually with an elected or appointed head, as in America and Australia. However, it is also in use in the People's Republic of China. Parliamentary democracy, a special form of representative democracy, is the most common in northern hemisphere nations. Often there are two major parliamentary parties, almost evenly balanced (Britain, Germany, the United States) and in effect the majority rules. There is restricted scope for the smaller voices.

### Deliberative democracy

For deliberative democracy, authentic deliberation and not mere voting, capacity is the primary goal. Considerable effort is made to provide complete and accurate information on a topic, as well as fruitful opportunities for open discussion among all the interests involved. James Fishkin,[18] an advisor on deliberative democracy for many countries, lists five characteristics of authentic deliberation: accuracy of information, balance, diversity, conscientiousness and sound evidence.[19]

In deliberative democracy there is an assumption that whatever the issue, somewhere there is an answer. A selected or random sample of citizens participates in the deliberation, making it a subtype of direct democracy. One exercise in deliberative democracy involves the country's electoral commission reproducing a statistical sample of the voting population of the whole country.[20] Others apply the label of deliberative democracy to the contributions of representative bodies. If decision makers cannot freely reach consensus after careful deliberation, then they vote on the proposal, so in the end the majority rules. In short, a deliberative democracy seeks consensus and the one right answer from an informed populace. It may take the road of being elitist (majority rule from the top down) or populist (crowd-sourced from the bottom up).

One claim for the benefits of deliberative democracy is that it incorporates scientific opinion and research. Another is that it generates ideal conditions for impartiality, rationality and knowledge transfer. These claims reflect the priorities and values of the Enlightenment, so that deliberative democracy can be considered as belonging to the scientific era of privileging rational thought. There has even been an argument that the more these conditions are met, the greater the likelihood that the decisions reached are morally correct, a confusion between the different evidence bases for facts and values left over from the scientific era.

### Deep democracy

Deep democracy was developed as a means of approaching the relationships among individual, organisational and social transformational change which support collective governance. Amy[21] and Arnold Mindell's world work framework draws on relativity concepts from physics to heighten awareness of the relationship element in all experience.[22] A central concept is the validity of subjective inner and observable outer experience as two sides of the same coin. This is reflected in the inward-directed and outward-directed questions in the suite of seven questions which underpin collective knowledge.

In reflecting on democracy the Mindells use the term consensus reality for the form of reality that has general agreement in the central culture. They use the term non-consensus to describe experiences that do not correspond with general consensus and are especially likely in times of radical change. This includes non-conscious or more-than-conscious reality,[23] with its individually subjective experiences. Deep democracy awareness welcomes inner voices and makes use of diversity and existing tensions to access subjective experience, deeper vision and tangible results of the participants.

The work of Parker Palmer also adds to the more usual social and ethical debates on the 'true' nature of democracy.[24] Generated as an antidote to what was considered the too formal and impersonal approach of representative government, deep democracy is a fresh current running throughout the world's modern states. Small group meetings, workshops and discussion circles have emerged in a range of countries under titles such as New Democracy, Democracy Now and Worldwork. Most of these are returning democracy to its original ethical basis of valuing the deep commitment of each individual at the heart of democracy. For deep democracy the integrity of each individual citizen's contribution to collective governance is the essential unit of a democratic world.

Parker Palmer offers his dream of the pathways that allow people in any community to become a coherent collective. Rather than laws and rules he suggests that taking part in social relationships is normal for each community. Existing social spaces can act as crossroads where people can meet: streets and footpaths, community gardens, buses, libraries, sports events, street parties, shopping malls, workplaces, public parks and social media. All these can provide the potential essence of a social self for that community. Christopher Alexander would add the need for each living place to have strong centres that include the diversity of understanding of all who use the spaces.[25]

### *Direct democracy*

Today it may seem strange to propose a direct and all-inclusive democracy to support collective governance. Direct democracy asks for a full and effective contribution to governance from every member of a community. In the face of a global population of nine billion and rising, it might seem more practical to consider an expanded form of representative democracy, one that covers ever larger groups of people. For a collective mind, however, that argument can be put into reverse. The more people, the more their full contribution is necessary, both for their own sake and for the public good. Ideally, on both counts no one should be left out of governance of their world, whether it is large or small. With the creation of cyberspace and the communication cloud, for the first time in history direct democracy at all scales is a practical possibility.

No previous democracy has had a universal franchise. In the classic Athenian model, slaves, youths and women were excluded. In the nineteenth century, even in the early enthusiasm for democracy, only landholders could vote. Two documents that are treated as the heart of democracy are the British Magna Carta and the American Constitution. The Magna Carta empowered the knights of the realm, and included neither freedmen nor serfs. For the American Constitution it was only hard-won amendments that admitted slaves and women to the rights of citizens.

Thinkers who have examined the suitability of direct democracy for the current era include Hanna Arendt's[26] *The Human Condition*, and Pierre Clastres'[27] *Society Against the State*. Both support direct representation to the greatest extent possible. Both wish to optimise the value of each citizen's contribution to escape the potential tyranny of the state. Both authors question the automatic connection between the principles of a political system such as direct democracy and the management of the state. Arendt suggests that political action takes place in the open public realm, while the construction and administration of laws belongs in the organised social realm. Clastres holds that the state is a necessary evil, in the same way Paine considered the need for an organised democracy as initially a failure of moral virtue.

On the other hand, despite the United States being a federal republic with no direct democracy at the federal level, the majority of the states and many localities hold citizen-sponsored ballots. Even in states where direct democracy components are scant, there are often local options for deciding matters, such as whether a county should allow the sale of alcohol, and whether to permit capital punishment or abortions. In the New England region of the US, most municipalities decide local affairs through the direct democratic process of the town meeting.

### *Participatory democracy*

Yet another label for the principles that recognise the collective nature of democracy is participatory democracy. Participatory democracy emphasises the mutual learning from widespread contributions to decision making, and recognises the existence of the wider community as separate from the state. Small but effective participation groups translated into small world networks[28] are increasing in number the world over, supported by the Internet. This approach to democracy falls within the domains of social learning and civil society. It is based on the belief that a strong non-governmental public sphere is a precondition for the liberty and autonomy of its people.

In 2011, participatory democracy emerged into the public eye through the international Occupy Movement.[29] From London to New York and in between, citizens moved into public spaces that they had identified as excluding civil society. Wall Street[30] and the City of London[31] were high on the list. Camps were set up in central public spaces. Crowds gathered as attention centred on these public places. A general assembly made group decisions on every aspect of the action. The emphasis on being leaderless, using consensus to make decisions and behaving non-violently and convivially was core to the understanding of the occupy groups and very difficult for civic authorities to understand.

---

### *Box 9.1* **Ethical dilemmas for e-democracy as addressed by e-democracy**

Facebook recently announced that the billionth user has signed up, making it an important avenue for e-democracy. It has a voting system where users can vote for or against major privacy changes. Under rules of the website, for the votes to have an effect, at least 30 per cent of its user base has to take part in the vote. Recently, Facebook sent an email to all the users saying that it wants a much more meaningful method for the users to provide feedback. The social media giant also sent round a proposal to combine the information across the other services, like Instagram photo sharing. Under existing rules, if there are at least 7,000 comments on the topic, there will be a vote to decide. A campaign opposed the changes to the privacy policy and called for further transparency. 'Click here to cast your vote on the changes to the privacy policy of Facebook.'

---

## *E-democracy*

The Internet has become an integral part of human communication all over the planet and so becomes an integral part of a democracy. Not only is it accessible all over the world, the so-called digital divide is rapidly narrowing as the hardware becomes ever cheaper and more readily available. Since democracy is a matter of human-to-human communication, then any form of democracy has to be reconsidered in the light of this potential revolution. The Internet's literally unlimited capacity for generating an inclusive language, new physical discoveries, changing social structures, ethical dilemmas, aesthetic satisfaction and sympathetic understanding is only just emerging (Box 9.1).

This emergence of the Internet as a collective democratic medium was not inevitable. A whole series of decisions in the direction of open collaborative communication led to Web 1, the world of email, data storage and websites. First the technical online initiatives of research universities decided to keep their networks open, without centralised control. The sharing culture that developed led to the US National Science Foundation banning commercial takeovers. This opened up the capacity for software such as Linux to be open source, available to everyone. Chat rooms, newsgroups and email groups opened up cyberspace for individuals. This in turn forced newspapers and radio to open up to public voices. This took 20 years until about 2000. However, it was only the beginning.

Web 2, 3 and 4 have followed, with wikis (pages that anyone can edit), blogs (commentaries which anyone can comment on), YouTube (free video-sharing sites) and Facebook (free social networking sites). The world has suddenly opened up to voices that were silenced before. Democratic representatives are not only now directly reachable by all the citizens, they are using these channels themselves to talk to those who they represent. This use of the World Wide Web was the basis for Barack Obama's successful presidential campaigns, and is now standard procedure. Many countries now have online democratic processes (Box 9.2). Alexander's pattern language has inspired patterns for a wide variety of strategies and tools enabling marginalised voices.[32]

---

**Box 9.2 Countries working for direct democracy via e-democracy**

Australia: Senator Online,
Canada: Online Party, electronic direct democracy party
Finland: Change 2011, political party
International: ¡Democracia Real YA! (Real Democracy NOW!)
Britain: Occupy City of London
Russia: Autonomous Action – a communist and anarchist movement
South Africa: Abahlali base Mjondolo – shack dwellers' movement
Spain: Internet Party, a liquid democracy system
Sweden: Demoex, direct democracy party
US: The National Initiative for Democracy; Occupy Wall Street

(Source: Wikipedia)

---

## Resolution: including all the democracies

Any search for the one 'true' collective democracy is bound to fail. The goal of being democratic can be better understood as a wicked problem. A wicked problem is a complex problem that has been produced by the society that needs to resolve it. The resolution of the problem of a failing democracy will require major changes to society. There will always be multiple interests to reconcile. In the end there can be no final solution since democracy will always need to respond to changing conditions. For this planet and this century it seems clear from the foregoing that the many versions of democracy belong together in one collective process.

First, there is a need for each person to access their own deep democracy, the energy for and commitment to democracy that comes from the power of the collective self.[33] Then there is a need to revive direct democracy, with every individual having their own voice through e-democracy. Direct democracy will need representative democracy for some purposes in a world population of nine billion. Deliberative democracy and parliamentary democracy are forms of representative democracy aimed at bringing accessible information and transparency of process to direct democracy. Finally there is a need to ensure participatory democracy at every one of these stages, from the inner person, to the individual, to all public citizens, to their representatives and in the end to the system of governance (Figure 9.1).[34]

The difference between government and governance becomes apparent as shown in Figure 9.1. Government is a series of representative steps formalised in a hierarchy. Governance is the concerted contributions of the individuals at successive scales of population. In collective governance, the entire system is participatory, that is, individuals communicate from their own understanding, across scales and between roles. For collective governance, the collective questions are as follows:

### Introspective questions

Who am I when I cast my vote? A parent? A businessman? An environmentalist? How do I contribute to the collective for myself, my community and my country? Answer: Feeling at home in each of these selves is the source of the power that allows each person to take their full place in the collective, regardless of age, wealth or formal education. The Quaker saying 'telling truth to power' is accessible to every citizen who can find their own voice.

### Physical questions

What structures support collective governance systems? Answer: Beyond the social systems of government and law comes the need for a space safe for a collective democracy: safe tollbooths, campaign funding limits, compulsory voting, bridging the digital divide, secure websites.

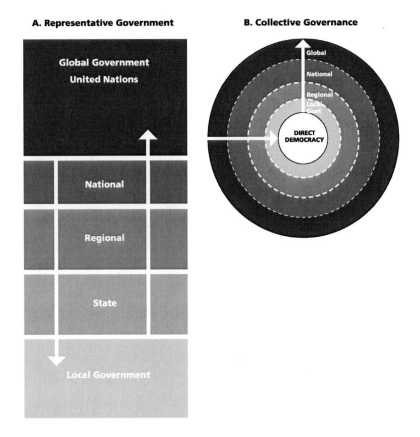

**A. Representative Government**

Global Government

United Nations

National

Regional

State

Local Government

**B. Collective Governance**

Global

National

Regional

Local Govt

DIRECT DEMOCRACY

*Figure 9.1* Democracy: A. top-down, bottom-up and B. inside out

## Social questions

What are the social rules, customs, symbols and celebrations that generate a collective democracy? Answer: Any of those that treat the tensions between the individual and the group as the yeast that keeps democracy rising. It is treating strangers as friends, not enemies, treating language as a dialogue rather than an information transfer, and celebrating a success with the whole community rather than one leading individual. It will include all avenues for democracy: deep, direct, participatory, representative and parliamentary.

## Ethical questions

What are the ethical rules for relating to other living things, including other people? Answer: Human beings seem to need a personal framework for living meaningfully in a human history full of violent disputes. The suggested capacities are humility, respect and openness, and taking responsibility for the actions of oneself and for others. Vehicles can be spiritual, religious, philosophical and aesthetic. Ethics for human rights has expanded in Western cultures to include rights for all living things. For many first peoples this has always been the case.

### Aesthetic questions

What is deeply felt as beautiful and ugly for collectives of human relationships? Answer: Social structures that allow tensions to be held creatively; designs that allow people to embrace tensions and transcend issues into a different plane of felt meaning. Icons, symbols and works of art (painting, music, dance, literature) that carry felt meaning across boundaries. Examples are the transdisciplinary works of William Blake, Shakespeare, the Breughels, Walt Whitman, Abraham Lincoln and Leonardo da Vinci.

### Sympathetic questions

How can members of a collective, from the individual to the entire human species, deeply understand others? Answer: First of all, through valuing difference and embracing the other. This has been expressed as 'to walk a mile in their moccasins'. There are three connected worlds to which every human being belongs. One is a consensus reality of what the members of a community call the real world. A second world is constructed through everyone's imagination, ideals and expectations. These may not normally be shared although they are interwoven into an unspoken fabric. The third space is the essence of human thought in which every human being joins, generated by what has gone before. For example, Arnold Mindell's *The Deep Democracy of Open Forums*, Teilhard's noosphere and Bateson's more-than-conscious world.

### Reflective question

Can democracy be understood as a system of collective governance? Answer: Democracy as proposed by Abraham Lincoln is essentially collective. The foundation is direct democracy, aided by deep democracy and deliberative democracy and made possible by e-democracy. Practically, the size and scope of the human population means that representative and parliamentary democracy are needed as an added dimension, although certainly not the whole. Together, these forms of democracy supply the sense of identity, physical capacity, social structures, ethical rules, transformative vision and the sympathetic voice of humanity needed to bring a collective democracy into being. That this is not impossible is demonstrated in the many attempts at collective democracy around the world.[35]

## Examples: collective democracy working across local, national and international scales

Summary examples of collective democracy are the Swiss national governance framework and the international policy instrument of the Earth Charter. Each of these examples operates simultaneously at the local, national and global scales.

### *Collective democracy in Switzerland*

Citizen law-making in Switzerland began in the thirteenth century. Swiss political events since then have given the world a valuable experience in participatory democracy. Switzerland is often regarded by political scientists as a political oddity. It is more appropriate to regard it as a pioneer. The Swiss political system, with its direct democratic devices in a multi-level governance context, becomes increasingly interesting for scholars of European Union. Switzerland is divided into the administrative areas of cantons, which act as an important vehicle for direct participatory democracy.

The Swiss constitution may be changed if an overall majority of the electorate agrees in a referendum and if the electorate of a majority of the cantons agrees, or if 100,000 citizens request it. Minor changes to the Swiss constitution are quite frequent without affecting the stability of Switzerland's political system.

All federal laws are subject to a three to four step process:

1. A first draft is prepared by experts in the federal administration.
2. This draft is presented to a large number of people in a formal opinion poll which includes canton governments, political parties, non-governmental organisations and associations of civil society.
3. The result of the poll is presented to parliamentary commissions of both chambers of the federal parliament, discussed in privacy then debated in public sessions of both chambers of parliament. Members of parliament take into account the results of step 2, because if they do not, step 4 will be taken.
4. The electorate has a veto-right on laws: If 50,000 citizens sign a form demanding a referendum within three months, a referendum must be held. Referendums on more than a dozen laws per year are not unusual in Switzerland.

Corresponding rules apply for referendums at canton and community level. While referendums over budgets are not possible at federal level they are common at communal level. The number of citizens that may demand a canton or community referendum is 1 per cent of the electorate.

### *The Earth Charter*[36]

The Earth Charter is an international declaration of fundamental values and principles considered useful by its supporters for building a just, sustainable and peaceful global society in the twenty-first century (Figure 9.2). Created by a global

*Figure 9.2* The Earth Charter

consultation process, and endorsed by organisations representing millions of people, the Charter 'seeks to inspire in all peoples a sense of global interdependence and shared responsibility for the well-being of the human family, the greater community of life, and future generations'. It calls on humanity to help create a global partnership at a critical juncture in history. The Earth Charter's ethical vision proposes that environmental protection, human rights, equitable human development and peace are interdependent and indivisible. The Charter attempts to provide a new framework for thinking about and addressing these issues. The Earth Charter Initiative organisation exists to promote the application of the Charter.

The idea of the Earth Charter originated in 1987, when the United Nations World Commission on Environment and Development called for a new charter to guide the transition to sustainable development. In 1994, Maurice Strong and Mikhail Gorbachev, working through organisations they had each founded (the Earth Council and Green Cross International, respectively), restarted the Earth Charter as a civil society initiative, with the help of the government of the Netherlands. The drafting of the text was done during a six-year worldwide consultation process (1994–2000), overseen by the independent Earth Charter Commission, which was convened by Strong and Gorbachev with the purpose of developing a global consensus on values and principles for a sustainable future. The Commission continues to serve as the steward of the Earth Charter text.

The Charter has been formally endorsed by organisations representing millions of people, including UNESCO, over 250 universities around the world, the International Union for Conservation of Nature (IUCN), the Indian National Capital Territory of Delhi, the 2001 US Conference of Mayors, and dozens of youth organisations. The approximately 2,400-word document is divided into sections (called pillars), which have 16 main principles containing 61 supporting principles. The document opens with a preamble.

**The Earth Charter:**

Preamble
We stand at a critical moment in Earth's history, a time when humanity must choose its future. As the world becomes increasingly interdependent and fragile, the future at once holds great peril and great promise. To move forward we must recognize that in the midst of a magnificent diversity of cultures and life forms we are one human family and one Earth community with a common destiny. We must join together to bring forth a sustainable global society founded on respect for nature, universal human rights, economic justice, and a culture of peace. Towards this end, it is imperative that we, the peoples of Earth, declare our responsibility to one another, to the greater community of life, and to future generations.

Principles: The four pillars and sixteen principles of the Earth Charter are:

**I. Respect and Care for the Community of Life**
  1. Respect Earth and life in all its diversity.
  2. Care for the community of life with understanding, compassion and love.
  3. Build democratic societies that are just, participatory, sustainable and peaceful.
  4. Secure Earth's bounty and beauty for present and future generations.

**II. Ecological Integrity**
  5. Protect and restore the integrity of Earth's ecological systems, with special concern for biological diversity and the natural processes that sustain life.
  6. Prevent harm as the best method of environmental protection and, when knowledge is limited, apply a precautionary approach.
  7. Adopt patterns of production, consumption and reproduction that safeguard Earth's regenerative capacities, human rights and community well-being.
  8. Advance the study of ecological sustainability and promote the open exchange and wide application of the knowledge acquired.

### III. Social and Economic Justice

9. Eradicate poverty as an ethical, social and environmental imperative.
10. Ensure that economic activities and institutions at all levels promote human development in an equitable and sustainable manner.
11. Affirm gender equality and equity as prerequisites to sustainable development and ensure universal access to education, health care and economic opportunity.
12. Uphold the right of all, without discrimination, to a natural and social environment supportive of human dignity, bodily health and spiritual well-being, with special attention to the rights of indigenous peoples and minorities.

### IV. Democracy, Nonviolence, and Peace

13. Strengthen democratic institutions at all levels, and provide transparency and accountability in governance, inclusive participation in decision-making, and access to justice.
14. Integrate into formal education and lifelong learning the knowledge, values and skills needed for a sustainable way of life.
15. Treat all living beings with respect and consideration.
16. Promote a culture of tolerance, nonviolence and peace.

## Notes

1 Following the political turmoil associated with the 1973 Watergate scandal, Richard Nixon became the first US president to resign from office. Woodward, B. and Bernstein, C. (1974) *All the President's Men*, New York: Simon & Schuster. More recently, Sussman, B. (2010) *The Great Coverup: Nixon and the Scandal of Watergate*, Santa Ana, California, US: Seven Locks Press.

2 The last words of Abraham Lincoln's First Inaugural Address as American President, 4 March 1861, http://www.bartleby.com/124/pres31.html [accessed 9.5.13]. See also Palmer, P. J. (2011) *Healing the Heart of Democracy: The Courage to Create a Politics Worthy of the Human Spirit*, San Francisco, US: Jossey-Bass.

3 In the political tradition of the west, the beginnings of the idea of democracy are linked to the city-states of ancient Greece. The derivation of the word is from the Greek *demokratia*, from demos, 'the people' and *kratos*, 'rule'.

4 See https://en.wikipedia.org/wiki/Representative_democracy [accessed 28.5.13].

5 Edmund Burke (1729–97), the Irish statesman and philosopher. He opposed the doctrine of 'natural rights' and advocated the idea of a social contract, attaching to it a divine sanction. His book, *Reflections of the Revolution in France* (1790) was read all over Europe. He is considered by many today as the father of modern conservatism. See also Ayling, S. (1988) *Edmund Burke: His Life and Opinions*, London: John Murray.

6 Thomas (Tom) Paine (1737–1809) is the English radical political writer who wrote powerfully of his discontent with law and order in England, America and France. In 1774, he met Benjamin Franklin who helped him immigrate to America just before the American revolution (1775–83). His famous pamphlet, *Common Sense* (1776) outlined the background to the war and spurred on the revolutionary cause. He wrote *The Rights of Man* (1791–92) in reply to Edmund Burke's *Reflections on the French Revolution*. In his book he supported both the French Revolution and an overthrow of the British Monarchy.

7 Voltaire is a pseudonym for Francois Marie Arouet (1694–1778), the French writer and historian and the embodiment of the eighteenth century Enlightenment. His book

'Candide or Optimism' in *Candide and other stories* (tr.) R. Pearson, London: Oxford University Press, is a famous satirical portrayal of the human condition.

8 Paine, T. (1776/2004) *Common Sense*, London: Penguin, p. 8.

9 Ibid.

10 See http://www.australianhumanitiesreview.org/archive/Issue-May-2003/goot.html [accessed 29.5.13].

11 Chapter 3.

12 The Court is the principal judicial organ of the United Nations. It was established in 1945 by the Charter of the United Nations and began work in 1946. The seat of the court is at the Peace Palace in The Hague (Netherlands) http://www.icj-cij.org/court/index.php?p1=1 [accessed 29.5.13].

13 The famous 272 word Gettysburg Address on 19 November 1863 on the battlefield near Gettysburg, Pennsylvania, US. See http://rmc.library.cornell.edu/gettysburg/good_cause/transcript.htm [accessed 29.5.13].

14 Chapter 4.

15 See Schmidt, E. and Cohen, J. (2013) *The New Digital Age: Reshaping the Future of People, Nations and Business,* New York: Alfred A. Knopf. The authors interviewed Julian Assange.

16 Edmund Burke, speech to the Electors of Bristol, 3 November 1774. http://press-pubs.uchicago.edu/founders/documents/v1ch13s7.html [accessed 29.5.13].

17 Ibid.

18 James Fishkin established the Centre for Deliberative Democracy in Stanford University, California, US. Fishkin in collaboration with Robert Luskin has pioneered a model of polling called Deliberative Poll. http://cdd.stanford.edu/ [accessed 30.5.13].

19 Fishkin, J. and Luskin, R. C., 'Experimenting with a Democratic Ideal: Deliberative Polling and Public Opinion', *ActaPolitica*, **40**, 2005, 284–98.

20 That country is Australia. See Drysek, J. (2010) *Foundations and Frontiers of Deliberative Governance,* UK: Oxford University Press. Uhr, J. (1998) *Deliberative Democracy in Australia: The Changing Place of Parliament,* Cambridge, UK: Cambridge University Press.

21 Amy and Arnold Mindell's website address is www.aamindell.net [accessed 31.5.13].

22 Mindell, A. (1992) *The Leader as Martial Artist: An Introduction to Deep Democracy. Techniques and Strategies for Resolving Conflict and Creating Community,* San Francisco, US: HarperCollins. Mindell, A. (2002) *The Deep Democracy of Open Forums: How to Transform Organizations into Communities: Practical Steps to Conflict Prevention and Resolution for Family, Workplace and World,* Charlottesville, US: Hampton Roads.

23 Called 'dreamland' by Amy and Arnold Mindell who noted that 'a group is experienced not only as a group of people discussing pressing issues but also as a field with a particular atmosphere'. In Mindell, Amy (2012) 'Bringing Deep Democracy to Life: An Awareness Paradigm for Deepening Political Dialogue, Personal Relationships, and Community Interactions', p. 6. See http://www.aamindell.net/ [accessed 30.5.13].

24 Palmer, P. J. (2011) *Healing the Heart of Democracy: The Courage to Create a Politics Worthy of the Human Spirit,* San Francisco, US: Jossey-Bass.

25 Chapter 7.

26 Hanna Arendt was a United States philosopher and political theorist whose work focused on the moral issues raised by the catastrophic events of the twentieth century. Arendt, H. (1958) *The Human Condition,* Chicago, US: University of Chicago Press. See http://isocracy.org/node/62 [accessed 1.6.13].

27 Clastres, P. (1974/1989) *Society Against The State* (tr.) R. Hurley and A. Stein. New York: Zone Books. Pierre Clastres was a French anthropologist and ethnographer.

28 Barabási, A-L. (2002) *Linked: The New Science of Networks,* Cambridge, US: Perseus.

29 http://www.guardian.co.uk/world/occupy-movement [accessed 1.6.13].

30  http://occupywallst.org/ [accessed 1.6.13].
31  http://occupylondon.org.uk/ [accessed 1.6.13].
32  Schuler, D. (2008) *Liberating Voices: A Pattern Language for Communication Revolution*, Massachusetts, US: MIT Press.
33  Chapter 12.
34  Brown, V. A. (2005) 'Leadership in the Local Government sector: working from the inside out' in Hargroves, K. and Smith, M. (eds) *The Natural Advantage of Nations: Business Opportunities, Innovation and Governance in the 21st Century*. London: Earthscan, pp. 289–98.
35  The Transition Towns movement is considered in Chapter 8.
36  See http://www.earthcharterinaction.org/content/pages/read-the-charter.html [accessed 2.6.13]. It is not only the outcome of the Earth Charter itself but also the comprehensive dialogue and decision making worldwide that inspires confidence in the potential of the collective mind.

# 10  Collaborative economy and gift relationships

**Pattern:** the collective economy as a successful commons.

**Context:** the world's economy is dominated by a market economy established on the basis that humans are primarily self-centred, competitive and rational, a perspective that masks the gift relationships that operate on the basis that humans are connected, cooperative, and creative.

**Issue:** models of economic management such as the tragedy of the commons and the prisoner's dilemma maintain a monopoly of mixed market and planned economies and block the way to a collaborative economy.

**Resolution:** the guidelines for collective action proposed by Elinor Ostrom in her Nobel Prize-winning work on managing common pool resources are based on collaborative relationships that include gift relationships.

**Examples:** whole-of-community economic collaboration in couch surfing, the Totnes Pound and micro loans.

## Context: market economics meet gift relationships

As you walk through a shopping centre you may be met by someone begging. Do you give them anything? If you do, why? Because you are sorry for them? Because you have so much and they so little? Because you do not believe that your community provides an adequate safety net? If you do not give them anything, is it because you think that they are no concern of yours? That they should solve their own problems and get back on the road? There are social services and welfare to take care of them and you pay for those with your taxes? Do you walk past feeling unconcerned, guilty, sad, angry or sympathetic? The best way to discover how an economy shapes everyone in it is to reflect on our own direct experiences.

Deeper ethical questions lie behind each of those experiences. An economic system allocates a community's resources, that is, who gets what, how much and for how long. Do some people deserve more than others? Are some people more worthy than others? Is everyone entitled to special treatment, or only some people, such as children or the gifted or the aged? And, crucial to the system, how are the people in the system expected to treat each other? Steal what they can from each other or give everything away? Keep all they can get or share everything they have? If there are fewer people in the world will everyone get more? At some level of consciousness everyone holds a position on each of those questions.

Unfortunately for those looking for a different economic system to the dominant market and planned economy, inquiring about choices brings only that one answer. Whether you consult an economics textbook, an encyclopaedia or a financial advisor, you will find only references to a mix of market and centrally planned economies. Adam Smith[1] and David Ricardo[2] are exemplars of this. In *The Wealth of Nations* Smith wrote, 'it is not from the benevolence of the butcher, the brewer, or the baker that we expect our dinner, but from their regard to their own interest'.[3]

In the market-based economic framework human beings are regarded as selfish and competitive rational beings, who in all circumstances will calculate how they can achieve the biggest advantage to themselves. A wave of economists in the late nineteenth century,[4] built mathematical models based on these assumptions. The market economy has indeed brought great social gains. The advantages of the market brought an entire middle-class into being, first in the United States, then Europe, followed by Japan, India and China. Food availability, health services, housing and life expectancy reached levels previously unknown.

In a democracy, decisions about national defence, health, education and welfare, and the taxes to pay for them, are a planned part of the economy, supposedly controlled by a government for the public good. In recent times these planned decisions have increasingly been put back into the market. Competitive bidding for services often has a requirement to accept the lowest price, leaving in doubt the quality of the service. Welfare functions are outsourced to commercial services, taking them away from long-serving philanthropic services. This may increase efficiency but breaks long-established sympathetic connections.

The dominance of the market economy persists in spite of the diminishing returns from continual social disruption and episodes of market failure. Averages of financial gains hide another story. The gap between rich and poor, having narrowed during the twentieth century, is now widening. In the United States, the top 1 per cent of the citizens own 35 per cent of the wealth. Globally, in 2000, the richest 1 per cent of adults owned 40 per cent of global assets.[5] The 1945 establishment of the International Monetary Fund and the World Bank were meant to maintain economic equity on a global scale. The introduction of market-based, structural adjustment programs to developing countries by the International Monetary Fund in the 1980s was accompanied by increased child mortality, malnutrition and lower life expectancies.[6] In industrially developed countries, reliance on the market brought about the disasters of the Great Depression of the 1930s, the global financial crises of the 2000s, and many glitches in between.

Advocates for environmental security and social justice who seek a sustainable economy constantly point out that their concerns are omitted from the market economy. The economists' reply is that they can be considered as 'externalities', in other words as optional extras, which is hardly the case. Further, the market economy's interpretation of the ways in which people actually behave is far from being realistic. The market approach of competition and selfishness stands in stark contrast to the everyday life of most human beings, whose lives depend on others, as partners, family, friends and colleagues. People do share, to a greater or lesser extent. People do get satisfaction from helping others for no monetary reward. Many human activities cannot be undertaken alone and that collaboration forms a non-monetary economy at least as large as the market. The three sorcerers selected as collective thinkers (Darwin, Lovelock and Wiener) freely shared the gift of their minds with their collaborators across their diverse fields.

At the time of the 1930s Great Depression, a considerable step was taken towards an economy that was concerned with people's well-being. John Maynard Keynes[7] broke ranks with other economists and advised the British government that, even in times of government deficit, it was necessary to pay the workforce from government funds to prime the economy. While this is still a matter for debate among market economists, the advice was taken at the time and has been since. This action was not entirely linked to the need for continued production. The unemployment queues of the 1930s and the homelessness of the 1990s were unacceptable to fellow citizens. Democratic and Labour governments with an interest in social well-being came into power in North America and Europe in the 1930s and 1990s.

A shift in economic policy in many countries came during the 1970s, including in Britain, Canada, Europe and Australia. The allocation of welfare to people disadvantaged by radical change moved from a charitable exercise (a limited gift), to meeting their entitlement as fellow citizens (an inescapable duty). Although the shift was less marked in the US and then-developing countries like Japan, the ethical principles of mutual respect and entitlement began to infiltrate mixed economies with social values. Again in the 1970s, sustainable development emerged as an influence on an economy, as predictions of increasing environmental degradation, climate change and resource depletion were fulfilled.[8] Social movements for sustainable lifestyles and community ways of living emerged all over the planet, although only a few prevailed over the majority economies such as Findhorn[9] in Scotland, Nimbin[10] in Australia and Lost Valley[11] in the US.

This increased attention to the cooperative, sympathetic, social sharing and caring aspect of human existence underpins the emergence of collective responses to economic issues. This behaviour cannot be explained in terms of the 'rational economic man' model espoused in Western formal economic thought. In a collective economy gifts can be found as a strand in all resource exchanges, physical, social and interpersonal. In giving gifts, the utilitarian value of things and actions is renounced for less tangible social rewards, and so ethical, aesthetic and sympathetic values can transcend economic values and yet still contribute an important dimension to the economic system.

Anthropologist Marshall Sahlins[12] found that gift-giving ranges from an unwanted gift at one pole to an exploitative relationship at the other. In between there is a range of socially approved and socially influential positions. The highest category of free gift-giving, the European ideal, is not to give in order to receive; a return gift may be customary, but it need not be close in time, quality or quantity, or even expected. A second category of generalised gift-giving is custom-directed and usually within a kin or friendship network. Birthdays, festivals, and life events such as births and funerals spark customary gifts. A third category, balanced gift-giving, acts to preserve social relations. In this form, equivalents may be exchanged within a relatively short timescale, as with the buying of drinks in a bar, or neighbourly gifts of food. The proportion of gift-goods in the modern West has been found to be as high as in more traditional societies.[13]

Sahlins' fourth category of gift-giving is a negative exchange where each party looks to maximise his or her own advantage at the expense of another. One example is gifts that the receiver knows the giver cannot afford to return. Gifts of money in Western societies are problematic, since they may focus attention upon the economic value of the gift, rather than its symbolic meaning. For instance, in most Western societies money as a Christmas gift is acceptable only if it passes down and not up a status hierarchy. For a younger generation to give an elder money would risk the elder losing face and risk turning affection into a commercial transaction.[14]

In market and planned economies exchanges become visible in the form of nations producing their own tokens: shells in the highlands of New Guinea and paper money and coins in most of the rest of the world. Gift exchanges are often invisible, although their effects are usually observable. Parental gifts in their caring for their children routinely go far beyond their caring duties. Helping a stranger in the street has been marked as a significant gift since biblical times. For some, although certainly not all in the market economy, accumulation of the tokens for money is a gift to the self. For others, money offers the opportunity for gift exchanges and is a passport into participation in all the activities of the society. With the arrival of the online e-dollar,[15] money does not even have to have a physical equivalent at all. What one can buy with money has been described rather contemptuously as 'stuff'. However, this includes the essentials of life such as food, shelter, companionship and health services, and clean air and water.

If the focus moves away from the market-planning economy to the economy as a whole, there are some surprises. First, the black economy,[16] which evades the taxes of the planned economy, has grown so large that it has plunged the European Union countries into debt and put the Union at risk.[17] Second, there is the all but invisible contribution of women. Marilyn Waring,[18] who was responsible for the national accounts of New Zealand, calculated that the contribution to the gross domestic product (GDP) from the unpaid and underpaid work of women was two-thirds of the GDP.[19] The same effect was then found in other industrially developed economies.

Third, in economic accounting the difference between events that increase and events that decrease social well-being and national wealth is not well recognised. A massive suburban fire increases the size of the city's economy due to the salaries of police, firemen and ambulance, hospital costs and rebuilding programs. There is no avenue by which to subtract the costs of pain, stress, loss, replacement labour and reorientation of resources, thereby seriously distorting the impact on the local, and sometimes the national economy.

Fourth, in many areas the market economy is being replaced by collaborative processes. In addition to the socially embedded gift exchanges of marriage/partnership, parenthood, neighbourhood and friendship, there is a whole new world emerging in collaborative consumption. There is an explosion in swapping, renting, gifting, sharing, lending, trading, bartering and anything else people can think of that can allow them to take part in their own creative cooperative initiatives. This world is building rapidly on the innate human capacity for person-to-person collaboration coupled with the person-to-person dialogues made possible by the Internet. Online purchases are threatening the profits of those palaces of the market economy, the shopping malls and the department stores. Online gifting is also partly about saving money and time. As the examples below demonstrate, it is also a great deal about personal relationships, choice, identity, ideas and experiences.

The stimulus of a gift relationship has driven people online to join networks that share cars, books, bikes, offices, accommodation, holidays, hospitality, travel, furniture, paintings, children's clothes, commercial equipment, gardens, laundries and relationships. Many of these have a small access fee or none at all; they may depend solely on further gifting. The communication itself can be almost free, thanks to the arrival of social media. All major cities now have cheap car booking and free bike sharing, so as to reduce traffic congestion. Families who swap or share houses regularly become extended family with shared support networks. Bartercard, UExchange and Swaptree by which anything can be swapped for anything else, have ballooned. Rachel Botsman and Roo Rogers, who have founded and advised many different gifting relationships, group them into three separate systems of exchange: distribution of new products, redistribution of existing products and changes in lifestyle. Each of these is being carried by the social media throughout the world.[20]

In summary, in the majority of countries there is now a very mixed economy, with market, planned, black, relationship, sustainable and collaborative economies all functioning largely independently. A gift relationship is one consistent thread that runs through them all. Human beings are biologically and culturally social beings and that shows in all the economies. Even in the market economy the exchange can be represented at least in part as a gift. Television advertisements confirm this undercurrent of buying and selling: 'This product is a gift'. In the planned economy, political representatives and public servants project their self-image as serving their community as a gift out of their public responsibility, not for money.

The gift economy cannot be properly recognised without asking the set of collective questions. The physical exchange of gifts is a social language, often only understood from within the society itself. Even the black economy has an undercurrent of a gift to their community by citizens, a refusal to give the state what they ethically consider belongs to the community. The relationship economy is the realm where humans in sympathy with one another, kin and friends, share their lives and their goods. It is often called the true gift economy because there are no formal exchanges in this realm, all interactions fall into the category of a free gift. The aesthetic contribution to the economy is both central to any society and ill paid. Artists in all creative fields contribute their work to their society regardless of the level of reward. In exchange they are largely supported by the relationship and collaborative economies. Thus the organisation and dispersal of a community's resources cannot be understood without recognising the pattern of gift relationships which act as an undercurrent to both the competitive and collaborative economies.

## Issue: incompatible economic systems

The issues arising from multiple economies are quite different from those for multiple democracies. The several versions of democracy share a common driving ethic of collaboration. While the several forms of democracies together make up a cohesive whole, the various economies either pretend each other does not exist or act in conflict with each other. Taken separately, none of the multiple economies are functioning well even on their own terms. The dominant economy, the market, became uncontrolled and dramatically broke down in the global financial crisis of 2007–08.[21] A planned economy is often not strong enough to resist the pressures of the market, as with the lapsed Kyoto protocols to reduce global warming and the faded ideal of equitable taxation. The black economy is currently disrupting the governments of Greece and Italy. The market economy puts pressure on generational relationships, parenting and the family. The sustainable economy remains a gleam in green activists' eyes. The online collaborative economy is expanding exponentially with only internal supervision.

The different economies continue bubbling along in parallel, attempting to manage the same set of resources serving the one group of people. In its own way, each of those economies adds something to the society it serves. Yet their different ethical systems of good practice, and their different interpretations of the nature of human beings, mean that for them to work together will indeed require transformational change. However, as we found with the transformative ideas of our three collective minds, Darwin, Lovelock and Wiener, the existing dominant interests can be expected to move to block the introduction of new ideas. In the case of a mixed market-planned economy, folk tales have been widely used to justify a monopoly of the planned and the market economies, and to dismiss even the possibility of a collective economy.

Misleading stories that shore up market and planned economies and reject the collective economy outright include the tragedy of the commons, the prisoner's dilemma, economics as a science and the ideal of being objective. Each of these maintains the four paradoxes that we have argued in Chapters 5 and 6 are fading truths of the scientific era. They separate the multiple factors that affect the commons, use models of simplistic self-replicating systems as the prisoner's dilemma, discount community and society as mere aggregations of individuals, and treat the human mind as innately competitive and rational. All four reject the complexity, dynamic exchanges, cooperative human relationships, self-organising environmental systems and collaborative components of the existing economy.

## The tragedy of the commons

The influential paper 'The Tragedy of the Commons' was first published in the journal *Science* by economist Garret Hardin in 1968.[22] The title refers to ancient English law that recognised that certain resources should not be allocated to any one individual or special group, but always remain the common property of all. For many centuries it meant common grazing lands, and included the extensive northern lands of nomadic peoples. Today it is applied to the wide range of environmental commons currently threatened with overuse, such as water, forests, fishes, oceans and fossil fuels. The idea of the commons also includes social commons as varied as public spaces, the human population, open source programming and social services, although not yet cyberspace itself.

Hardin's argument is that left to themselves, those with access to common resources will inevitably exploit them for their own gain and without regard for others. The story is that without regulation, the villagers who collectively own a town common will keep increasing their personal use of their common land until it is entirely barren and no use to any of them. Hardin argues against relying on conscience as a means of policing commons, since this favours selfish individuals, or on personal choice since the more powerful will inevitably overuse the resources. According to Hardin, the rate of depletion of the resource depends on the number of users, the rate of consumption, and the relative robustness of the common. This narrow framing of the issue takes the most pessimistic view of human nature, and bypasses the inventiveness of users, the different forms of collective use, the different technical options, and the social and environmental context of each particular commons.

Despite the narrowness of its logic, 'The Tragedy of the Commons' is still quoted as an over-riding imperative for policy, legislation, social services and environmental planning. The particular risk that concerned Hardin and his associates was overpopulation. In practice, the commons offers a valuable metaphor for the strength of the need for a collective economy, in a reversal of the way 'The Tragedy of the Commons' tells the story. For example, justification for rejecting the commons is drawn from the overfishing of the Grand Banks fishing grounds and the production of greenhouse gases from everyone driving cars. Each of these is an outcome of the market and the planned economies themselves. Collective alternatives had always existed, ranging from modern democracies to the potlatch give-away cultures of North America.[23] The tragedy is rather that the story of the tragedy of the commons has been used to reject the social, ethical, aesthetic and sympathetic principles that have long supported the sustainable and equitable use of a commons in all cultures.

## The prisoner's dilemma

The prisoner's dilemma is another story used to maintain the dominance of the current market and planned economies. It purports to establish that people are primarily self-interested and thus competitive, and that a collaborative economy would be impossible. The story became popular in games theory in the 1950s and has held a prominent place in market economics ever since. One version of the issue of competition as opposed to collaboration was grounded in a prison context and named 'prisoner's dilemma' by Albert Tucker.[24]

The story goes: The police are interrogating two suspects in separate rooms. Each suspect can either confess, thereby implicating the other, or keep silent. No matter what the other suspect does, each can improve his own position by confessing. If one confesses for the reward of a lighter sentence, then the other would do better to do the same. If one confesses and one keeps silent, then the silent one could receive a heavier sentence. Thus, from the point of individual gain, confession is the best strategy for both. But when both confess, the outcome is worse than if both keep silent, since there is no need to reward either by a lighter sentence. If neither confesses, they may escape conviction or receive lighter sentences. The story is used to argue that individuals are always self-interested and so will always take an advantage over the other, even though the best option for both is always to support each other.

The prisoner's dilemma has applications to economics, business and everyday life. Cooperation between superpowers in an arms race, or individuals in an examination, offers examples of the dilemma. Members of both groups are better off in terms of their respective goals of peace and of performance when they withdraw from competition to collaborate. Yet the arms race continues due to the high cost of losing and exam candidates compete because of the rules of the game. To prevent collaboration, orthodox thinking calls arms agreements 'disloyalty' and examination cooperation 'cheating'.

In real life, humans are collaborative, sympathetic and creative as well as self-centred, competitive and rational. As Gregory Bateson points out, social rules develop which allow people to cope with the range of competing conditions that they face. Each strategy evolves according to the context of the time and place, not by following an eternally fixed rule. For instance, game theorists point out that the prisoner's dilemma changes dramatically according to the degree to which the participants know and trust each other, the extent to which they are under others' control as in jail or in examination rooms, or acting as free agents. Elinor Ostrom wrote 'By referring to natural settings as tragedies of the commons, prisoner's dilemmas, or open access resources the observer frequently wishes to invoke an image of helpless individuals caught in an inexorable process of destroying their own resources'.[25]

## 'There is no such thing as society'

Discussion of economic matters as an essential part of society frequently draws biological parallels such as the human response to economic pressures of flight or fight. This is hardly the same biological response as that, say, of a lobster or a snake, in which the flight or fight response is automatic and immediate. In all mammals there is a learnt intervention between the challenge and the response. Sigmund Freud opened up a Pandora's Box of possibilities when he identified the more-than-conscious mind as a driver of human decisions. Using Freudian terms, an economic decision can be determined by an ideal, a compromise, displacement behaviour (i.e., replacing one ideal with another) and repressed desire for power, influence or dominance. While Freud's work has been questioned, it remains an example of the complex thinking that lies behind relationships among humans.

It is therefore a mistake to suggest that humans make economic decisions through biological programming, for fight (investment in the market) or flight (selling out of the market). Humans are a social species. They are programmed to relate to other members of their own species, in language, in emotions and behaviour, although not in any predetermined way. British Prime Minister Margaret Thatcher[26] developed policies that placed all aspects of the economy onto a commercially competitive basis. She is on the record as saying in response to the many pleas to consider the social consequences that 'there is no such thing as society'.[27] Her economic policies moved economic support for industry from the poorly performing north of Britain to the more successful south. She thereby introduced a chasm of disadvantage that is still dividing Britain to this day.

Compare Thatcher's response to that of US president John Kennedy, who made history in his 1961 inauguration speech by saying, 'Ask not what your country can do for you, ask what can you do for your country'.[28] This assumption of national collaboration as a key driver for how the country is managed is still quoted as often as Lincoln's Gettysburg address,[29] which was also concerned with people from all parts of society working together. Perhaps more to the point, in playing out their life as a social species, humans cannot survive without collaboration, from their conception to their childhood to their education, employment, family support and aging. It is therefore a completely irrational statement to suggest that humans can manage their resources, that is, their economy, without acknowledging the necessity for collaboration among those involved.

## 'Economics is an objective science'

The standard economics of the market and planned economies claims to be objective and thereby claims the privileges of an empirical science. This is a difficult claim to sustain when the criteria for a science are the objectivity of the evidence and use of quantitative measurement to known standards.[30] The proposition is also expected to be falsifiable, that is, able to be proven false and so rejected. The sections above contain many economic propositions that have easily been proven false, but have not been rejected.

The other criterion, quantitative measures to known standards, is indeed a major feature of standard economics. However, since the measures are in the main derived from economic theory and so are not independent measures, it is not surprising that they become self-fulfilling prophecies. It is therefore difficult to accept economics as a science. It is even doubtful that it is in the interest of the economic community to make that claim, given the argument in Chapter 8 on the need for multiple sources of evidence in Transformation Science.

The set of five reality-check questions: physical, social, ethical, aesthetic and sympathetic, are increasingly being included in the science of the twenty-first century. We have presented the case for a Transformation Science in Chapter 8. If Transformation Science were to be applied in economic practice, then economics could indeed claim to be a science.

While making the claim to being objective, the author of 'The Tragedy of the Commons', Garret Hardin, summarised the solution to the issue as 'mutual coercion, mutually agreed upon'.[31] This solution he based on cases as narrowly defined as in the stories reviewed above. His strategy was to either privatise or set up an external regulatory agency for the commons. His co-editor John Baden went even further to condemn the commons, in his comments that the arguments for managing resources based on equity 'often resemble religious arguments conducted by non-theologians'.[32]

## Resolution: the triumph of the commons

In 1999, Nobel Prize-winning economist Elinor Ostrom[33] and her husband Vincent reviewed the ideas contained in the tragedy of the commons in theory and in practice. They described the commons dilemma as follows: management of a resource where the ownership is held in common, some of the users have independent rights, no one user has complete control and the total demand on the resource exceeds the supply. This description fits most of the social and environmental issues of today and is all-embracing enough to account for an economy of almost any size. It covers renewable and non-renewable natural resources from forests to uranium mines and social resources such as population, roads and urban planning.

The Ostroms' work explores the relative risks for an individual and for a group in Garret Hardin's solution of 'mutual coercion, mutually agreed upon' and his solution of a centralised planning authority. The Ostroms noted that neither was individual management a solution. An individual may be tempted to over invest in their use of the commons to improve their outcome, thereby challenging other users to do the same. The escalation of costs will then disadvantage everyone unless there is external regulation. However, external regulation may be to the benefit of the regulator; it may be a short-term solution to the immediate problem; and it may be made in ignorance of the versatility of the participants to find other solutions. It may lead to undue influence on the regulator from different users, or even to corruption of the regulator. The Ostroms noted that once a competitive common pool develops, users will feel they have social permission to vie for influence on the regulator.

Another outcome is that the regulatory agency will need to either develop a decision-making structure or adopt one already in existence. The structures in existence are almost all confrontational and competitive and so not particularly helpful. Establishing a different structure and procedures has opportunity and administrative costs that can exceed the benefits and could lead to some users paying for decisions with which they disagree. Members disagreeing with the decision-making process is a common cause of organisational breakdown. An avenue developed for the design and conduct of a shared enterprise by the users of that enterprise is a pattern language, applied in this book. Its use by urban planners, software designers and project engineers has been explored in Chapters 4, 5 and 6.

Three aspects of governing a commons apply to any management regime: the setting of boundaries; responding to change; and meeting the information needs of all the interested parties. Very few commons are discrete and have firm boundaries. Even fewer collect information on the effects of change on the full reach of the commons' concerns. For instance a uranium mine has concerns with anti-nuclear protests. A city trying to conserve the health of its lake also has some responsibility for those living on the rivers draining that lake. Rarer again is the open communication of that information among all the members. Even with the vast increase in information flow with the Internet, it is far easier to guarantee an open information flow in a cooperative environment than it would be in a competitive one. Part of that cooperative climate is the capacity for dialogue, for reaching a mutual understanding of the issues among the members, discussed in Chapters 5, 6 and 12.

The Ostroms adopted the reoriented positions on the paradoxes outlined in Chapter 6: that commons are always both wholes and parts of a larger enterprise; subject to both fixed rules and uncertain events; a social enterprise and so rest on collaboration and cooperation; and require both subjective and objective information on the state of the commons. While the Ostroms decided that there are no utopian solutions, they uncovered many practical ones.

For her 2009 Nobel Prize, Elinor Ostrom demonstrated that collective management of common pool resources gives an economic advantage equal to or better than markets. She established that a successful collective economy is based on: an increase in the likelihood of self-organisation; enhancement of the capabilities of individuals to continue to be a part of self-organised efforts over time, and so maintain commitment and critical loyalty; and serve to ensure that the self-organisation remains free of external control to the greatest degree possible. This last excludes external control from any of the economies: market, planned, black, relationship, sustainable and collaborative, while taking account of all of them.[34] Responding to the suite of collective questions is a useful way of exploring the Ostroms' set of key variables at any scale.

### Introspective questions

These questions reposition the individual thinker on the four perspectives that reorient the way we see the present compared to the recent past. The collective thinker needs to consider the effects of the relationships between parts and wholes, stability and chaos, individuals and society and creativity and rationality (the four dimensions explored in detail in Chapter 6). That world includes the individual's own role in gift relationships.[35]

### Physical

The commons is a useful metaphor for the physical basis of an economy. It assumes that all a society's physical resources are in some way held in common. The visible evidence of the amount of possessions of the community is stuff: house, land, vehicle, clothes, ornaments and people as workers and citizens. Also, physical evidence of the state of the economy is the demographic profile, the population as residents, tourists (strangers), migrant clusters, health status, homelessness and all other aspects of living. It also includes the stuff of gift relationships: what do people give to whom?

### Social

The social dimension of a commons covers the lifestyle arrangements and interpersonal relationships that keep the community together. The social structures that support a collective commons are a combination of a collective language, science, governance, economics, education and their social identity. In the economic sphere, certain gift relationships form a common thread that binds collective governance.

### Ethical

The basis for ethical decisions is divided between the market-planned economic systems based on humans as competitive and self-centred, and a collective economy based on humans as sharing, caring and collaborative.

### Aesthetic

New and inspirational ideas are generated by the challenge of change. This is particularly the case in the shift from a competitive to a collaborative economy. Innovative ideas have been listed above and in the examples below. The products of everyone's creativity can be transmitted worldwide.

### Sympathetic

Connections between members of a commons develop on the basis of cooperative personal relationships. People coming together to govern the commons may be quite negative about each other. So for a collective economy, there will be work to be done in bringing people together. Ostrom has also shared her experience here.[36]

### Reflective

Reflecting on the potential for collaborative governance in any one example of the commons draws on the answers to all these questions. It can also draw on the powerful work of the collective thinkers we have been presenting. Once the full suite of evidence is collected, it will include all segments of the economy. Whole-of-community governance will need to take account of all existing economies, market, planned, black, relationship, sustainable and collaborative, with gift relationships running through them all.

Elinor Ostrom established that the key conditions for effective collective governance are not size or administrative level, they are the conditions that actively support cooperation among the interests involved.[37]

## Examples: Gift relationships in couch surfing, Totnes Pound, and the Grameen Bank

### *Couch surfing*[38]

Throughout the world a moving population is creating a new consumer group. People have always moved around their local regions staying with friends or relations, or paying for their accommodation. With modern transport and the movement of whole populations, travellers have expanded to a global dimension. The movement of people around the world has spread ever more widely and in larger numbers through a gift relationship: couch surfing. The thought of sleeping in a stranger's home would be expected to arouse fear of exploitation and fears for safety in both host and guest. It seems that a combination of trust in the gift relationship and the use of social media have managed to overcome both.

The pressures on accommodation during big conventions and conferences gave three friends the idea of offering their spare room at a minimal rent during a design conference in their town in 2007.[39] They expected a few students, used to crashing in other people's apartments. They were inundated with requests from families, holidaymakers and business travellers. The reasons the people gave were not only saving money. They wanted the experience of meeting residents of the city, while the hosts enjoyed meeting the travellers. The three set up a website, offering rooms for rent, and by 2010 they had 85,000 registered users, and more than 12,000 rooms in 3,234 cities.

At first the network notices were for modest rooms, although the offerings quickly rose to sites such as a castle in Ireland, a village in Thailand, and an apartment in New York. Success was so immediate that other similar websites from within special interests such as clubs or occupations quickly followed. How were the issues of trust and exploitation resolved? The system proved from the first to be self-policing. The only fixed rules are that travellers must be able to ask the host questions before they book, and the rooms must be a personal possession, not a commodity, as with a hotel. While the host holds their credit card, payment is not extracted until the guest has been in place for 24 hours. The booking company does not vet rooms or renters. There are usually photos and detailed descriptions and other users' reviews. If these are not accurate, the room vets itself. There have been no reports of theft, and very rare reports that a room was not clean or someone has not turned up.

It turned out that couch surfing was a revival of an idea from before the hotel era. The communication chain was then a network of friends and relations, now it is carried by the Internet, although still as a person-to-person communication. Couch surfing is only one aspect of the unbounded field for peer-to-peer exchanges; between producer and consumer, seller and buyer, lender and borrower, neighbour and neighbour. With the withdrawal of consumers from the market after the global financial crisis, there were predictions that the economy would not recover. On the contrary, consumption became wider and more general, with much smaller profits over a much larger population, and many positive side effects. The sharing of cars and bicycles in the world's major cities also reduces traffic congestion and air pollution. Freecycle, a worldwide online registry, circulates free items for reuse and recycling.[40] More than 12,000 items are gifted on this website every day. Shared Earth[41] links people with unused land with those who do not have gardens. The sheer size of collaborative consumption, the low capital investment, and the contribution of the ethical commitment to a gift relationship make this an economy of its own.

### The Totnes Pound[42]

A collective community network that spread around the world from the small English town of Totnes is described in Chapter 8. Among the many innovative steps created within that network was the invention of the Totnes Pound. Advice to the Transition Town Totnes project[43] was that the locality could only function collectively and sustainably if it had an internal economy that fitted into the surrounding economy. The project built on the Local Exchange Trading Systems (LETS)[44] scheme already in action in Canada. The Totnes group decided that LETS formed a mini-economy of its own, allowing only for exchanges among members of LETS groups. Totnes wanted to change the local economic system as a whole towards a collective, and so decided to develop a currency that would become a part of the general currency. The idea was to keep money circulating within the community and to build new relationships, with people thinking and talking about how they spend their money and using local trade.

The Totnes Pound was launched in 2007 with the motto 'Local money. Local skills. Local power'. The notes were printed by the Totnes Transition Towns project, copying a 1810 Totnes banknote from a time when local banks printed their own money. Sample notes were given to each of the town councillors and 21 shops signed up immediately. More shops followed and placed 'Totnes Pounds accepted here: Totnes Pounds as good as real money only better' in their windows. The Totnes project took advice on a number of matters. First, printing your own

*Figure 10.1* The Totnes Pound

currency was perfectly legal, as long as it was used locally and it did not claim to be sterling. The pounds could be traded back to the Totnes project subject to a five per cent discount for administration. This small discount helped keep the notes in circulation; otherwise they were exchanged for goods, services and English Pounds. The full printing of Totnes Pounds was a common pool resource, guaranteed by Totnes Transition Town members, who in turn are the majority of the population of Totnes.

The Totnes project confirmed Ostrom's findings. The Totnes Pound did better when the person recommending them was locally respected, when the shops advertised them on their own behalf, and when the shops put up a notice appealing to the residents 'Ask for Totnes Pounds in your change'. Within six months more people had heard of the Totnes Pound than had heard of the Transition Towns project itself. An unexpected dimension was the explosion of tourists buying the pound notes as keepsakes. Townspeople used them as presents and mementos, inside and outside the town. The most successful similar examples the project could find were in the Southern Berkshires region of Massachusetts and on Salt Spring Island near Vancouver. Both issued the full range of currencies $1 to $50 dollars. In all three towns the notes were immensely popular, and acted as marketing devices for the shops and the town, as well as a valid currency within the towns.

### The Grameen Bank[45]

The Grameen Bank has an enviable track record of turning the age-old vicious circle of 'poverty, no capacity to save, no capacity to borrow, no capacity to earn' into a virtuous circle of 'poverty, capacity to borrow, capacity to earn, capacity to save, end of poverty'. Starting with the rural poor of Bangladesh in 1976, the Bank demonstrated to the world that individuals deeply trapped in poverty have the ability and the will to use their creativity and determination to enter the economy on its own terms. In an action research program at the University of Chittagong, Muhammad Yunus designed a system of banking services that supplied micro credit to the very poor, mostly women. To everyone's surprise, the program was not only a social success, it was a commercial success.

People who had never had access to any resources, had no guarantees or security, and no record of independence, flooded into the program to borrow money for a bicycle, a sewing machine, cleaning materials, shoes, anything that might help them earn money. Not only did they repay their debts, they repaid them faster than the average bank loan is repaid. The model of micro loans without security and with moral support for the borrower spread throughout the world that is dependent on development funds.

By 2006 Yunus had been awarded the Nobel Peace Prize and was being honoured by organisations all over the world. By 2012, Yunus was under political attack in his home country of Bangladesh. Disapproval of his Nobel Peace Prize, political turbulence and envy led to government pressure for him to resign from the Grameen Bank, the micro lender he had founded, and let the government take it over. Another difficulty in introducing the transformational change is the number of copycat lending institutions that sprang up in the Grameen Bank's wake, on more commercial principles and without the trust in the borrowers. Not surprisingly they tended to fail.

So far the Bank and its founder survive as a shining example of Elinor Ostrom's principles of collective organisation in practice. The commons is the earning capacity of the poorest of the poor in Bangladesh, at first almost non-existent, now the basis of a full-funded, well-established bank. The Ostrom design principles are, first, clear boundaries, and rules congruent with local conditions; the loans are small and require no guarantee. The arrangements between bank and borrower are open-ended and not competitive, and so can be fitted to individual conditions and applicants can collaborate. Monitoring is more in the style of consultation than judgment and sanctions hardly ever have to be applied. There have been very few defaults. Conflict resolution mechanisms involve relationships rather than formal structures, based on a basic recognition of mutual rights in each transaction. The final principle, multi-level governance seems to be where the project is vulnerable. At the heart of the project the governance is sound. It is at the higher levels that trust and cooperation failed.

## Notes

1 Adam Smith (1723–90), Scottish economist and philosopher who, in examining the consequences of economic freedom, came up with the division of labour as the main component of economic growth, rather than land or money.

2 David Ricardo (1772–1823), British political economist who advocated free trade among countries and individual specialisation.

3 Smith, A. (1776/1986) *The Wealth of Nations, Books I-III,* New York: Penguin classics, p. 119.

4 For example, Francis Edgeworth (1845–1926), Professor of Political Economy at Oxford who was the first editor of the *Economic Journal* (1891–1926), an outstanding mathematical economist who wrote *Mathematical Physics* (1881). William Jevons (1835–82), Professor of Logic at Owen's College, Manchester and later Professor of Political Economy at London. He introduced mathematical methods into economies and wrote *Theory of Political Economy* (1871) and the posthumous *Principles of Economics* (1905). Léon Walras (1834–1910), French mathematical economist who formulated the marginal theory independently of others and pioneered the development of general equilibrium theory. Vilfredo Pareto (1848–1923), an Italian economist and sociologist, was Professor of Political Economy at Lausanne who wrote economic textbooks with a mathematical approach.

5 Reported in a study of the World Institute for Development Economics Research at United Nations University. See http://en.wikipedia.org/wiki/Economic_inequality [accessed 7.6.13].

6 See https://www.oxfam.org.au/ [accessed 7.6.13].

7 Keynes (of Tilton), John Maynard Keynes, 1st Baron (1883–1946), English economist, pioneer of the theory of full employment. See Keynes, J. M. (1936) *General Theory of Employment, Interest and Money*, London: Macmillan, where he argued that full employment was not an automatic condition, expounded a new theory of the rate of interest and set out the principles underlying the flows of income and expenditure. Keynes theory on a planned economy influenced Franklin D. Roosevelt's 'New Deal' administration in the US.

8 Daly, H. E. and Cobb Jr., J. B. (1989/1994) *For the Common Good: Redirecting the Economy toward Community, the Environment and a Sustainable Future*, Boston, US: Beacon Press.

9 See http://www.findhorn.com/ [accessed 7.6.13].

10 See http://nimbin.nsw.au/ [accessed 7.6.13].

11 See http://lostvalley.org/ [accessed 7.6.13].

12 Sahlins, M. (1972) *Stone Age Economics*, Chicago, US: Aldine-Atherton.

13 It is interesting to note that in the US during the 1950s almost twice as many Christmas cards were sold and delivered as there were people in the US: five hundred million during one Christmas. Gopnik, A. (2011) *Winter: Five Windows on the Season*, Toronto: Anansi, p.125.

14 T. Caplow, 'Christmas gifts and kin networks', *American Sociological Review*, 1982, pp. 383–92.

15 See http://www.e-dollar.ng/ [accessed 8.6.13]. E-dollar was founded in 2010 with the mission: 'Digital Currency for Every One'. Bitcoin is another bank and government-free digital currency.

16 See http://en.wikipedia.org/wiki/Black_market [accessed 8.6.13].

17 See http://www.cnbc.com/id/100787222 [accessed 8.6.13].

18 Marilyn Joy Waring (1952– ) New Zealand feminist, activist for female human rights, environmental issues and development consultant and United Nations expert. Member for the New Zealand Parliament for Ragian (1975–78) and Waipa (1978–84). Seen as principle founder of feminist economics. See http://en.wikipedia.org/wiki/Marilyn_ Waring [accessed 18.7.13].

19 Waring, M. (1988/1999) *Counting for Nothing: What Men Value and What Women are Worth*, Toronto: University of Toronto Press.

20 Botsman, R. and Rogers, R. (2010) *What's Mine is Yours: The Rise of Collaborative Consumption*, New York: HarperCollins.

21 Shiller, R. J. (2008) *The Subprime Solution: How Today's Global Financial Crisis Happened and What to Do about It*, New Jersey, US: Princeton University Press. See also http://en.wikipedia.org/wiki/Financial_crisis_of_2007%E2%80%9308 [accessed 8.6.13].

22 *Science*, **162**, 1243–48. See also http://en.wikipedia.org/wiki/Tragedy_of_the_commons#cite_ note-9 [accessed 8.6.13].

23 See https://www.mint.com/the-history-of-potlatch-and-native-american-currency/ [accessed 16.8.13].

24 Poundstone, W. (1992) *Prisoner's Dilemma*, New York: Doubleday.

25 Ostrom, E. (1990) *Governing the Commons: The Evolution of Institutions for Collective Action*, Cambridge, UK: Cambridge University Press, p. 10.

26 Margaret Thatcher, Baroness Thatcher (nee Roberts) 1925–2013 was Britain's first female Prime Minister from 1979–90 and Leader of the Conservative Party from 1975–90. See Moore, C. (2013) *Margaret Thatcher: The Authorized Biography, Volume One: Not for Turning*, London: Allen Lane.

27 This phrase is attributed to Margaret Thatcher during her third term as Prime Minister. See http://en.wikiquote.org/wiki/Margaret_Thatcher [accessed 8.6.13].

28 See http://www.ushistory.org/documents/ask-not.htm [accessed 8.6.13].

29 The famous 272 word Gettysburg Address on 19 November 1863 on the battlefield near Gettysburg, Pennsylvania, USA. See http://rmc.library.cornell.edu/gettysburg/good_ cause/transcript.htm [accessed 29.5.13].

30 Popper, K. (1963) *Conjectures and Refutations: The Growth of Scientific Knowledge*, London: Harper and Row; Popper, K. (1972). *Objective Knowledge: An Evolutionary Approach*, Oxford, UK: Oxford University Press.

31 Hardin, G. 'The Tragedy of the Commons', *Science*, **162**, 1968, 1243–48.

32 Hardin, G. and Baden, J. (1977) (eds) *Managing the Commons*, San Francisco, US: W H Freeman, p. 137. A second edition was published in 1998. See Baden J. A. and Noonan, D. S. (1998) *Managing the Commons*, 2nd edn, Indiana, US: Indiana University Press.

33 Elinor Ostrom (1933–2012) an American political economist was the first woman and, to date, the only one to win the Nobel Prize for economics with Oliver Williamson in 2009. A key aspect of her research was on how individuals and communities can often manage 'common pool resources' (i.e. 'manage the commons') ranging from fisheries to information systems as well as, or better than, markets, companies or state through collective action, trust and cooperation and thus demanded a separate school of public choice theory.

34 Ostrom, E. (1990) *Governing the Commons: The Evolution of Institutions for Collective Action*, Cambridge, UK: Cambridge University Press, Chapter 2.

35 Hyde, L. (1983/2007) *The Gift: How the Creative Spirit Transforms the World*, Edinburgh, UK: Canongate Books. Mauss, M. (1950/1990) *The Gift: Forms and Functions of Exchange in Archaic Societies* (tr.) W. D. Halls, London: Routledge. Patel, Raj (2009) *The Value of Nothing: How to Reshape Market Society and Redefine Democracy*, New York: Picador.

36 Poteete, A. R., Janssen, M. A. and Ostrom, E. (2010) *Working Together: Collective Action, the Commons, and Multiple Methods in Practice*, Princeton, New Jersey, US: Princeton University Press. See also Brown, V. A. and Lambert, J. A. (2013) *Collective Learning for Transformational Change: A guide to collaborative action*, London and New York: Routledge.

37 Ostrom, E. (1990) *Governing the Commons: The Evolution of Institutions for Collective Action*, Cambridge, UK: Cambridge University Press.

38 Based on Botsman, R. and Rogers, R. (2010) *What's Mine is Yours: The Rise of Collaborative Consumption*, New York: HarperCollins.

39 Ibid, pp. x–xiv.

40 See http://en.wikipedia.org/wiki/Freecycle [accessed 10.6.13].

41 See http://www.sharedearth.co.uk/ [accessed 11.6.13].

42 Hopkins, R. (2008) *The Transition Handbook: from oil dependence to local resilience*, UK: Green Books. See http://www.totnespound.org/ [accessed 10.6.13].

43 See http://www.transitionnetwork.org/projects/totnes-pound [accessed 10.6.13].

44 See http://www.lets-linkup.com/ [accessed 10.6.13].

45 The Grameen bank was established in 1976 by the Nobel Laureate Muhammad Yunus. Grameen means 'rural' or 'village' in Bangla language. See http://www.grameen-info.org/index.php?option=com_content&task=view&id=19&Itemid=114 [accessed 18.7.13].

# 11 Life-long education
## Learning without limits

**Pattern:** seven ages of learning.

**Context:** there is a growing appreciation of learning patterns that reflect the life-stage of the learner and include the conscious and the more-than-conscious mind, individuals and groups.

**Issue:** confining learning to different compartments, such as separating thinking from doing, subjective from objective and inner-directed from other-directed minds, blocks the way to collective learning.

**Resolution:** expanding the reach of open-ended collective learning in each of Shakespeare's seven ages of man.

**Examples:** collective learning that brings inner-directed questions into the context of field studies and social learning.

## Context: seven stages of human learning

We know from experience that human learning has the creative capacity to cross any of the boundaries erected by humans. The boundaries between individual, community, specialist, organisational and creative knowledges have also divided learning across time, space, language, culture and the brain itself. The capacity for collective learning across all these human-made boundaries is exemplified by the shining examples of master thinkers we have already discussed, such as Darwin, Lovelock, Wiener, Teilhard de Chardin, Bateson, Alexander, Mindell, Ostrom and many more. Each has made transformational leaps within their own collective learning capacity that they have then shared with the world. However, any transfer of their collective thinking has to take place afresh inside each learner's head.

From the emergent field of neuroscience comes the realisation that we can change the patterns of neurons in our brains throughout our lives. However much the left hemisphere of brain may have been developed in a construction engineer or a mathematician, the right hemisphere has been absorbing new ideas as well. However much our rational minds present our arguments on important matters in careful linear logic, our ethical, aesthetic and sympathetic ways of understanding have also laid down patterns in our brains.

In 1958, Michael Polanyi[1] drew attention to the crucial importance of tacit knowledge in all learning, that is, the knowledge we do not usually bring into our consciousness, the knowledge that we do not know we know. In the 1990s neuroscience gave us a figure for our tacit knowledge: 95 per cent of our thinking draws on tacit knowledge,[2] or as Gregory Bateson wrote, the more-than-conscious mind.[3]

Another new field of learning has opened up in cyberspace. Television, the personal computer and telephone have all converged into one device. The capacity to spread the most recent and varied views about climate change, stem cells and political unrest has opened up a new dimension to our experience of the world. At the same time, ideas can go around the planet in words in a blog,[4] or as pictures on YouTube. Ideas and events can flash around the world; in the language of the Web, 'going viral'. Content can be extracted from almost anywhere and sent almost anywhere. Learning no longer has physical or personal limits, or even content limits; the size of the file can be megabytes or more.[5] Yet this is also a time in which language can be reduced to one word: 'like' on Facebook, 60 words at a time on Twitter and a phonetic jumble on SMS.[6]

The capacity to learn has long been recognised as a mark of the existence of life itself. Charles Darwin, James Watson and James Lovelock have all linked the origins of life to a capacity for learning. Albert Einstein earned his doctorate by observing the movements of single cells responding to their environment, learning at the simplest level of life, before he took to calculating the movement of celestial bodies.[7] We have already noted that when James Lovelock was commissioned by NASA (National Aeronautic and Space Agency)[8] to advise them on how astronauts could recognise signs of life, he suggested that they looked for a different pattern in the overall pattern. That would be a sign that there is something there that can think for itself. For the whole of their evolutionary history, the hallmark of humans is their distinctive capacity for learning. The discussion on Transformation Science in Chapter 8 concluded that it is the capacity to reflect on their own reflections, to draw on their explicit and tacit knowledge together that distinguishes human minds as human.

One of the ways humans find help with communicating complex ideas is in the form of a myth, an allegory or a story. Shakespeare's account of the seven ages of man has found resonance in people's minds across the centuries.[9] His story offers a benchmark for changes in learning patterns from the English Renaissance through the time of the Enlightenment to the present Anthropocene. Since human learning is cumulative, to this day learning contains the creative language of Shakespeare's day, the focused compartmentalised learning of the scientific era and the unbounded lifetime of learning that is the mark of today.

> one man in his time plays many parts, his acts being seven ages: At first, the infant, mewling and puking in the nurse's arms;

> And then the whining school-boy, with his satchel and shining morning face, creeping like snail unwillingly to school;

> And then the lover, sighing like furnace, with a woeful ballad made to his mistress' eyebrow;

Then a soldier, full of strange oaths and bearded like the pard, jealous in honour, sudden and quick in quarrel, seeking the bubble reputation even in the cannon's mouth;

And then the justice, in fair round belly with good capon lined, with eyes severe and beard of formal cut, full of wise saws and modern instances, and so he plays his part;

The sixth age shifts into the lean and slipper'd pantaloon, with spectacles on nose and pouch on side, his youthful hose, well saved, a world too wide for his shrunk shank, and his big manly voice, turning again toward childish treble, pipes and whistles in his sound;

Last scene of all, that ends this strange eventful history, is second childishness and mere oblivion, sans teeth, sans eyes, sans taste, sans everything.

*William Shakespeare 1623*

In this poem, each learning stage of today has been transformed to the point we seem to belong to an almost different species, yet each stage is still recognisable. In 1614 universal education was not even on the horizon. Infants were farmed out at birth to wet nurses and returned to their parents at about three years old. Children were at work as young as nine. Shakespeare's lover and soldier advanced into life within a social framework that held them to a strict social hierarchy. Few people held a respected position unless born into it, so the judge also tended to be a product of a certain inheritance. Women's lives were, of course, invisible. With an average life expectancy of 38, aging began at 30, and by the time someone was in their 40s they were among the old and infirm. Overall, learning was contained in a short life within a predetermined social framework.

Leaping forward 400 years, we now know that it is in infancy that children lay down the patterns needed for a lifetime of learning. Parents no longer hand their babies over to others for their first three years. It is in the first three years that the brain lays down the uniquely individual pattern of sight, hearing, touch, smell, taste and body image that is the basis for the owner's identity and all their later learning. The rate of learning in these early years far exceeds anything that comes later. Two-year-olds learn about 14 new words a day. The strength of the social context in influencing infant learning was scarcely realised until Jean Piaget demonstrated that African potters' children saw the world in a physically different way from children of hunters from the same tribe.[10]

The rapid increase in support for infant learning is no longer confined to expert advice and specialised texts. On the Internet, parents have access to the same information as the experts and often greater motivation to pursue it. Social pressures and socially provided incomes place mothers and sometimes fathers at home to make sure those infant years lead to the best equipped citizen. Elaborate programs such as the television program *Sesame Street* are designed to ensure that early development of literacy, numeracy and language is open to all. As a result, infancy can become almost a forcing-house, dedicated to the social value of competition for individual excellence and cognitive enhancement, even in the early years. In contrast, there is a parallel body of thought that holds that all infants need is a constant caregiver and a stimulating environment and freedom to learn for themselves.

For most children, school is no longer a matter of 'spare the rod and spoil the child'. A culture of child-centred education, where the individual and social development of the child is the guiding principle, has had notable leadership in Maria Montessori,[11] Rudolph Steiner[12] and John Dewey.[13] John Dewey, working in the United States in the 1920s, revolutionised mainstream education worldwide. He introduced the idea that school is a social world of its own, where each school acts as its own model of democracy. The teacher can become a friend and a guide, rather than the fount of all knowledge. Overall, fewer children creep like snails to school.

In the nineteenth century Montessori and Steiner linked the child, their society and the natural world in a dynamic web of collective learning. Although a minority choice for schooling, their thinking still influences mainstream education. In the West we would celebrate a seventh birthday by promoting the importance of each individual by singing 'Happy birthday to you' and 'For she's a jolly good fellow'. A Montessori birthday is marked by children holding hands and dancing around a globe, singing 'Seven times round the sun, seven times round the sun, Jenny Jones has been seven times round the sun'. The celebration of the individual includes connection with her peers and the physical world. Steiner's Waldorf schools concentrate on ensuring the innate capacities for growth of each individual are not separated from their own inner-self and their natural world.

Jerome Bruner[14] opened up the idea of education to far beyond the school walls, to the entire culture in which the growing child was immersed. He described how each person constructs their own narrative of who they are. The narratives they have available are shaped by the models of identity and agency supplied by their culture. Bruner pointed out that the narrative is not from any single discipline, it encompasses introspective, physical, social, ethical, aesthetic, sympathetic and reflective ways of being. From this perspective a classroom becomes a mutual learning culture, a microcosm of the potential of the society itself.[15]

Adolescence has been claimed as a twentieth century invention, with time to develop as an individual before being absorbed into society. Shakespeare gave this stage to the lover, and it is still the stage when relationships become important and sexual activity begins. Eighteen years is the current standard age for permitting alcohol consumption, driving, marriage and voting. At this stage, teenagers are testing their body, their self-respect, their social identity, their brain, their capacity to think abstractly, and their emotional connections to others. At the same time their surrounding culture is judging them as potential citizens. It is not surprising that this is the life-stage of protest songs and unpredictable behaviour.[16]

This is the stage that keeps sending messages of protest to the so-called ordinary world. 'Just another brick in the wall' from Pink Floyd, 'Gotta keep swimmin' or you'll sink like a stone' from Bob Dylan and 'But I might die tonight' from Simon and Garfunkel are all messages from over the fence that separates adolescence from adulthood. The 1970s counter culture blossomed among this age group, as did the student unrest that led to the cessation of the Vietnam War and beginning of the United States civil rights movement.

Shakespeare's soldier has been re-created in our era as the citizen, someone emerging from adolescent turmoil turning into a member of their society. As recently as the late twentieth century there was an unwritten assumption that 35 was the limit for learning; postgraduate courses and research institutions did not accept applicants older than this. Serious work on adult learning first began to appear around the 1970s.[17] Two of the leaders were educator David Kolb,[18] who worked on learning from personal experience as discussed in Chapter 6, and David Bohm,[19] who gave us adult learning as the mutual learning of dialogue, explored in Chapters 7 and 12.

The wisdom of the elder citizen, the judge, has changed as dramatically as the other stages of life. The end of the scientific era still found the expert and the authority figure as all-knowing and not to be questioned. Dictionaries and encyclopaedias defined terms for almost everything, and these definitions usually went unchallenged. There has been a dramatic change in access to knowledge and with it a change in access to power.[20] Transformational changes in the entire social context bring changes to learning at all ages, and particularly the citizen and the judge. The computer era has made the information on which knowledge is built accessible to everyone on Earth. Even villages in the poorest parts of Africa have access to television and someone will probably have a wireless computer. It has come to the point where the world's senior universities are offering free online courses. Teaching can be almost content-free, with the information needed freely available on the Internet and in many e-books. Adult education's future is in promoting critical review, teasing out relationships between ideas, and collective thinking. Power has become access to new ideas. It has also become the capacity to package them for maximum impact in the direction one chooses – the 'spin'.

Marshall McLuhan, a prophet of the digital age[21] in which all this is now happening, wrote 'When the globe becomes a single electronic computer, with all its languages and cultures recorded on a single tribal drum, the fixed point of view of print culture becomes irrelevant and impossible, no matter how precious'.[22] Today the tribal drum beats ever louder. There is Project Gutenberg which aims to digitise all books that have ever been in print. The crowd-sourced Wikipedia makes new ideas available immediately.

There is a computer program called 'The Voice of Humanity', with which its developers hope to link all the computers on the planet in a single consultation on global issues. A global solution has been proposed by the International Simultaneous Policy Organisation in the form of their global Simultaneous Policy campaign.[23] Voters in each country save their votes for politicians who have signed the Simultaneous Policy pledge. When a tipping point of serving politicians worldwide has been achieved, simultaneous policy can be negotiated between nations and then implemented.

The ideal of a collective global policy looks distant as the world fails to address climate change, civil war and the oppressive rule of tyrants. On the other hand the towering figures of our time have become familiar to us in a fashion unknown to generations without the tribal drums of Facebook and YouTube. The contributions of Lincoln, Gandhi, Churchill and Roosevelt are known to following generations, not just their own. For social models of success such as winners of the Nobel Prize and the Olympic marathon, it is becoming more common to acknowledge supporting teams, and the winners become household names.

Shakespeare's last two stages of aging have effectively been collapsed into one. The increase in average life expectancy to over 80 years in the industrialised countries, coupled with maintaining health and the capacity to think until the last few months of life has changed the profile of aging. In the West, people are living independent lives into their 90s; the need for care is deferred until the end of life. This is not to deny the surge in the incidence of dementia that has come with longer lives. Even then the capacity to postpone and to treat dementia is emerging from the health field. Seventy has been called the new 60 and 90 the new 80.

Looking back over the seven ages, a surge in both the quality and the quantity of human learning can be observed at every stage. The surge has been from the limited, the contained and the authoritarian to the open, the unbounded and the collective of the electronic age. Between Shakespeare's time of the Renaissance and the present Anthropocene, respect for the human capacity to reflect independently on the world that they are a part of shaping has increased. Two fresh dimensions of learning have been added to that independence. One is the collective learning among diverse peoples enabled by travel and by the World Wide Web. The other is each individual's internal collective learning enabled by more open social frameworks and the ability to reflect on their reflections.

## Issues: the reduction of ways of knowing and the rejection of ignorance

The wide-open space for learning created by the Internet on the one hand, and the move to collective thinking on the other, has generated is own problems. The dramatic emergence of the open-ended communication of the World Wide Web has been the special realm of the visionary Marshall McLuhan. He wrote 'the medium is the *massage*' to emphasise that the pathway through which the learner gains access to knowledge determines what they learn and how they learn it.

McLuhan compared the use of the new mass communication media to a blind or deaf person adjusting to the loss of sight or hearing by heightening the use of other receptors. There are changes in the proportional allocation of learning to each of the five (or six including the feelings) senses. Over time, the emphasis has moved from feeling (the theatre, art and creative thinking of the Renaissance) to print (the logic of books, newspapers and journals of the Enlightenment) to the all-embracing electronic media (the social, aesthetic and interpersonal communications of the Web).

Both print and radio seemingly carry the full meanings conveyed by speech but miss the emotion and creativity of face-to-face speech, and magnify logic and rationality. Later Western thinking became specialised, fragmented knowledge, making it harder to make full use of the all-encompassing environment of the electronic age. So although there are now fresh avenues for people to bring together all the ways of knowing, and there are excellent precedents, the continuing division of knowledge into disciplines still stands in the way. Pope's *Dunciad*[24] makes the point:

> O! Would the Sons of Men once think their eyes
> And Reason given them but to study flies!
> See Nature in some partial narrow shape,
> And let the Author of the whole escape:
> *Alexander Pope, pp. 453–56*

The advances in collective thinking and the openness of the Internet could have been expected to lead to a transformational expansion of the boundaries of formal education. On the contrary, the formal construction of knowledge in educational institutions past primary school is likely to be contained in its pre-electronic era compartments. Curriculum design, library resources, administrative departments and agencies at all scales remain firmly allotted to standardised knowledge divisions. The chances are high that any inquiry on the nature of change will be directed to the biological or physical sciences, sociology or philosophy. The situation improves in higher education, where whole universities are dedicated to transdisciplinary education and most campuses have some transdisciplinary courses.

While adolescence may be a peak time of introspection, of thinking about oneself, the next stage, the soldier and the citizen, is exposed to the peak of social pressure to conform. The need for a job, for economic self-reliance, and to support a family are on record as leading to a loss of youthful dreams to be different. As life continues, the successful citizen, the judge, is more likely to have been rewarded for conforming to existing societal standards than learning how to change them.

The routine blocking of creativity has long been confirmed by Thomas Kuhn's 1962 *Structure of Scientific Revolutions.*[25] This seminal work differentiates between normal or plodding learning that examines the parts and follows the rules, and revolutionary learning whose creativity extends the whole understanding and breaks the rules. This same pattern extends to all occupations. In skilled trades, past methods of operation are supported by strong union action, long after more productive and effective methods have been developed. The printer's union sticking to handset type long after electronic typesetting was available is a case in point.

In later life, comparative health and longer life expectancy are leading to the pantaloons and the gaffer still being at work. The age of retirement is rising in most Western countries, as is the size of the volunteer workforce sourced from the retired. This era is divided between those who feel they are free to think as they like and those who see their role in society as defending the traditional values.

One of the most powerful mechanisms for dismissing challenges to divided ways of thinking is the allocation of ignorance. Anything that does not fit into the classical division of knowledge can be labelled ignorant and so dismissed from serious consideration. The chief categories for allocating ignorance are that a contribution to knowledge is irrelevant, nothing to do with the topic in hand; taboo, a matter which it is not proper to discuss; and error, what you are claiming is wrong.[26]

All forms of collective learning can readily be proved guilty of ignorance. Since the collective mind draws on multiple realities, to standard disciplinary learning all but one must be irrelevant at any one time. In collective learning, there is considerable effort needed to draw on the introspective, physical, social, ethical, aesthetic, sympathetic and reflective ways of knowing. The advantage is that, coming from the outside, a non-specialised perspective makes it easier to see each knowledge area in perspective and to take account of the inevitable areas of ignorance.

To a practitioner of reductionist science, it is misleading and presumptuous to claim to be able to capture the whole. In science the whole is regarded as the sum of the parts. In collective thinking, combining the ways of knowing brings not only a whole, incomplete as it must always be, it brings more than the whole that is greater than the sum of the parts. It brings the promise of a new whole, one that includes the diverse understandings of the parts and produces a new vision for the future. The new vision will fall outside present experience and so introduce a fresh and fruitful area of ignorance. Thus one of the major differences between a knowledge monoculture and a collective knowledge is in accepting the value of ignorance.

## Resolution: learning with a collective mind

The electronic communication age offers a multitude of ways in which learners can access information and make it their own knowledge. It also offers innumerable ways to share this knowledge. McLuhan insisted on his own writing being a mosaic of symbols and stories so that readers could experience both the parts and the whole. The idea of learning as constructing a mosaic is very close to the metaphor of a collage used throughout this book to describe the working of a collective mind. A mosaic creates a fresh picture out of pre-existing pieces, although the material for the pieces can be as rich and varied as the creator of the mosaic chooses. A collage goes one step further, with the pieces that build up to the final message remaining distinct and continuing to carry their own original messages while together creating an entirely new one.

Across all the Shakespearean stages, there has been a clear development from an externally directed and divided mind towards an independent collective mind. In infancy there is an unprecedented parental interest in developing the mind of a newborn child. In childhood, Dewey advocated for the school as forming a microcosm of an ideal society, with equality among students and staff. In the Sudbury School model,[27] schools are run via school meetings where students and staff participate equally. Everyone who wishes to attend can vote, and there are no proxies.

Summerhill School[28] in England has operated a direct democracy approach to decision making for over 80 years. In 1999, after it was threatened with closure by the government, the school won an appeal to the High Court. The school argued that government inspections must consider the full breadth of learning at the school. Learning was not confined to lessons; it included the collective learning that took place among the students themselves.

*Figure 11.1* A collage by Juan Gris (1887–1927) *Breakfast* (The Museum of Modern Art, New York/Scala, Florence)

Other schools have established deep democracy as their educational philosophy. For teachers to change a school's philosophical foundations from the outer-directed learning in which the teachers themselves were reared, to the inner-directed learning that underlies deep democracy, most teachers will need help. The work of Amy and Arnold Mindell described in the chapter on collective governance (Chapter 9) has been widely recognised as providing this pathway. The Mindell's thinking is based in process philosophy, a position that holds that reality is best understood as a process of change, a process of becoming, rather than as a fixed or a stable state. This approach moves schools further towards the goals of Alfred North Whitehead[29] and John Dewey, the architects of the child-centred school, and towards Transformation Science, a science of change.

A philosophy based on a changing rather than a stable world reconciles objectivity and subjectivity and assumes that all seven collective questions are needed to interpret reality. One objective is to reconcile the inner-directed and outer-directed learning of a continually changing self. This requires access to all ways of knowing and includes imagination, intuition, dreams, altered states of consciousness, compassion for others and synchronicities. Mindell[30] suggested there are three worlds which contribute to becoming: consensus reality, which is the reality that each society agrees is there; dreamland, where the 95 per cent of our more-than-conscious thought resides; and a sentient essence that lies in the mind of every human being. This sentient essence was called on by Teilhard de Chardin in his vision of the noosphere of combined human thought.[31]

A student of the Mindells, Myrna Lewis, translated their work into an educational strategy that would enable collective learning.[32] She proposed five steps to learning to value dissent. First, move the discussion from majority to minority democracy. When the minority voice is encouraged to express itself, then everyone thinks more deeply about alternative ways to achieve multiple goals. Two, encourage the dissent. It needs to be safe for people to express their dissent and not feel afraid to say 'no'. Three, open up the dissent for everyone's consideration. This encourages others to agree with aspects of the no case and widens the dialogue. Four, investigate the wisdom of the no case, pursuing the implications of all the collective questions. Fifth, when people keep having the same small arguments like a broken record, or keep avoiding the issues, a facilitator is needed to work with dialogue.

During the 1960s adolescents were brought into the sphere of adult rather than childhood education, dramatically changing the identity of the learner. Student revolutions seeking student responsibility for their own learning echoed round the world, from the Sorbonne in Paris to Harvard in the United States. While higher education claims to have changed in response, expert-based curricula continue to be the rule. Nevertheless, avenues for collective learning have begun to appear sporadically in many universities.

Physicist turned philosopher David Bohm has developed ideas of dialogue[33] as a mutual teaching and learning strategy. Bohm perceives the construction of reality as the unfolding of an implicate order already present in the world.[34] Each person and each event draws on this order for their very existence. The space in which this happens is a dialogical space. In the dialogical space, speakers come together, hear each other, and generate their own synergy. Once again, very like Teilhard de Chardin's noosphere.

Parker Palmer summed up the essence of what he calls integrative education,[35] and what we are calling collective learning, as follows:

> There is a new community of scholars in a variety of fields now who understand that genuine knowing comes out of a healthy dance between the objective and the subjective, between the analytic and the integrative, between the experimental and what I would call the receptive [i.e. received wisdom]. So I am not trying to split the paradoxes apart; I am trying to put them back together.

## Examples: transformative learning for individuals and for groups

### Co-learning in a science program

*Course designer:* This example is from an undergraduate environmental science degree course that specialised in co-learning. In this program, everybody, including myself and other staff, were both teachers and learners. On the extended field trips that were the foundation of the course, everyone was invited to bring their whole selves to the learning. Jerome Bruner[36] wrote 'The human ability to understand the minds of others, whether through language, gesture or other means … is not just [in] words, but [in] our capacity to grasp the whole of the settings in which words, acts, and gestures occur …' The following comments come from graduates of the course.[37]

*Student:* 'The field trips made a big impression. The experience of being miles away from your normal environment and the chance to have other limitations disappear as you went away – the camaraderie is a big aspect of it. Once you get out in a vehicle and go out into a natural area, particularly if you're a long, long way away from other things that shaped your life, you lose a lot of the associated trappings. You're no longer a person with a name and a role, you're just you.'

*Course designer:* Students on field trips developed a strong sense of camaraderie and goodwill towards each other and staff, especially on long trips to remote locations in the Australian bush. Students and staff were pitched out of their ordinary everyday world to experience each other and the world anew. Accompanying this shared experience is an overwhelming feeling of one's common quest for knowledge and understanding of their world.

*Student:* 'On all the field-trips you were reminded that there was a real world out there and that's what we had to connect with. That connectedness is important because if you can connect with the environment you can then connect with other people because you realize the interdependence and interconnectedness of everything. I think that's got to be better for us all.'

*Course designer:* Knowledge is something people construct by talking together. It is the way environmental science students can be emboldened to cross the disciplinary boundaries of science. Acknowledging such a position also helps to pull the sciences back from their privileged position as objective knowledge and allow other ways of knowing some reasonable legitimacy.

*Student:* 'There was a great attitude towards the trips and they set up a great bonding amongst us such that the whole social values became more permeated within the group. The things that became important were the attitudes and values that we had to change in order to do something significant for the environment.'

*Course designer:* The small groups working on specific projects became transition communities that provided the support that students needed as they went through the risky business of becoming members of new knowledge communities. Students first vested authority and trust tentatively and for brief periods in other members of their group. Finally, they came to accept their own authority and trust themselves as individuals conducting research.

*Student:* 'What comes to mind is the phrase "go away and think about it". It made me realize that not only do I have the capacity to work things out but that I should be doing it. "You can do it!". It not only forced one to think but also gave that extra confidence in oneself, which was a really important thing.'

*Course designer:* Reflection involves thinking carefully about the meaning and personal relevance of knowledge: how what we learn changes the way we think. It is difficult to teach reflection and is likely to require one's time and quietness. It was enhanced through camaraderie and good interpersonal communication.

Source: John A. Harris, Lecturer in Environmental Studies.

### Community co-learning – singing one's heart out

> Talk for our planet's sake
> Talk with heart and reason
> Care for nature, care for humans
> Care for our children's future
> > *One of the songs sung by A Chorus of Women at Canberra Conversations.*
> > *Words and music by Johanna McBride*

A Chorus of Women was formed in March 2003 when 150 women gathered to sing in the national Parliament House on the day that Australia joined the American war with Iraq. The singing was not a protest – it was a lament for what was about to happen to the Iraqi people. As in ancient Greek theatre, it was a chorus of citizens commenting on the drama – stating what would happen as a result of our nation's actions that day. Expression of the emotional underpinning of what will happen as a result of our personal, local, national or international action, or inaction, is sadly rare in public discourse anywhere in the world. This unique action resonated deeply with many people.

This first event was entirely spontaneous. A small women's choir used email and word of mouth to canvas the idea of singing the lament as the politicians debated their entry into war. These women then went on to sing, compose music and meet weekly to develop a unique brand of philosophy and the arts to bring an authentic emotional and ethical voice into public discussions. The singers included musicians, business women, scientists, artists, public servants, teachers, community workers, gardeners, a Jungian psychotherapist, a naturopathy practitioner, mothers, daughters and grandmothers.

In 2007 and 2008 the Chorus of Women gave two artistic and scientific presentations about climate change in National Science Week supported by several prominent scientists: 'On the Edge of Silence' and 'Longing for Wisdom on our Changing Climate'. These presentations included conversations with the audience. The conversations highlighted two things: the ability of artistic expression to connect people from diverse perspectives and create space for deeper reflection; and the frustration of participants with the usual adversarial carry-on in politics and the media.

It became clear that people wanted opportunities for proper dialogue where opinions could be examined, fears expressed, uncertainties explored and creative ideas nurtured. We have since held eight Canberra Conversations. Each has been three hours and topics have ranged across Canberra's energy future, transport, reducing carbon emissions, sustainable development and urban infill. The 60–80 participants at each conversation have included business people, scientists and other academics, artists, politicians, senior ACT (Australian Capital Territory) and Australian public servants, members of community organisations, activists and other members of the public. Most of the conversations have been held at the ACT Legislative Assembly – symbolically, a good place for this form of grass roots democracy.

Discussions with Chorus helped me join the dots in my head about what was missing from public discussion of science issues and from public discourse in general. The intellectual content was there – the facts and the figures – but not the emotional context. Writing in the early 1970s, Australian poet Judith Wright said: 'Our feelings and emotions must be engaged, and engaged on a large scale. Whether scientists like it or not, it is *feeling* that sways public opinion, far more than reason; and it is feeling that spurs us to protest and act'.[38]

Each conversation starts with some information sharing by people who bring particular perspectives and experience, followed by small group discussions and a final 'circle' discussion where people deepen the conversation based on what has been emerging during the evening. Musical expression of the issues provides an opportunity for participants to reflect on key issues and connect with the emotional and ethical dimensions of the topics. The music is composed by members of the Chorus and we have even been known to sing lyrics created during the conversation!

In this safe space, we have been inspired to see people opening up to different perspectives and embracing the diversity and complexity of issues. In our last conversation (Filling in Canberra: Can a denser city still be a home among the gum trees?), participants did not agree on the type of urban infill or even the need for it, but they did agree that there should be respect for good design.

Source: Dr Janet Salisbury, a member of A Chorus of Women and the facilitator of Canberra Conversations.

## Notes

1   Polanyi, M. (1958) *Personal Knowledge: Towards a Post-Critical Philosophy,* Chicago, US: University of Chicago Press.
2   Lackoff, G. and Johnson, M. (1999) *Philosophy in the Flesh: The Embodied Mind and Its Challenge to Western Thought*, New York: Basic Books, p. 13.
3   Chapter 3.
4   Blog or weblog, a personal site on the World Wide Web consisting of a series of entries. The information can be written by the site owner, other websites or users.
5   Yottabyte is the largest unit of digital data, equal to one trillion terabytes. See https://en.wikipedia.org/wiki/Yottabyte [accessed 17.7.13].
6   Short Messaging Service.
7   In 1905, Albert Einstein studied Brownian motion. See Clark, R. W. (1973) *Einstein: The Life and Times*, London: Hodder and Stoughton.
8   Chapter 3.
9   In *As You Like It* by William Shakespeare, which is thought to have been written around 1600 and published in the *First Folio* in 1623. In Act II, Scene VII 'All the world's a stage' begins the famous monologue comparing the world to a stage and life to a play, and cataloguing the seven ages of a man's life.
10  Children's stages of development were an unknown until Jean Piaget identified shifts in the reality that the early child experiences. First, reality lies within the child's own perception. Around three years, their attention shifts to an external world. Around seven, the capacity to abstract from their world to the general world begins. These stages have been questioned for their order but not their existence. See Piaget, J. (1951) *The Child's Conception of the World*, London: Routledge, Kegan Paul. Ginsburg, H. and Opper, S. (1969) *Piaget's Theory of Intellectual Development: An Introduction*, Englewood Cliffs, New Jersey, US: Prentice-Hall.
11  Maria Montessori (1870–1952), an Italian physician and educationist, founded a school for children with learning difficulties (1899–1901) and developed a system of education for three to six year olds based on spontaneity of expression and freedom from restraint. The system was later worked out for older children and applied in Montessori schools worldwide.
12  Rudolf Steiner (1861–1925) was an Austrian social philosopher and founder of anthroposophy, who aimed at integrating the psychological and practical aspects of life into an educational, ecological and therapeutic basis for spiritual and physical development. His first school was founded in 1919 for the children of the Waldorf Astoria factory that became the first of many hundreds of Waldorf or Steiner schools worldwide.
13  John Dewey (1859–1952), US philosopher and educationist began his professional career as a high school teacher but became a university academic and eventually Professor of Philosophy at Columbia University from 1904 until his retirement in 1930. He was a leading exponent of pragmatism and his philosophy of education stressed the development of the individual, understanding of the environment and learning through experience. See http://www.britannica.com/EBchecked/topic/160445/John-Dewey [accessed 17.7.13].
14  Jerome S. Bruner is a US psychologist and educationist who wrote *The Process of Education* (1960) Cambridge, Massachusetts, US: Harvard University Press. Bruner

stressed the centrality of teaching for underlying cognitive structure and the usefulness of the 'spiral curriculum'. His humanities program 'Man: A Course of Study', described in *Toward a Theory of Instruction* (1966), Cambridge, Massachusetts, US: Belkapp Press, was significant for curriculum development. See http://infed.org/mobi/jerome-bruner-and-the-process-of-education/ [accessed 17.7.13].

15  Bruner, J. (1996) *The Culture of Education*, Cambridge, Massachusetts, US: Harvard University Press. Also see Bruner, J. (1990) *Acts of Meaning*, Cambridge, Massachusetts, US: Harvard University Press and Bruner, J. (1986) *Actual Minds, Possible Worlds*, Cambridge, Massachusetts, US: Harvard University Press.

16  See Roszak, T. (1968/1995) *The Making of a Counterculture: Reflections on the Technocratic Society and Its Youthful Opposition,* Berkeley and Los Angeles, US: University of California Press.

17  Knowles, M. (1973) *The Adult Learner: A Neglected Species*, Houston, Texas, US: Gulf Publishing Company.

18  David A. Kolb (1939– ) is a US educational theorist with a focus on experiential learning, the individual and social change, career development and professional education. Building on the work of Dewey, Lewin and Piaget, in the early 1970s, Kolb and Ron Fry developed the Experiential Learning Model (ELM) composed of four elements: concrete experience; observation of and reflection on that experience; formation of abstract concepts based on reflection; testing the new concepts (repeat learning cycle). Kolb is also known for his Learning Style Inventory (LSI) that is built on the idea that learning preferences can be described using two continuums: active experimentation-reflective observation and abstract conceptualisation-concrete experience. The result is four kinds of learning styles: the convergent, divergent, assimilative and accommodative styles. See Kolb, D. A. (1984) *Experiential Learning: Experience as the Source of Learning and Development*, Englewood Cliffs, New Jersey, US: Prentice-Hall.

19  David J. Bohm (1917–92) was a US theoretical physicist who worked on the Manhattan Project and subsequently developed a great interest in quantum mechanics. His book, *Quantum Theory* (1951) New York: Prentice Hall, was an exposition of the quantum field. Bohm's breadth of vision and concern for humanity led him to investigate many philosophical issues associated with modern physics, as well as the nature of thought and consciousness. His books include *Science, Order, and Creativity* (1987) with co-author F. David Peat, New York: Bantam Books, *Thought as a System* (1994) London and New York: Routledge and *On Dialogue* (1996) London and New York: Routledge.

20  Foucault, M. (1969/2002) *The Archaeology of Knowledge* (tr.) A. M. Sheridan Smith, London and New York: Routledge.

21  Chapter 4.

22  McLuhan, M. (1962/2011) *The Gutenberg Galaxy*, Toronto: University of Toronto Press. Quoted in the essay of W. Terrence Gordon for this edition, p. xiv.

23  The Simultaneous Policy requires governments in all jurisdictions at once, worldwide, to implement a policy shift at once, so that no one is disadvantaged or unfairly disadvantaged. See http://en.wikipedia.org/wiki/Simultaneous_policy [accessed 9.6.13].

24  Pope, A. (1902) *The Complete Poetical Works of Alexander Pope,* (ed.) Boynton, H. W., Boston, New York: Houghton, Mifflin and Company. See the full text of Pope's *The Dunciad*, Book IV at http://www.bartleby.com/203/166.html [accessed 19.8.13].

25  Kuhn, T. (1962/1970) *The Structure of Scientific Revolutions,* Chicago, US: University of Chicago Press.

26  See Smithson, M. (2010) 'Ignorance and Uncertainty' in *Tackling Wicked Problems: Through the Transdisciplinary Imagination* (eds) Brown, V. A., Harris, J. A. and Russell, J. Y. London: Earthscan, pp. 84–97.

27  See http://en.wikipedia.org/wiki/Sudbury_model [accessed 18.7.13].

28  An independent boarding school. See http://en.wikipedia.org/wiki/Summerhill_School [accessed 18.7.13].

29  Alfred North Whitehead (1861–1947), an English mathematician and philosopher, was Professor of Applied Mathematics at Imperial College, London (1914–24) and Professor of Philosophy at Harvard University (1924–37). While at Harvard, Whitehead presented the Gifford Lectures rejecting materialism and mechanism for an organic view of the universe arguing that entities that make up life are events or processes. See Whitehead, A. N. (1929/1978) *Process and Reality* (corrected edition) (eds) Griffin, D. R. and Sherbourne, D. W., New York: Free Press. This way of thinking is called process thought, which provided the framework for *On Purpose* (1990) Kensington, Australia: NSW University Press, written by Australian ecologist and philosopher Charles Birch (1918–2009). See http://science.org.au/scientists/interviews/b/birch.html [accessed 18.7.13].

30  See Mindell, Amy (2012) 'Bringing Deep Democracy to Life: An Awareness Paradigm for Deepening Political Dialogue, Personal Relationships, and Community Interactions'. See http://www.aamindell.net/ [accessed 18.7.13].

31  Chapter 2.

32  Lewis, M. and Woodhull, J. (2008) *Inside the No: Five Steps to Decisions that Last,* self-published in South Africa.

33  Bohm, D. (1996) *On Dialogue,* London and New York: Routledge.

34  Bohm, D. (1987) *Unfolding Meaning,* London: Routledge.

35  Palmer, Parker J. and Zajonc, A., with Megan Scribner (2010) *The Heart of Higher Education: A Call for Renewal*, San Francisco, US: Jossey-Bass, p. x. See also Boyer, E. L. (1990) *Scholarship Reconsidered: Priorities of the Professoriate*, The Carnegie Foundation for the Advancement of Teaching, San Francisco, US: Jossey-Bass. In Chapter 2, 'Enlarging the Perspective', four kinds of scholarships are considered: Discovery, Integration, Application and Teaching and Boyer wrote 'they dynamically interact, forming a dynamic whole', p. 25.

36  Bruner, J. (1996) *The Culture of Education*, Cambridge, Massachusetts, US: Harvard University Press, p. 20.

37  Harris, J. A. (2009) *The Change Makers: Stories from Australia's first environmental studies graduates,* University of Canberra, Canberra, Australia, ISBN 9781740883092.

38  Wright, J. A. (1975) 'Nature is much to wreck', in *Because I Was Invited*, Melbourne, Australia: Oxford University Press, p. 206.

# 12 The collective self

## Asking introspective questions

**Pattern:** parts and wholes.

**Context:** collective minds that are both inner-directed (able to make the internal connections that lead to a collective self), and outward-directed (combining with each other to become parts in a collective world) are the basis for a collective future.

**Issue:** the previous tradition of a divided mind has long impeded the development of a collective self.

**Resolution:** connecting inner-directed and other-directed collective minds allows the emergence of a collective identity.

**Examples:** finding an individual collective self through raising consciousness and individual adult learning.

## Context: connecting collective minds

I am large. I contain multitudes …
Failing to fetch me at first keep encouraged,
Missing me one place search another,
I stop somewhere waiting for you[1]

*Walt Whitman 1855*

In Chapter 1, we warned of the dangers of confusing the multi-dimensional collective mind with the closed one-dimensional mass mind that has such tragic consequences. On the more positive side, whenever human beings meet there is the possibility of a collective mind. Global systems, spontaneous crowds, focused packs, formal organisations, social groups and close partnerships create contexts where individuals come together and can and often do operate as a collective mind. These occasions all have the capacity to generate the outer-directed collective mind that was predicted by Pierre Teilhard de Chardin as the next stage of human evolution.

All of these opportunities for forming a collective mind, however, depend on a collective self, an inner-directed collective mind that can at the same time connect with other minds (Figure 12.1). A collective mind is taken to be the potential of each individual to think as a whole person and also to connect with others to form a collective mind. That does not mean that everyone has to agree on any particular

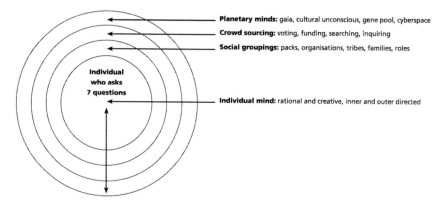

*Figure 12.1* The inner-directed and outer-directed collective mind

matter. It does mean that they are able to come together in a rich confluence of diverse minds. The fresh spark from the synergy in any one mind can supply the spark in other collective minds that leads to transformational change. The parts (the individual minds) are collective minds in themselves, and a microcosm of the whole collective mind.

The master thinkers who initiated creative leaps of transformational ideas, Charles Darwin, James Lovelock and Norbert Wiener, had collective minds that were both inner-directed, thinking across dividing boundaries, and other-directed, linking to other collective minds. The common threads that make a collective self possible have been variously identified by visionaries: by Pierre Teilhard de Chardin as the collective self of the noosphere; by Gregory Bateson as negotiating a collective social understanding; and by Christopher Alexander as ensuring vital collective centres as the core of all human designs for living.

The question arises: How does a collective mind form within a divided society? To heal the well-established divisions across ways of thinking, among competing goals and between individual and collective minds is not a simple task. The ability to develop a collective mind, to remain alert to the relationships between parts and wholes, to explore the links among the parts and to go beyond the whole rests in each individual human mind. People have come to accept that there are multiple realities and the inevitability of uncertainty and no one right answer. There remains the need to go further than acceptance and to welcome the synergies created through multiple ways of understanding the world, and the opportunities that can arise with an uncertain future.

The move to a collective mind is not a new direction; it is part of the inheritance of human evolution. We hold in common that each of us have our own unique program of our genes: signals from our nervous system, the product of at least two million years of evolution. None of these signals can be erased, since they are chemically coded in our genes, stored in our physical bodies and traced in the neurones of our minds. In our everyday experience of living, each of us is continually and effortlessly bringing all these signals into a collective whole that is uniquely our own.[2] This forms our identity, our sense of self.

In a compartmentalised world, it is possible that we will never fully access our own identity. On the other hand, we can access the whole of our identity by asking the introspective question that starts with the collective thinking process: *Who am I?* This means responding to the seven Herculean questions for ourselves. Once we have reflected on our sense of self, our physical status, our multiple social roles, our orienting ethical position, our aesthetic responses and our sympathetic relationships with others, we are in a position to know ourselves and to reflect on how we shape our own minds (Box 12.1).

In the conclusion to Part I, we concentrated on the asking of the final questions of the suite of collective questions, the reflective questions. In this conclusion to Part II, we are pursuing the opening question of introspection. Phenomenologists, cognitive and Gestalt psychologists, anthropologists, sociologists and historians of ideas have explored their own particular interests in introspection. Here we are concentrating on ways in which asking introspective questions can contribute to the individual collective mind. Here again a series of writers have pursued different lines of thought on the collective mind. In our treasure hunt we have found work on the participatory mind as a new philosophy, the meditative mind in neuroscience and Gestalt psychology, and the unbounded mind in organisational theory.

---

### Box 12.1 Knowing oneself: asking collective questions

| | |
|---|---|
| Introspective questions | Who am I? |
| Physical questions: | What do I look like? What is my state of health? Where do I live? |
| Social questions: | What roles do I play in my community? family? job? age cohort? |
| Ethical questions: | What ethical principles guide my actions? loyalty? equity? |
| Aesthetic questions: | Which designs and patterns bring me a feeling of delight? disgust? |
| Sympathetic questions: | Who do I feel sympathy for? Who do I feel responsible for? |
| Reflective questions: | What are my assumptions about the world I live in? Do I live in a connected or a divided world? |

---

In his book *The Participatory Mind: A New Theory of Knowledge and of the Universe*, Henryk Skolimowski argues that human beings are innately and primarily participatory. He goes so far as to paraphrase Descartes' 'I think therefore I am' as 'I participate therefore I am'. 'I do not participate therefore I am not'. This is presupposing that the human mind exists in itself and in the interaction with other minds at the same time, a confluence of parts and wholes. In moving on from a mechanical and compartmentalised world view, Skolimowski suggests that the collective mind is the major emerging influence on the transforming world.[3] To make full use of its spiral of learning, the mind requires healing after its centuries of fragmentation, and he uses the same set of collective questions as in Box 12.1.

A perspective on the inner-directed collective mind as complete in itself comes from *Towards a Nonviolent Mind* by Shri Ravindra Varma and Anna Alomes.[4] This is a positive story of how we can change our thoughts and reset our minds by practising meditation based on compassion, interdependence (inter-being) and non-violence. We can change the neural pathways of our brains in this way, away from the Western mind's concentration on anxiety, anger and violence. The goal is to change not only our thoughts but also the words we use in conversation as well as our actions. Research by neuroscientists with Buddhist monks who have meditated all their lives, focusing on compassion, the interdependence of all beings and non-violence found neural networks and brain structures quite different to those of the control group of Western students.

In all cultures and times, one consistent division between minds has been between men and women. While there is no doubt of the cultural division between male and female tasks in all societies, the notion of fixed physiological differences in the brain has undergone a transformational change. After decades of matching brain differences such as size and mental activities to socially-assigned responsibilities, each of the questions in Box 12.1 potentially had two sets of answers, males as structured and organised, women as creative and open. Cordelia Fine wrote that behavioural differences between the sexes are rarely fixed. In countries that subscribe less strongly to gender-stereotyped beliefs, women tend to perform well in organised tasks, men adopt caring roles.[5]

These findings remind us that over-generalising findings about gender differences risks setting up self-fulfilling prophesies. Men and women come to resemble unfounded stereotypes. Fine pointed out the close similarities between male and female brains are far more significant than the differences. As expectations of male and female equality in education, occupations and family roles increase, so do the records of female abilities in these areas. Since the social realities do not match the expectations, the division continues as a serious impediment to the collective mind.

Yet another interpretation of the collective mind is found in *The Unbounded Mind: Breaking the Chains of Traditional Business Thinking* by Ian Mitroff and Harold Linstone.[6] This time the collective thinking is based in transformational change in the business world, changing the core idea of addressing problems from within organisational interests to how the problem will affect and be affected by many different people with different orientations to the problem. The authors emphasise the ethical and aesthetic dimensions of a problem as critical to resolving all problems. They offer their ideals for a collective mind: a humane, whole person, not a perfect person; replenishment of the environment, not individual economic abundance; the dignity of the individual person as the unit of a collective mind; and implicit in each of the ways of knowing is the acceptance of the implied necessity of all the others.

In summary, human brains are evolving self-organising systems with increasing capacity for plasticity. By learning to rewire our individual brains we can change behaviour that feeds back to our brains. The question is: How does this work collectively? Is there a collective synergistic interaction of individual minds such that the future collective mind is evolving and self-organising as global networks and nodes arise? We can each transform our minds through dialogue with others in the third space holding compassion, interdependence and non-violence in our hearts and minds. Thus the collective mind emerges as a new trajectory for humanity.

## The multiple mind

Moving from the part to the whole, from the unit of collective thinking, the self, to the widest context of human life, the planet, there is already a strong foundation for the creation of a global collective mind. The planet-wide gene pool that shapes interdependent ecological systems provides the basis for Darwinian natural selection. The interchange between the universe and the web of all life on Earth inspired Lovelock's Gaia. Wiener's electronic extension of minds reaches all human minds in the so far unlimited world of cyberspace. The entire social history of humankind, from the formation of the first social group about 100,000 years ago, is contained in our social responses. The essence of our ancestor's thinking is carried forward in Jung's account of cultural consciousness. Each of us will draw on our learning from experience up to the immediate moment. Generations still unborn carry the potential for the humankind of the future. These all-pervading influences give humankind a sense of unity and cohesion, and so form a sympathetic context for the development of a collective mind.

Crowds have long provided opportunities for a collective mind to drive transformational change. Elias Canetti,[7] who won the 1981 Nobel Prize for literature, proposed that individuals come together spontaneously as a crowd, a pack, and a crusade.[8] He found that four characteristics generate the vigour of a crowd: growth, there being no limit to the size; density, with people in close touch with one another; equality, in that everyone in a crowd is equal for that space of time; and direction, in that there is a serious purpose behind the gathering. Where power is shared equally among all members and their shared purpose bridges the divisions between them, there is the potential for a collective mind. Gandhi's mass Salt March to the ocean was to mark independence from the British salt tax and eventually the British did leave India. The crowd that tore down the wall that divided East and West Berlin was so large that the guards dared not shoot. Both the salt marchers and the dancers on the wall, each group combining many agendas of their own, were acting as a collective self for that time.

Canetti used the word 'pack' for a smaller, more intense group than a crowd. The growth is in commitment, not in size; there is a tight and cohesive core membership; equality lies in that shared commitment; and the purpose is well-developed. A pack can arise either spontaneously or from established practice such as a church or an academic discipline. Canetti suggested three origins of collective thinking in packs, each including the others. A hunting pack forms to deal with a quarry too big for any one person. War is a special case of two hunting packs with competing purposes. A lamenting pack grieves for a loss of a member or a key resource; marking the loss renews the strength of the pack. An increase pack is formed to expand a resource base. A rain dance is an increase pack and so is a Nobel Prize committee welcoming fresh examples of creative minds. The third type of crowd, a crusade, is distinguished by passion, commitment and a moral purpose. Since a crusade demands loyalty to a single purpose and has a single unifying idea, it is rarely a vehicle for an open mind.

A crowd and a pack, however, can and do act as sites where a collective mind can flourish. The power of crowds is demonstrated in the increasing use of crowd sourcing, sending out calls for services, ideas, resources and support from an open-ended and anonymous community. Coined by *Wired* magazine in 2006, the term crowd-sourcing includes crowd voting for a certain decision, crowd funding for a creative initiative, and crowd searching for a missing person or lost document. While the requests for help are sent out globally, the rewards lie in the individual response and in the exercise of power. While there is sometimes some minor financial reward, in general crowd-sourcing works as a gift relationship. Humans are prepared to help other humans simply out of sympathy with other humans.

There are many cases where a group of people is more knowledgeable than an individual alone. Collective intelligence proves particularly effective on the Internet because people from diverse backgrounds can contribute to a forum in real time. A notable example of the wisdom of crowds is the making of the *Oxford English Dictionary*, compiled through an open call to volunteers. They were asked to identify all words in the English language and provide sample quotations for each one. It received over six million submissions over a period of 70 years.[9] The United States' Defense Advanced Research Projects Agency (DARPA)[10] project challenged teams to report on the location of ten balloons randomly distributed across the United States. The winning team (Massachusetts Institute of Technology) established its own 'collaboracompetitive' environment to find all the balloons in nine hours.

Doubts about crowd sourcing include questioning the quality of the outcome and the denial of rights to intellectual property. On the first point, we have already noted that evaluations of crowd-sourced Wikipedia and expert-based *Encyclopaedia Britannica* found them to be comparable.[11] Mathematical calculations by a crowd can turn out to be closer to the mark than those of any single group of the contributors, including mathematicians. On the second point, much intellectual property is open source, that is, available to everyone within the quality controls set by the designer and with acknowledgement of the originator. The cybernetic world of social media would not exist if there had not been software designers willing to generate open source programs on which anyone can draw. Indeed, there would not be an Internet if the consortium of universities who co-founded the first linkages of research data had not agreed to leave it in the public domain.

The organisation is a social environment especially designed to bring minds together to fulfil shared tasks. Often categorised as impeding collective goals through a fixed agenda and tightly controlled boundaries, an organisation still holds the potential for nurturing the open collective mind. The boundaries of the organisation are usually strongly defined and reinforced by regarding all other organisations as competitive, and even threatening; even the sub-divisions within organisations can be set to compete with each other. The extreme form is Taylorism, where tasks are broken down into their smallest parts and allocated to individual workers. On the other hand, there can be learning organisations, as described in Peter Senge's *The Fifth Discipline.*[12]

The pyramid of power relationships, with the chief at the apex and layers of responsibility underneath has become so common that people tend to forget that the pyramid, like the organisation, is a human invention, not a permanent form of human interaction. Research on organisations differs as to the value of the social contribution they make. One sociologist, Max Weber,[13] considered the bureaucratic organisation the most efficient and satisfying vehicle for people to combine to perform complex tasks. Another sociologist, Robert K. Merton,[14] identified the deficits of the bureaucratic organisation. Members are expected to give their personal loyalty to the organisation. Giant organisations such as IBM and DuPont have company songs, t-shirts, and regular group bonding sessions. Under these conditions there is little place for a collective self.

In summary it would seem that, while there is not yet the critical mass of collective minds hoped for by visionaries, there is a marked trend in that direction. At the same time, there is a long history of the further development of individual collective minds, through advances in collective principles for the design of language, governance and education.[15]

## Issues: divided minds and multiple realities

In developing a collective mind, the principal problem is not dividing wholes into parts. The flexible human mind can create and dissolve divisions in all elements of experience, personal, physical and social. The difficulties lie in that, once divided, the parts remain separated from each other and from their whole. A doctor is regarded as a separate person from their patients, parents from their children, food from its origins, and a town from its landscape, when it is the connections that create the context for the parts to exist. The relationships between the parts give the parts their shape and form. In these cases, the whole is a medical practice, a family, a meal and a dwelling place. They are each, of course, parts of still larger wholes. The human mind appears to relish making divisions, and comes to believe that the parts exist in their own right. The observer may fail to remember that the whole and its parts were a human construct in the first place.

So far in this pursuit of the collective mind, we have found that new ideas that change the pattern and make the boundaries permeable run the risk of being ignored or rejected. When new ideas call for a significant change in thinking, a new interpretation can generate real anger. Darwin's ideas crossed the boundaries that once separated humans from other forms of life, and he was denounced in British pulpits as an anti-Christ. When Lovelock established that the physical planet and its life forms together form a single self-organising system, his fellow scientists subjected him to orchestrated ridicule. Wiener saw the implications of electronic signals linking minds as well as physical brains and was socially isolated as a difficult troublemaker.

On the other hand, ideas that cross existing divisions have consistently been awarded Nobel prizes. Examples are the Ostroms with common pool resources, Barbara McClintock with 'jumping genes',[16] and Canetti with the wisdom of crowds. The awards came after decades of the proponents being ignored, and the new ideas have only been partly assimilated many more decades later. The difficulty is that new ideas bridging the boundaries fail to take hold in a thinking environment that has adopted parts as sufficient basis for interpreting reality.

Our inquiries in the previous five chapters have confirmed that clinging to divided thinking is still the dominant use of the mind. Yet those chapters also uncovered opportunities for collective thinking in the structures that create contemporary society. In every case, there was the potential for collective thinking to become the mainstream, with successful examples already in practice. Yet, while the collective options were increasingly being recognised, they were not yet in everyday thinking.

There is an apparently unlimited human capacity for learning available to make the transition from the divided to the collective mind. However, the transition is not without its problems. One major difficulty is the conflict that inevitably comes with change. Changing from the divided to the collective threatens power relationships established to protect the sovereignty of the parts. In the previous five chapters these power bases were the specialist languages, empirical sciences, representative democracy, the market economy and expert education. Thus the change from divided to collective thinking requires answers to the collective questions in an open environment protected from the knee-jerk responses from the past. This would indeed be a Herculean task without the tools that have been developed for the very purpose of maintaining an open mind to new ideas and collective relationships.

## Resolution: dialogue, pattern language and collective learning

The first task in collective thinking is to bring together all the minds concerned with the issue. Answering the set of questions together in an open group gives each of the contributors an insight into everyone else's introspective, physical, social, ethical, aesthetic and sympathetic understanding. Bringing the diverse positions together to reflect on the answers to these questions is the major challenge, as we have explored in Chapter 6.

In previous chapters we have suggested a number of avenues for collective minds to expand into new domains of thinking, both individually and through combining with other collective minds. These avenues have included asking the suite of collective questions, following the spiral of collective learning, designing environments with energy for living, expanding into cyberspace and employing Bohmian dialogue. It is now time to consider how and when these avenues relate to one another and how they can be best put into practice. When established, Bohmian dialogue is part of a sense of self, a way of thinking that permeates everything we do. It is a capacity that is central to the success of the other tools for collective thinking. Once dialogue is established, the use of the seven collective questions automatically calls into question the strengths and weaknesses of the traditional authorities: the social and physical sciences, social leadership, spiritual messages and aesthetic conventions.

## Practising dialogue

The dialogue developed by the physicist and philosopher David Bohm has already been mentioned as crucially important for developing a collective self, as a personal way of life rather than a temporary tool. In Chapter 7, we discussed the everyday rules of dialogue. William Isaacs of the Massachusetts Institute of Technology described what he called four dialogic practices that make up the dialogic space: listening, respecting, suspending and speaking out (for Isaacs this is voicing). The use of the Bohmian approach to dialogue is practised in many change-oriented programs that seek to develop both the inner-directed and the other-directed collective mind.[17] The individual undertakes a dialogue with their self as they answer the Herculean questions on their own behalf. They undertake a dialogue with others in the place of the more usual discussion or debate.

Listening to yourself is not easy, since your preconceived ideas usually fill up the available space. To listen properly is to develop an inner silence that allows deeper feelings to emerge. A rewarding way of putting yourself in touch with the natural environment is practised in environmental education. The individual is asked to put on a blindfold and sit under a tree, allowing the sounds they hear to enter into their more-than-conscious mind. A whole new experience takes over. To do this in concert with other people brings a collective experience, each contribution is unique and yet able to be shared with others. Hearing the tone of others' voices as well as, or even instead of, the words also brings another world of experience.[18]

Respect also starts with the self. There is a world of difference between making dogmatic statements in a knee-jerk fashion and putting forward an opinion based on your own respect for your ideas. Once you have established the grounds for respecting yourself, there is no longer any need to spring to the defence of a prejudice or prejudge others. It opens the way to seeking out respect for others, and interpreting their communications as revealing their potential as well as the immediate message. In the collective learning cycle, an exercise helps establish an atmosphere for creative thinking. In small groups, members are asked to share something about themselves that would surprise the others in the group. One member described dancing on the Berlin wall as it came down, and another, known to be a pacifist, had been employed as a powder monkey (setting explosives). These were only a couple of the surprising responses. After this exercise, the increase in respect for each other could be clearly felt in the group.

Speaking out in your own authentic voice assumes that you are speaking with respect and after having listened to the others. It involves the importance of recognising the power of not speaking until the time is ripe. It may be that what you wanted to say has already been said, that you are not yet sure of what you want to say, or that the dialogue is continuing and you do not wish to interrupt. An important contribution from David Bohm is the idea that in all conversations, when encouraged, implicate order will unfold from the thinking already in the room.[19] Dialogue is part of the unfolding, not separate from it, and so any contribution will need to consider how it will help with the unfolding. A contribution solely from your own need to speak will almost certainly be disruptive. A contribution that comes after listening and suspending judgment will open creative new channels of thought in the speaker and the listeners.

Often from the very openness of a dialogue come topics that had been suppressed. This is sometimes called bringing out the elephant in the room. When the speaker speaks about the elephant with their authentic voice, instead of shock and rejection, there can be silence and then a great sense of relief. The dialogue flows more intensely in the new direction. This has happened in practice in the hundreds of workshops of the Local Sustainability Project.[20] It happened with the naming of an organisational head as the inhibitor of new thinking. It occurred when a group recognised that they had come to the end of their abilities and needed to bring in someone new from outside. Authentic voicing can lead, not to further conflict, but to an 'aha', a collective recognition of something that the whole group had learnt from one another.

## Pattern languages and transformational change

Dialogue and a pattern language lie at either end of the process of collective learning. Dialogue gives access to a deeper level of understanding that allows people to share diverse ideas. A pattern language offers a framework that allows diverse interests to generate a collective solution to a shared problem. Living and non-living systems are made up of patterns. Networks, webs, trees, circles, spirals, pairs, waves, music, static, scents, mathematics and history are all patterns. The human mind is so eager to find patterns that it invents them to explain events such as the cycles in history. Work on chaos theory has discovered the mathematics that underlies fractals: patterns in nature that are scale invariant, that is, the shape of the pattern repeats itself at every scale. Examples are coastlines, weather patterns and the brindled pattern on cows and seashells.[21]

Christopher Alexander used this ubiquity of patterns to develop the basis for individuals and communities to share ideas when creating living and built environments that satisfy physical, social, ethical, aesthetic and sympathetic human needs. He insisted that beautiful, comfortable and flexible environments could best be designed collectively by the people who will inhabit those environments. Once designed, both built and social environments would be mutually supportive living places inhabited by people who could defend their chosen design and challenge any other solution forced upon them.[22]

Pattern language has been used extensively in innovative design in architecture, community development, software design and engineering. In the preceding chapters of this book, we have applied the elements of pattern language, title, context, issues, resolution and examples to transformational change in the fields of language, science, government, economics and education. After extensive experience in the applications of pattern language, Alexander evolved criteria that made it possible to design a successful pattern language. He concluded that all significant experience arises from being in touch with the authentic self, often hidden from us by social rules about how we should think. Alexander wrote that the sign that we have found that centre in ourselves is when we tap into strong centres that have life, the 'I' of every person. In a steel and concrete bridge, a song, a shared experience, a cumulus cloud, we can recognise life – and recognise the same sense of sharing in life in humans everywhere. Alexander proposed that the foundation of this sense of life will always include the pattern that connects. For Alexander, a boundary is the site of a connection not a point of division. You can find a list of potential connections in Table 7.3.

In a world accustomed to being defined by difference, a sense of sharing life at points of connection may require some help. Programs for peace studies, cross-cultural awareness and non-violence offer pathways to identifying and making connections. In *Towards a Nonviolent Mind*[23] Shri Ravindra Varma and Anna Alomes tell a positive story of how we can change our thoughts and reset our minds to compassion and caring for others. The authors pointed out that this is not to give entry to weakness, these give entry to strength.

## Examples: community consciousness raising and individual adult learning

### Community consciousness raising

#### Context

Paulo Freire was working in community development in Brazil in times of great oppression of marginalised communities. One rural community on the point of starvation was displaced to the edges of a city, with no provision of food or services of any kind. Their shelter and food was anything they could scavenge from the local rubbish dump. Physical health and community morale was at a low ebb. There was no energy left even to protest at their state or to help one another. Life was merely survival.

Freire arrived at the community, assessed the situation – and acted in a way that brought transformation. He bought a number of the then new Polaroid instant cameras and distributed them among the community members. Freire asked each person to take a picture of whatever was most valuable to them. The reaction brought energy back into the community. The photographs the people took were of beloved people and self-made shelter. The degradation of both became clearly visible in the photographs and entered the consciousness of the beholders. Freire called this 'conscientisation': the raising of the level of sympathetic response to injustice, cruelty and degradation.

Once the people in this community had their consciousness aroused, they turned to each other to think about what could be done. There was much that could be done, and Freire could help. Together they could protest to whatever authorities there were, initiate political action with a stronger group, and work together even with their scavenging to increase their minimal resources. Freire used many such examples to confirm that this is the collective mind, the conscious and the more-than-conscious mind together that is the source of self-respect and identity.

Freire became a hero in Brazil, generating so much political action from the raised consciousness of communities that he was banished. Decades later a political change allowed him to return. When his boat pulled in, the wharf was packed with cheering people as far as the eye could see. As he reached the wharf his welcomers said to him 'Now you can tell us what we should do'. According to the news report Freire sat down on the wharf and said 'Only you can tell what you can do. I am only here to listen'. His belief in the inner capacity of all people, no matter how limited they may appear to others and to the people themselves, never wavered.

Source: Paulo Freire, *Pedagogy of the Oppressed.*[24]

### Individual adult learning

A course on adult learning in the local technical college spontaneously generated the following learning about the self.

Fernando, a large, bluff, Italian-born teacher of bricklaying in the local technical college was in a class on adult learning that discussed Jean Piaget's stages of cognitive development in children. Piaget found that children up until seven cannot separate their world of inner experience from the outer world of others. In that class Fernando had tears in his eyes. A month later he came to my room and told me he had three small children, all under seven. Like his father before him, he had beaten them if they 'misbehaved'. Misbehaving meant not doing what he told them to do. He had no idea that they had their own different construction of the world. Now, he said, he had found a whole new world. He was taking the greatest delight in experiencing the world afresh through their eyes, and his learning was as great as theirs.

Patrick, an indigenous environmental manager from a remote island came to my office to resign from an environmental studies course because he 'could not understand a word the lecturers were saying'. Since he was extremely articulate, well-read and intelligent, there was something strange here. Since I knew that his cultural background was a tightly interwoven personal, physical, spiritual and social culture on a tropical island, I said 'But they are describing your island. Every word they are saying applies to your island. Apply the material to your island'. That is all it took. After two sessions, Patrick was advising the tutor about the ecological systems of his island.

Sarah, an experienced public health practitioner, considered that she already knew most of the course material and tended to instruct other students rather than discussing the issues with them. Sarah knew all about adult learning in relation to disease, or thought she did. During the course her mother was diagnosed with uterine cancer. Her distress at her mother's illness and treatment changed her orientation to the course. The material she was learning was no longer for her to use with clients – it was to help her mother. Her language, professional practice and even her body language underwent a radical change, from self-sufficient expert to sympathetic advisor.

Jason, a successful builder failed to submit assignments although he took an active and apparently well-informed part in class discussions. He confessed that he had left school at 14, and had never read a book or been inside a library. Yet his work included designing houses, managing complex projects and dealing with people. In other words, he often made major decisions and drew on multiple sources of evidence. He was able to make a model of a complex roof system in a flash, revealing a high-level understanding of geometric forms. After we talked about this, drawing the connections, Jason experienced a major readjustment of his own identity. The 'aha' that his own competencies could be translated directly into academic competencies gave him access to, in his words 'a whole new idea of who I was, what I could do'.

Source: Valerie A. Brown, Lecturer in adult learning.

## Notes

1 Walt Whitman, *Song of Myself*, 1855, p. 14.
2 Humberto Maturana and Francisco Varela tell this story of individuals continually 'bringing forth a world' through the process of living in detail in Maturana, H. and Varela, F. (1987) *The Tree of Knowledge*, Boston, US: Shambhala. See also Capra, F. (1996) *The Web of Life: A New Synthesis of Mind and Matter* (1996) UK: HarperCollins and Capra, F. (2002) *The Hidden Connections: A Science for Sustainable Living,* New York: Random House, where Fritjof Capra presents a clear interpretation of the research of Maturana and Varela and its significance.
3 Skolimowski, H. (1994) *The Participatory Mind: A new theory of knowledge and of the universe*, London: Arkana. Henryk Skolimowski (1930– ) is a Polish philosopher. See http://en.wikipedia.org/wiki/Henryk_Skolimowski [accessed 20.8.13].
4 Varma, R. and Alomes, A. (2012) *Towards a Nonviolent Mind,* Dharamsala: Library of Tibetan Works & Archives. Anna Alomes is a British-born Australian philosopher who works for the promotion of compassion and the reduction of violence with the Mind and Life Institute. See http://www.mindandlife.org/ [accessed 20.8.13].
5 Fine, C. (2010) *Delusions of Gender: How our Minds, Society, and Neurosexism Create Difference,* New York: W.W. Norton & Company.
6 Mitroff, I. I. and Linstone, H. A. (1993) *The Unbounded Mind: Breaking the Chains of Traditional Business Thinking*, New York: Oxford University Press.
7 Elias Canetti (1905–94) was born into a community of Spanish-speaking Jews in Bulgaria. From 1938 to 1970 he lived in Great Britain. He was a novelist and playwright whose works explore totalitarianism, crowds and the psychology of mass behaviour as well as individuals at odds with society. He wrote in German and won the Nobel Prize in literature in 1981. See http://en.wikipedia.org/wiki/Elias_Canetti [accessed 19.7.13].
8 Canetti, E. (1960/1984) *Crowds and Power* (tr.) Carol Stewart, New York: Farrar, Straus and Giroux. See http://en.wikipedia.org/wiki/Crowds_and_Power [accessed 19.7.13].
9 Winchester, S. (1999) *The Surgeon of Crowthorne: A Tale of Murder, Madness and the Oxford Dictionary*, Harmondsworth, Middlesex, UK: Penguin.
10 See http://en.wikipedia.org/wiki/DARPA [accessed 19.7.13].
11 See http://en.wikipedia.org/wiki/Reliability_of_Wikipedia [accessed 19.7.13].
12 Senge, P. M. (1990) *The Fifth Discipline; The Art and Practice of the Learning Organization,* New York: Currency Doubleday.
13 See http://en.wikipedia.org/wiki/Max_Weber [accessed 20.8.13].

14  See http://en.wikipedia.org/wiki/Robert_K._Merton [accessed 20.8.13].
15  Chapters 7, 9 and 11.
16  Chapter 2.
17  See for example the Local Sustainability Project at The Australian National University. Brown, V. A. and Lambert, J. A. (2013) *Collective Learning for Transformational Change: A Guide to Collaborative Action*, London and New York: Routledge. Another example is the Institute for Educational Studies (TIES) at Endicott College in Massachusetts, US. See https://organis.facebook.com/TIESEndicott [accessed 20.7.13].
18  Brown, V. A. and Lambert, J. A. (2013) *Collective Learning for Transformational Change: A Guide to Collaborative Action*, London and New York: Routledge.
19  Bohm, D. (1980) *Wholeness and Implicate Order*, London: Routledge. See also Bohm, D. (1994) *Thought as a System*, London and New York: Routledge.
20  Brown, V. A. and Lambert, J. A. (2013) *Collective Learning for Transformational Change: A guide to Collaborative Action*, London and New York: Routledge.
21  Mandelbrot, B. (1982) *The Fractal Geometry of Nature*, San Francisco, US: W. H. Freeman & Co. See also Briggs, J. and Peat, F. D. (1990) *Turbulent Mirror: An Illustrated guide to Chaos Theory and the Science of Wholeness*, New York: Harper & Row.
22  Chapter 4.
23  Varma, R. and Alomes, A. (2012) *Towards a Nonviolent Mind,* Dharamsala: Library of Tibetan Works & Archives.
24  Freire, P. (2006) *Pedagogy of the Oppressed*, 30th Anniversary edn., New York: Continuum.

# Part III
# Changing worlds

# 13 Utopian thinking in a connected world

**Synopsis:** in hoping for a just and sustainable future, the planet can best be thought of as a continually changing four-dimensional world in which the human collective mind has accepted responsibility for its own actions. Usual predictions are in the form of a dystopia or a utopia, a hopeless or a hopeful world. Such predictions will always be unrealistic since utopias are models of perfection and dystopias models of disaster. A more practical option is to use the phrase 'utopian thinking' for a search for positive and practical ideas on moving towards an unknown future. This means accepting the reality of the dynamic connections between parts and wholes, stable and chaotic systems, individuals and groups, and creative and rational thinking. This continually changing world can best be understood through reflecting on the suite of questions that involve all ways of knowing. Introspective, physical, social, ethical, aesthetic, sympathetic and reflective questions are core to any hopeful and realistic consideration of the future.

## Context: a divided world

There are many ways to imagine what the future might hold for a collectively governed planet. The transformational changes happening all around the world make anything possible. Options include a utopia[1] in which all ills have been remedied; a dystopia in which the worst has happened; and a prediction projected from the current state of the world. Given the rate of transformational change, projections and predictions of the future are destined to be extremely unreliable. Another possibility, utopian thinking, asks 'what if' and 'what might be' rather than trying to guess what will be. However, before going along that path it will be useful to consider the dystopias and utopias on offer for the present century.

The most common form of future telling is to threaten a dystopia, with doom-laden warnings against continuing present lines of action. A few approaches, such as the annual State of the World Report[2] and the United Nations Millennium Development Goals[3] consider the future as a dynamic interaction between the physical and the social worlds. More often, descriptions of a looming dystopia use different sources of evidence and different languages to describe the physical and the social worlds. As a result there are two sets of answers to the suite of introspective, physical, social, ethical, aesthetic, sympathetic and reflective questions posed by the collective mind.

The dystopian message for the physical planet is a rise in temperature of five degrees that could devastate life on Earth.[4] Even if this can be prevented, there is no hope of removing the threat altogether. It is already in train, although global action before 2020 could reduce the rate of increase to three degrees.[5] Three degrees would change plant fertilisation patterns, climate and sea level rise, but could still support many forms of life. The dystopian forecast for a social future assumes that the world's human population will continue its rate of exponential increase until it reaches nine billion. By that time food scarcity and starvation will control the population. Although we have avoided a global war for over two generations, the number of small wars and imminent civil wars is unprecedented, and presents hardly a desirable means of population control.[6]

The double forecast on the future state of the world continues through the rest of the suite of collective questions. Environmental scientists, climatologists and biologists tackle the social aspects of food security, population displacement and risks to health from their physical perspective. Economists, sociologists, political scientists and anthropologists answer the same questions from the social side. Both streams tend to ignore the exciting work reviewed in Part II on social structures based on the interdependence between the physical and social worlds. Little consideration is given to the world as a single self-organising system created by the interdependence among its three dimensions of living and non-living worlds, and the human mind, with a feedback loop of the synergy created by their interactions.

Ethically, the future of the biophysical planet is expressed as the need to maintain ecosystem services, that is, humans managing natural systems for positive human ends. Ethical concern for the social state of the world is usually about humans living at peace with one another. In legal systems of the Western world, natural systems have only recently been recognised as part of human ethical responsibility. The question 'Should trees have [legal] standing?' dates only from the 1970s.[7] Aesthetic questions appear to be answered from different wellsprings of creativity. Predictions of doom for the planet are in the form of films such as *An Inconvenient Truth*[8] and photographic collections of polar bears and melting ice-floes. The social side has produced Thoreau's *Walden Pond*,[9] Wendell Berry's love of community,[10] Aldo Leopold's *Sand Country Almanac*[11] and Walt Whitman's 'Leaves of Grass',[12] bringing the answers to all of the seven collective questions together in a creative leap.

Sympathetic relationships also differ between those who regard the state of the world as primarily biophysical or primarily social. Proposed management of the physical future takes the form of a hierarchical administration system led by experts. Proposed methods of governance of the social future are usually collaborations between different interest groups at different scales. When it comes to reflective questions, the division of the state of the world into two different realities is so deep that it stands in the way of collective understanding. Whether as a dystopia or utopia, as a hopeless or a hopeful perspective on the future, any scenarios generated from divided physical and social perspectives are inevitably a distortion of whatever may be happening in the actual world.

Another difficulty with accepting any particular form of utopia or dystopia as a solution to the world's ills is that, however original it may seem, it is set in pre-existing conditions. The very perfection of the biblical Eden,[13] Plato's *The Republic,*[14] Thomas More's *Utopia*[15] and Huxley's *Island*[16] means that each were repairing the inadequacies of the social and physical conditions of their time. They are unlikely to meet the needs of an, as yet, unknown future. In particular, a fixed utopia cannot meet the needs of a collective mind that is based on the diversity and creativity that arises from valuing difference. Humans living their distinctively different ways of life do not seek the same ideal world. A fixed-goal utopia is unlikely to satisfy the restless human spirit and its capacity for learning without limits.

Philosopher of ideas, Isaiah Berlin,[17] pointed out that every description of dystopia implies a possible utopia.[18] Thus every prediction of disaster for the Anthropocene implies that there is a parallel desirable world. From this perspective, if only the world was not wracked by wars; full of starving people; facing higher temperatures and disrupted food supplies; put at risk by a rising aging population's need for resources – there would be a perfect world. Under these scenarios utopia becomes the absence of risks rather than a promise of a different way to live.

Science fiction is a medium that often explores worlds made up of all four dimensions and answers each of the collective questions. For instance, *The Hitchhikers Guide to the Galaxy,*[19] *The Matrix Trilogy,*[20] and *Animal Farm*[21] are dystopias in the form of an allegory, a simulation and a satire. Each generated a cult following. Each offers a vivid example of the issues that face the future of a four-dimensional world: the living, non-living worlds, the power of human ideas and the synergy that arises from the interconnections of the other three. *The Hitchhiker's Guide* tells the story of a human adrift in the universe after Earth has been destroyed for an intergalactic highway. The universe's combined supercomputers spend centuries calculating the answer to a crucial question about the future of the world. The answer turned out to be 42. But what was the question?

*The Matrix Trilogy* offers a world that is an imagined reality that never in fact existed. The apparently real world is built from advertising, Internet and educational programs that replace the world they are pretending to describe. Only the few people who remain in touch with the underlying real world can return people to it. In *Animal Farm,* animals that have been exploited by humans have taken over the farmyard. As the animals exercise their new power, the original principles of their revolution, freedom, equity and sympathy for others, are forgotten. The animal victors replace the previous domination and cruelty of the human regime. Their propaganda line was 'Four legs good; two legs bad'.

Taken together the three dystopias describe a world where the invented world has become more real than the reality on which it was based, and the power of self-interest and misinformation can subvert even the best-intentioned attempt at social transformation. This is uncomfortably close to the real world of the twenty-first century.

## Collective questions for utopian thinking

An invented utopian world is almost always founded on expectations of humans as peaceful, loving, inventive, rational and caring beings. At the same time, being human, the same people carry the potential for conflict, misery, injustice, greed, and violence. In a stochastic, kaleidoscopic self-organising world, a potential utopia would need to find ways to mediate this paradox. In the stories reviewed so far it has emerged that a collective future requires some image of a future world that recognises the value of difference, helps divisions to become gateways, replaces competition with collective thinking and structures the social world in that vein.

Healing the divisions between a physical and a social world and repairing the fragmentation of knowledge and of interests would be an impossible task without access to a different system of thought and a vision of a world not so divided. Yet a dystopia is self-defeating and a utopia is unrealistic. Rescue from this impasse comes again from philosopher of ideas Isaiah Berlin.[22] He suggested that utopian thinking is a quite different process from accepting a utopian ideal. Rather than looking for an impossible perfection, utopian thinking is hopeful, but not single-minded. It holds dreams of avoidance of disaster and a brighter future while being able to deal with disappointment and surprise. With the contribution of collective thinkers, the range of experience and ideas can provide many surprises. The future may lie in an unexpected direction and so it becomes important to be open to innovation and new ideas, as well as open to the hopes and fears of our human fellow travellers.

The famous utopian, Thomas More, brings our attention to some crucial aspects of utopian thinking. One aspect is the sometimes urgent desire to establish the utopia in practice whether the conditions for it are supportive or not. The ruins of many a settlement and commune confirm the disastrous results. On the other hand, without some notion of how things would work for all seven elements of human experience there is no path to follow. The strength of the interconnections between the introspective, physical, social, ethical, aesthetic, sympathetic and reflective ways of being means that if one is missing, all will fall.

On the same grounds, if the utopian thinking does not in some measure embrace the ideals of all those concerned then, once again, the dream will fail. More coined the phrase 'utopia' to describe a vision of a country that works in practice with the full approval of all its citizens. This is the same vision that led Christopher Alexander to develop his pattern language for collective design which has proved a practical aid for crowd-based structures from neighbourhoods, to urban planning, to computer software.[23] More, being pre-Newton and pre-Einstein, deals quite differently with the physical world than we would today. He endorsed utopian thinking thus 'Everywhere one may hear of ravenous dogs and wolves; but it is not so easy to find states that are well and wisely governed'.[24]

The transformational thinking with which this story began has foreshadowed the potential ethical basis for an interdependent world of the future. Darwin's work on the evolution of human emotions implies a world in which all individual human beings are, or could be, in close sympathetic communication. James Lovelock's Gaia, with its self-organising system of living and non-living systems influenced by the human mind implies that the future is the responsibility of all humanity. Wiener's prediction of an electronic world included an urgent need for an ethic of collective responsibility, which is amply confirmed by the events of WikiLeaks and other whistle blowers. An ethical basis for utopian thinking is thus already in place: human responsibility for all other human beings.

Aesthetically, there could be a collective world where harmony and challenge exist side by side generating the creative leaps that permit transcendence from the present. Keats wrote "'Beauty is truth, truth beauty", – that is all Ye know on Earth, and all Ye need to know'.[25] The question remains, where do humans find beauty? There could be a world where people revert to their natural selves in perfect tune with nature, as Rousseau[26] longed for. There is Pierre Teilhard de Chardin's future world with one all-encompassing mind containing the thinking of all minds. The world could fulfil Gregory Bateson's hope that the pattern that connects is the basis for all thinking, rather than the barriers that divide. It could meet Christopher Alexander's ideal for people to generate collectively their own designs for how they will live. In a collective world, it could be all of the above. In utopian thinking they are not mutually exclusive.

Our treasure hunt has uncovered two preconditions for thinking about a collective future for humankind. One precondition is recognition that transformation along four lines of thought makes up our present world:

- In any dynamic system, everything is both a part and a whole.
- Living systems are both stable and chaotic at the same time.
- A society thrives on the collective learning of both individuals and the society.
- Human thought combines the creative and the rational, the body and the mind.

The other precondition is for a collective thinker to go about their Herculean task guided by the answers to the seven collective questions.[27] What follows is a review of the state-of-the-art collective thinking from the perspective of collective learning which has absorbed the transformation in thinking.

## Introspective questions

Every seeker for a collective world already has their assumptions about that world. We, the authors of this book, did not originally consider ourselves to be collective thinkers. As we uncovered the criteria for collective thinking that emerged from the life stories of collective thinkers, we recognised the same experiences in our own lives. We found that we had absorbed the full range of ways of experiencing the world into our thinking, struggled past self-doubt and the negativity of our peers. We had to go outside our training as ecologists to access other ways of knowing, found more commitment to collective thinking and collaboration than we had expected, and confirmed that it is the human mind that drives human actions and so has become the wellspring for global transformational change.

As members of the Enlightenment era, we ourselves had experienced the shocks from the shift from the specialised to the collective mind. Of the three master thinkers and the three visionaries whose stories make up Part I of this book, all were trained as physical scientists. This may have been a selection bias due to our scientific training. On the other hand, it was predictable after the 300 years of the Enlightenment that all the leading thinkers we chose would be science trained. As it turned out, all six master thinkers revealed an equal capacity to draw on all seven ways of thinking. The lesson is that a would-be collective thinker needs to reflect on their own journey.

## Physical questions

Accepting that we live in a self-organising four-dimensional world makes it impossible to think any longer of the world as static and divided. In the Transformation Science that is proposed for the era of transformation, an analysis of collective thinking divides the whole into seven questions, while at the same time keeping the whole in mind. Transformation Science continues to use the tools of traditional science: analysis, observation and measurement of the physical world. The seven questions that form the basis for the analysis are each grounded in human experience. Once having decided that the seven questions gave a fair representation of the workings of the human mind, they have been found to work in practice, as recorded in the examples found throughout this story. The previous era of the Enlightenment confirms that much of life can be described in physical terms, and how much is lacking when that is all there is described.

The response to the idea of a Transformation Science has often been confused about how to 'measure' ethical and aesthetic evidence, as well as the sympathetic. An inquiry can uncover physical signs of all ways of thinking. An ethical position is revealed in an individual or group's response to a human being in need. The answer to the biblical 'Who is my neighbour?' – 'Anyone with whom I have anything to do', gives objective data on an ethical stance. Someone's clothes, the objects they collect, and the way they go about their work are evidence of the aesthetic dimension of their thinking.

A frequent response to the idea of a Transformation Science has been to ask where do intuition, imagination, wisdom, judgment, common sense and reason fit in. Put simply, intuition is the synthesis of the evidence from all ways of knowing. Imagination is the precious capacity of the human brain to bring new ideas. Judgment is the bringing together of explicit and tacit knowledge that happens every time a complex decision is made. Common sense draws on the practical: 'Will it work?', 'Is it real?'. Reason is the use of the conscious mind, often mistakenly represented as a synonym for all thought. The hope for wisdom is a case of utopian thinking, going beyond the search for the right answer. All of these considerations apply to science and the study of the physical world equally as to other elements of thought.

## Social questions

Human beings are social beings. A human being cannot survive without the presence of other human beings, much less fulfil their potential. In the mother's uterus and for at least three years afterwards, humans require constant human support, the longest dependency of any animal. The technical word for this is neotony – birth as an incomplete individual. An evolutionary explanation for the long dependence is that it gives the large brain time and space to understand the patterns that make up the world. After childhood, humans continue to live collective lives through their relationships with parents, siblings, partners, peers, colleagues, friends and neighbours.

Social questions take priority in Part II of this book, in the accounts of key structures through which humans organise their society. An inclusive language develops a mutual understanding of the world. Transformation Science combines evidence from the seven perspectives into a collective interpretation of reality. A collaborative style of governance accesses avenues for collaboration at all scales and on all issues. A collective economy acknowledges traditional gift relationships and draws equitably on common pool resources. An open approach to education replaces the competitive with the collective at every stage of the human lifespan. Finally, the identity of each individual is forged in face-to-face relationships and by electronic communication with partners, families, groups and crowds.

The question is, 'Would a community with those social structures be a utopia?'. The answer is clearly no, since each of the structures is open to diversity and change, and its future form cannot be firmly predicted. The answer is also no because the collective world cannot be expected to be perfect when human beings are far from perfect. The collective structures demonstrate that a collective society is possible. The form of a collective society itself would be ideally determined by all the people present at the time.

The strength of the human capacity to think tends to overwhelm an understanding of the thinking capacity and collective structures of all other living things. This leaves a weak spot in our understanding of the relationships among the parts and wholes of the entire living world. The shock of the introduction of the ideas of Gaia is evidence of the extent to which this aspect of the world had been subdued during the scientific era. However, making up for lost time in the last 50 years has led to a realisation of the self-organising systems and presence of purpose in the more-than-human world, a realisation that began with Charles Darwin and continues in ideas of a symbiotic collaborative living world uncovered in Chapter 3.

## Ethical questions

Ethical questions are addressed to the relationships between living things. We have already discussed how all living systems, including humans, have a purpose in living. For humans, their purpose is intimately linked to their ethical position. Life scientists used to be told to avoid attributing purpose to any aspect of living, clearly an aberration of a time when only the observable was considered to exist. Now that complex living and non-living systems have been recognised as self-organising, it follows that there is a purpose behind the self-organisation, even if only for gathering food. We have come a long way from Aristotle's classification of living things by their usefulness to humans. For humans as individuals and in groups, a purpose is a self-fulfilling prophecy, a direction which people work towards.

We speak of a good or an evil purpose with reference to some ethical principle that is good if we share it and evil if we don't. This is not to say that all purposes are equally worthy of respect, only that respect comes from the eye of the beholder. With the powers humans have developed through learning to control energy and inventing new tools, they are likely to succeed in their purpose. Success has bred success, until human beings have influenced all parts of the living and non-living planet.

Iris Murdoch wrote of the issues implicit in equating good with God.[28] Teilhard de Chardin, as a Jesuit priest, saw the ultimate good for humankind as a collective mind that would become complete when it reached point Omega, one with God.[29] He also embraced the ideal of collective human minds informing each other in the mental environment of the noosphere.[30] On the other hand, philosophers of science have produced a whole literature on what they have called 'The God Delusion'.[31] Subsets of major human religions have created their own versions of a collective world by linking an inner-directed sense of conscience and collective minds. Options for following this path are the Quaker, the Buddhist and the Sufi commitment to the mind as 'the god within' as well as principles that support the coming together of those minds in a collective understanding.[32]

The Buddha-inspired collective mind is based on three commitments and five precepts.[33] The first commitment is to not cause harm, a commitment of kindness and compassion to all living beings. Contemplating one's individual and collective thoughts, feelings and emotions prevents acting in haste and confusion. The second commitment is to keeping the heart open to compassion and peace. The third is making a resolution to see the world just as it is. An individual's right path is the sum of their experiences of living in the world.

Quakers, also known as the Society of Friends, form a group within Christianity. Their openness to change and uncertainty, while cherishing each other as friends, makes the Quakers open to the development of a collective mind. Each individual has only their own self and their own conscience to bring to issues that confound their ideal path: peace, equality, truth, simplicity and care for Earth. For more than 300 years, Quakers have been making decisions without resorting to voting.[34] The aim for all decisions is to find 'a sense of the meeting', as a consensus[35] of all those present at the meeting.

Sufism is a Muslim movement whose followers stress respect for all believers, whether Muslim, Christian, Jewish, Hindu or Buddhist.[36] This commitment includes mutual civility and cooperation, regardless of religious or cultural background. The central doctrine of Sufism is the oneness of being that is the seamless garment behind all differentiation and manifestation. The chief aim of all Sufis is to let go of all notions of duality and realise the divine unity, which is considered to be the truth. The point being made here is not that these three groups have necessarily achieved their ideals; it is that substantial populations have persevered in developing conditions for a collective society.

## Aesthetic questions

The capacity for transcendence, for being lifted out of the ordinary, everyday world into the realm of awe, beauty and amazement is uniquely human. It gives humankind access to the new, the alternative, the inspirational which can change the person and the world. Leonardo da Vinci wrote 'The eye is the window of the soul. The eye is the chief organ whereby the understanding can have the most complete and magnificent view of the infinite works of nature'. Others give emphasis to the understanding and transcendence gained through the ear, the mind, and the body as in music, literature, poetry and dance. Yet others call on the combined senses in opera, theatre, musicals, and film. William Butler Yeats[37] recognised the human identity with the creative medium.[38]

> O body swayed to music, O brightening glance,
> How can we know the dancer from the dance?
> *William Butler Yeats*

From a collective thinking perspective the entire field of human understanding has been misinterpreted as a battleground between arts and science. The dualism of body and soul, matter and mind was taken to extremes and personified in the stereotypes of the scientist and the artist. At one extreme there is a self-effacing, unemotional and objective human being, loyal to their chosen discipline and their peers. At the other extreme is the dramatic, passionate and involved human, following the direction set by their muse. Stereotypes they may be, yet psychological testing found the personalities following the model.

Much energy has been spent on describing the polarisation of arts and science, from Greek scholar Archilocus's *Foxes and Hedgehogs*[39] to scientist Charles Snow's *Two Cultures*.[40] As Bateson[41] wrote, the new formulation of a human being as a whole person is neither a victory for the artist, nor a middle ground between the two poles. There have always been marriages between arts and science. Classic examples of inner-directed collective thinking are Leonardo da Vinci, painter, inventor and philosopher;[42] Goethe, mathematician, politician and poet;[43] and Winston Churchill, strategist, painter and writer.[44]

For outer-directed collective thinking, aesthetic experience is a strong bond whenever a group of people experience an aesthetic 'high' together. The mosh pit in a pop concert, the awed audience at a brilliant orchestral performance, the intake of breath at a beautiful picture exhibition, are all bonding experiences. The synergy between the people in the crowd emerges as a different way of being derived from their collective thinking.

## Sympathetic questions

The many avenues by which all humans are connected at the same time mark every human being as unique. The common gene pool, the global life-support systems of air and water, and the Internet are threads that both link all of humanity and are distinct for every individual. The common threads of humanity in speech and body language allow us to enter the private world of anyone, although only if they permit it. The extent to which speech, body language, shared emotions and stories allow an understanding of oneself and others gives validity to the answers to sympathetic questions. The Jewish philosopher, Martin Buber, wrote of the implications of the phrase 'I and thou', the mutual understanding that can only develop at a personal level.[45] He distinguished between sympathy, feeling for someone else, and empathy, which is feeling like someone else. Only mutual experiences can release empathy, while there are certain conditions that allow sympathy to develop among all individuals, which can also be valid for groups.

An essential condition for sharing a sympathetic understanding is trust. Human beings can protect themselves and their vulnerability by closing down or redirecting the channels that could give valid answers to sympathetic questions. The invented stories from the Pacific islanders about their sexuality that Margaret Mead published as anthropological research are famous examples.[46] Another prerequisite is critical loyalty, a shared commitment to a joint enterprise, which allows forthright and open communication among a group.[47]

David Bohm referred to the potential unfolding of all reality through each of us individually and around us collectively.[48] The world participates in each of us and we participate in the world. It is a participatory universe. The spirit of dialogue is an understanding that the essence of a common consciousness gives us the ability to perceive the deeper meanings of everybody in the dialogue. The mystery of consciousness was referred to by writer David Malouf as 'What else should our lives be but a continual series of beginnings, of painful settings out into the unknown, pushing off from the edge of consciousness into the mystery of what we have not yet become ...'.[49]

## Reflective questions

The final stage of a collective thinking process involves reviewing the answers to the previous six questions within their changing context of reoriented paradoxes. At the present time, the four reoriented paradoxes that are influencing our interpretation of reality are the interconnections between parts and wholes, stable and chaotic living systems, individual and social collective learning, and the different avenues of human thought.[50] Ways of applying these paradoxes in exploring the future proved to be to examine assumptions, apply Transformation Science, learn to combine diverse purposes, generate shared aesthetic experiences and communicate through dialogue.

Because a collective mind has evolved within other global cultures does not mean that it would be simple to establish that way of living in the West. The West was the cradle of the divided rational thinking that produced the technological miracles of the scientific era. Other cultures have had millennia to develop the subsets of their collective worlds, while the scientific era only took control comparatively recently. However, other collective realities offer tools and models to the West. For instance the ancient Chinese symbol of yin and yang[51] and the

Tibetan tradition of the Mandala[52] offer symbols that remind the user of the interchangeability of parts and wholes

The relationship between the one and the many, the individual and their society, has been a matter for discussion from the time of the Western roots in the Greek tradition. The tensions in this relationship have long been the foundation for legal systems, philosophical traditions and creative literature. Neuroscience has confirmed what philosophers have long proposed. All elements of human thought: conscious and more-than-conscious; rational and imaginative, inform each other within the one human mind.[53] The same neural processes can be found in different minds, so they can be linked together in a single web. Verbal, non-verbal, electronic, symbols and stories, and tacit knowledge are open channels that can connect any number of people. The tools for dialogue, extensively canvassed throughout this book, provide a very powerful unifying channel.

The fourth reoriented paradox contains the recognition that all people have the capacity to use all of their modes of thought: rational and creative, sympathetic and objective, supportive and critical, and ethically committed and detached. One of the essential capacities for collective learning is to be clear about which is which, and which is appropriate for which conditions. The collective questions call on all of these capacities. Well-developed schools of thought that can help expand the capacities that social conditions have not allowed to develop.

Obvious from this juxtaposition of the reoriented paradoxes that define the Anthropocene is that they are not independent. The paradoxes influence each other and become part of the social pattern in which they have arisen. The collective questions give us the thinking tools to address the issues arising from the social pattern of their time. As our sorcerers and visionaries concluded, there is already an interconnected world. Whether the next era is a new Enlightenment, recognition and development of that collective world remains to be seen. The next stage of the development of a collective world can be compared with a self-organised team of high-powered and restive horses, each with their own agenda, who are willing to be harnessed together in moving towards a common future.

## Conclusion

The evidence throughout this book confirms the emergence of a transformational change towards a collective world, affecting all of us as human beings and as members of a human society. The potential for that collective world has existed as long as the species itself. All peoples share the same genetic program; inherit a culture, talk to each other, ask questions, govern their social world, manage their shared resources, rear their young and match their identity to a particular group. The global distribution of populations, resources, finance and information is forcing open boundaries of space and time established over the two million years of human evolution. People are able to see and even take part in how other cultures live, thanks to the gift of global travel and the distress of displacement. Global trade is generating unprecedented distribution of physical and human resources. Information has become a free good thanks to the Internet and the whistle blowers.

The same principle of distinctiveness and connectedness, parts and wholes, applies to all four dimensions of the living planet. Earth's physical landscapes of valleys and deserts are physically distinct and climatically connected. Earth's rind of living things is so interrelated that any change affects an entire system, as in a previous quote, to pick an edelweiss in Switzerland is to make a polar bear tremble. The speed of the worldwide mental connection of one incident on YouTube has generated a new phrase 'gone viral'. The most challenging connectivity of all is the synergy between all four dimensions that generates a powerful force of its own. The 2004 Indian Ocean tsunami changed coastlines, decimated populations, caused a panic in science-policy circles at the lack of a warning capacity, forced a revision of coastal urban planning and, at some higher level, recalled the very interdependence of the other three dimensions.

While utopias and dystopias are ways of forecasting possible futures, they are not satisfactory guides to those futures; utopias because they are perfect and humans are not perfect; dystopias because they lead to avoidance of risk rather than moves to a better future. Both remain embedded in the present, since even human creativity has its limits. A sustainable humane future for life on Earth seems more likely to emerge from open-ended utopian thinking than from searching for a polished utopia. From the evidence in this book that future will rest on the harnessing of a collective mind made up of diverse independent minds.

## Notes

1  The famous Renaissance humanist and author, Thomas More, coined the word 'utopia' to describe a vision of a country that works in practice with the full approval of all its citizens.
2  Annual reports have been published since 1984 reporting on the state of the world by The World Watch Institute documenting the effects of the technological transformations on the social and physical aspects of the planet.
3  See http://www.un.org/millenniumgoals/ [accessed 30.7.13].
4  Flannery, T. (2005) *The Weather Makers: The History and Future Impact of Climate Change*, Melbourne, Australia: Text Publishing Company.
5  Adam, D. and Hickman, L. (2009) 'Scientists: Act now or face climate catastrophe – experts break tradition to comment on policy; Gore says political "tipping point" reached', *The Guardian Weekly*, 20–26 March, **180** (14), 1–2. See http://climate.nasa.gov/key_indicators#globalTemp for information on climate change at the time of publication [accessed 30.7.13].
6  See http://www.warsintheworld.com/?page=static1258254223 [accessed 30.7.13]. A documentary film, *Scarred Lands & Wounded Lives – The Environmental Impact of War* can be viewed on www.scarredlandsfilm.org. [accessed 31.7.13].
7  Stone, C. D. (1975/2010) *Should Trees Have Standing? Law, Morality and the Environment*, 3rd edn, New York: Oxford University Press. This is the thirty-fifth anniversary edition of the original book.
8  See Gore, A. (2007) *An Inconvenient Truth: The Crisis of Global Warming*, London: Bloomsbury. Adapted for a young person from the award-winning film.
9  Walden Pond is a small lake in Concord, Massachusetts in the US and a powerful symbol for many conservationists of the importance of living simply, attentively and caring for nature. US writer, activist, poet, philosopher and leading transcendentalist, Henry David Thoreau (1817–62) lived this 'simple life' close to nature on the edge of Walden Pond for two years from 1845. See Thoreau, H. D. (1844/1960) *Walden and Civil Disobedience*,

Boston, US: Houghton Mifflin. See http://transcendentalism-legacy.tamu.edu/authors/thoreau/ [accessed 1.8.13]. A recent book is Maynard, W. B. (2004) *Walden Pond*, New York: Oxford University Press.

10 Wendell Berry is a US farmer, writer, activist and academic living on a farm in Kentucky where he devotes his attention to the wellbeing of his family, community and Earth. Berry, W. (1977) *The Unsettling of America: Culture and Agriculture*, San Francisco, US: Sierra Club Books. See also http://en.wikipedia.org/wiki/Wendell_Berry [accessed 31.7.13].

11 Leopold, A. (1949/1981) *A Sand County Almanac and Sketches Here and There*, London: Oxford University Press. Recently there is Newton, J. L. (2006) *Aldo Leopold's Odyssey: Rediscovering the Author of A Sound County Almanac*, Washington, DC: Island Press, a Shearwater book.

12 Walter Whitman (1819–92) *Walt Whitman: The Complete Poems* (ed.) Francis Murphy, London: Penguin Classics.

13 As described in the book of Genesis, *The Holy Bible, King James Version*, Cleveland and New York: The World Publishing Company.

14 Nettleship, R. L. (1955) *The Theory of Education in Plato's Republic*, London: Oxford University Press.

15 More, T. (1530/1995) *Utopia* (tr.) Logan, G. M., Adams, R. M. and Miller, C., Cambridge, UK: Cambridge University Press. It is available as an eBook.

16 Huxley, A. (1962) *Island*, New York: Harper & Row.

17 Sir Isaiah Berlin (1909–97), British philosopher and historian of ideas, had a Russian and Jewish background.

18 Berlin, I. (1959/1990) 'The Decline of Utopian Ideas in the West' in *The Crooked Timber of Humanity: Chapters in the History of Ideas* (ed.) Hardy, H., Princeton, US: New Jersey Press.

19 Adams, D. (1979/2005) *The Hitchhiker's Guide to the Galaxy*, London: Picador, the film tie-in edition.

20 *The Matrix* is a 1999 American–Australian science fiction action film written and directed by Wachowskis. It depicts a dystopian future in a simulated reality called 'The Matrix', created by sentient machines to subdue the human population. It is based on Jean Baudrillard's Simulacra and Simulation and Lewis Carroll's Alice's Adventures in Wonderland. See http://en.wikipedia.org/wiki/The_Matrix#cite_note-Salon_philosophy-4 [accessed 31.7.13].

21 Orwell, G. (1946/1962) *Animal Farm*, New York: Signet Classics.

22 Berlin, I. (1959/1990) 'The Decline of Utopian Ideas in the West' in *The Crooked Timber of Humanity: Chapters in the History of Ideas* (ed.) Hardy, H., Princeton, US: New Jersey Press.

23 Chapter 4.

24 More, T. (1530/1955) *Utopia* (tr.) Logan, G. M., Adams, R. M. and Miller, C., Cambridge, UK: Cambridge University Press, Book 1, p. 1.

25 These are the last lines of the poet George Keats' (1820) Ode on a Grecian Urn. See http://englishhistory.net/keats/poetry/odeonagrecianurn.html [accessed 31.7.13].

26 Rousseau, Jean Jacques (1712–78) was born in Geneva and moved to France in 1741 where he made major contributions in political philosophy, education and literature. For his views on how society corrupts the basic goodness of human beings, which can be countered by living in tune with nature see http://infed.org/mobi/jean-jacques-rousseau-on-nature-wholeness-and-education/ [accessed 1.8.13].

27 Chapters 5 and 6.

28 Murdoch, I. (1970) *The Sovereignty of Good*, London: Routledge & Kegan Paul.

29 Teilhard de Chardin, P. (1955/1975) *The Phenomenon of Man* (tr.) B. Wall, New York: Harper & Row.

30 Discussed in Chapter 2.

31  For example, Dawkins, R. (2006) *The God Delusion*, London: Bantam.

32  Varma, R. and Alomes, A. (2012) *Towards a Nonviolent Mind*, Dharamsala, India: Library of Tibetan Works and Archives.

33  Chodron, P. (1012) *Living Beautifully with Uncertainty and Change*, Boston and London: Shambhala.

34  Hare, P. (1973) 'Group Decision by Consensus: Reaching Unity in the Society of Friends', *Sociological Inquiry,* **43** (1), 75–84.

35  The word consensus comes from the Latin, *consensus* (agreement), which is from *consentio* (literally 'feel together'). It describes both the decision outcome and the process of reaching a decision.

36  Varma, R. and Alomes, A. (2012) *Towards a Nonviolent Mind*, Dharamsala, India: Library of Tibetan Works and Archives.

37  Yeats, William Butler (1865–1939) Irish poet and winner of the Nobel Prize for literature.

38  The last two lines of stanza VIII, 'Among School Children', written in 1928 after Yeats visited a Montessori school.

39  See Berlin, I. (1998) *The Proper Study of Mankind: An Anthology of Essays*. London: Pimlico and discussion in Chapter 2.

40  Snow, Charles Percy, 1st Baron (1905–80) English novelist and physicist. Snow's warning that science and art are becoming two cultures was given in his 1959 Rede Lecture. See Snow, C. P. (2012) *The Two Cultures*, Cambridge, UK: Cambridge University Press, a Canto Classic.

41  Chapter 3.

42  Leonardo da Vinci (1452–1519) was an Italian painter, sculptor, architect and engineer. For insights into his contribution to the West see Kenneth Clark's 1969 television series of which there is a book made up of the scripts produced by the British Broadcasting Commission entitled, Clark, K. (1969) *Civilisation: A Personal View*, London: BBC and John Murray. The life and legacy of Leonardo da Vinci inspired a guide to collective action: Brown, V. A. (2008) *Leonardo's Vision: A Guide for Collective Thinking and Action*, Rotterdam, Netherlands: Sense.

43  Goethe, Johann Wolfgang von (1749–1832) was a German poet, dramatist, scientist, court official and one of the greatest figures in European literature. See http://en.wikipedia.org/wiki/Johann_Wolfgang_von_Goethe [accessed 31.7.13].

44  Churchill, Sir Winston Leonard Spencer (1874–1965), renowned Prime Minister of Great Britain during the Second World War, also won the 1953 Nobel Prize for literature. The eight volume biography by his son, Randolph, and Martin Gilbert entitled *Winston S. Churchill* is published by London: Heinemann, 1966–88. See also http://en.wikipedia.org/wiki/Winston_Churchill [accessed 1.8.13].

45  Buber, M. (1958/2000) *I and Thou*, 2nd edn (tr.) Ronald Gregor Smith, New York: Scribner Classics. Discussed in Chapter 5.

46  The famous US anthropologist Margaret Mead's field studies in Samoa on youth (predominantly adolescent girls) was published in 1928 entitled, *Coming of Age in Samoa: A Psychological Study of Primitive Youth for Western Society*, New York: William Marrow and Company. In 1983, after conducting his own field studies in Samoa, the Australian anthropologist, Derek Freeman, challenged some of Mead's research findings in his book, *Margaret Mead in Samoa: The Making and Unmaking of an Anthropological Myth,* Canberra: Australian National University Press. This book set off 'The Mead–Freeman Controversy'. See http://en.wikipedia.org/wiki/Coming_of_Age_in_Samoa [accessed 1.8.13].

47  Particularly valuable amongst postgraduate students undertaking research. See Cumming, F. (2010) 'Exploring the Doctoral Interface' in Brown, V. A., Harris, J. A. and Russell, J. Y. (eds) *Tackling Wicked Problems: Through the Transdisciplinary Imagination,* London: Earthscan, pp. 233–39.

48  Chapter 11.

49 Malouf, D. (1978/1999) *An Imaginary Life*, London: Vintage, p. 135.
50 Chapter 6.
51 Yin and yang are the two cosmic forces interacting with the five traditional natural elements of air, fire, water, metal and earth. It is a long-standing theory for understanding the relationships between the universe and humankind in terms of macrocosm and microcosm. Yin and yang cannot exist without each other and are in everything that exists.
52 The Mandala is a spiritual and ritual circle symbol in Hinduism and Buddhism and represents the universe. See https://en.wikipedia.org/wiki/Mandala [accessed 1.8.13].
53 See, for example, Damasio, A. (1994) *Descartes' Error: Emotion, Reason and the Human Brain*, New York: Penguin. Lackoff, G. and Johnson, M. (1999) *Philosophy in the Flesh: The Embodied Mind and Its Challenge to Western Thought*, New York: Basic Books.

# Bibliography

Adam, D. and Hickman, L. (2009) 'Scientists: Act now or face climate catastrophe –
experts break tradition to comment on policy; Gore says political "tipping point"
reached', *The Guardian Weekly*, 20–26 March, **180** (14), 1–2.

Adams, D. (1979/2005) *The Hitchhiker's Guide to the Galaxy*, London: Picador.

Alexander, C. (2002) *The Nature of Order. Book One: The Phenomenon of Life*, Berkeley,
US: The Centre for Environmental Structure.

Alexander, C. (2002) *The Nature of Order. Book Two: The Process of Creating Life*,
Berkeley, US: The Centre for Environmental Structure.

Alexander, C. (2003) *The Nature of Order. Book Three: A Vision of a Living World*,
Berkeley, US: The Centre for Environmental Structure.

Alexander, C. (2005) *The Nature of Order. Book Four: The Luminous Ground*, Berkeley,
US: The Centre for Environmental Structure.

Alexander, C., Ishikawa, S., Silverstein, M., Jacobson, M., Fiksdahl-King, I. and Angel, S.
(1977) *A Pattern Language: Towns, Buildings and Constructions*, New York: Oxford
University Press.

Andrewartha, H. G. and Birch, L. C. (1954) *The Distribution and Abundance of Animals*,
Chicago, US: University of Chicago Press.

Ansell, C. K. (2011) *Pragmatist Democracy: Evolutionary Learning as Public Philosophy*,
New York, NY: Oxford University Press.

Ashby, W. R. (1954) *Design for a Brain: The Origin of Adaptive Behaviour*, New York: Wiley.

Ashby, W. R. (1956) *Introduction to Cybernetics*, London: Chapman Hall.

AtKisson, A. (2010) *The Sustainability Transformation: How to accelerate positive change
in challenging times*, London: Earthscan/Routledge.

AtKisson, A. (2010) *Believing Cassandra: How to be a positivist in a pessimist's world*. 2nd
edn., London and New York: Earthscan/Routledge.

Ayling, S. (1988) *Edmund Burke: His Life and Opinions*, London: John Murray.

Baden, J. A. and Noonan, D. S. (1998) *Managing the Commons* (2nd edn), Indiana, US:
Indiana University Press.

Baker, G. (ed.) (2003) *Ludwig Wittgenstein and Freidrich Waismann, The Voices of
Wittgenstein: The Vienna Circle*, London and New York: Routledge.

Barabási, A. L. (2002) *Linked: The New Science of Networks*, Cambridge, US: Perseus.

Bateson, G. (1958) *Naven: a Survey of the Problems suggested by a Composite Picture of
the Culture of a New Guinea Tribe drawn from Three Points of View* (2nd edn), Stanford,
US: Stanford University Press.

Bateson, G. (1973) *Steps to an Ecology of Mind: Collected Essays in Anthropology,
Psychiatry, Evolution and Epistemology*, St Albans, UK: Paladin.

Bateson, G. (1979) *Mind and Nature: A Necessary Unity,* London: Wildwood House.

Begon, M., Harper, J. L. and Townsend, C. R. (1986/1996) *Ecology: Individuals, Populations and Communities*, (3rd edn), London: Blackwell Science.

Berger, P. L. and Luckmann, T. (1971) *The Social Construction of Reality: a treatise in the sociology of knowledge,* Harmondsworth, UK: Penguin.

Bergsen, H. (1907/2007) *The Creative Mind: An Introduction to Metaphysics* (tr.) M. L. Andison, New York: Dover.

Berlin, I. (1959/1990) 'The Decline of Utopian Ideas in the West', in *The Crooked Timber of Humanity: Chapters in the History of Ideas* (ed.) Hardy, H., Princeton, US: New Jersey Press.

Berlin, I. (1998) *The Proper Study of Mankind: An Anthology of Essays*, London: Pimlico.

Berry, W. (1977) *The Unsettling of America: Culture and Agriculture*, San Francisco, US: Sierra Club Books.

Birch, C. (1990) *On Purpose*, Kensington, Australia: NSW University Press.

Blake, W. (1803/2004) *The Pickering Manuscript*, Whitefish, Montana, US: Kessinger Publishing.

Bohm, D. (1951) *Quantum Theory*, New York: Prentice Hall.

Bohm, D. (1980) *Wholeness and Implicate Order*, London: Routledge.

Bohm, D. (1987) *Unfolding Meaning*, London: Routledge.

Bohm, D. (1994) *Thought as a System*, London and New York: Routledge.

Bohm, D. (1996/2004) *On Dialogue*, New York: Routledge Classics.

Bohm, D. and Peat, F. D. (1994) *Science, Order, and Creativity*, New York: Bantam Books.

Bohr, N. (1955) *The Unity of Knowledge,* New York: Doubleday.

Botsman, R. and Rogers, R. (2010) *What's Mine is Yours: The Rise of Collaborative Consumption*, New York: HarperCollins.

Boyden, S. (1987) *Western Civilization in Biological Perspective: Patterns in Biohistory,* London: Oxford University Press.

Boyden, S., Millar, S., Newcombe, K. and O'Neill, B. (1981) *The ecology of a city and its people: The case of Hong Kong*, Canberra: ANU Press.

Boyer, E. L. (1990) *Scholarship Reconsidered: Priorities of the Professoriate*, The Carnegie Foundation for the Advancement of Teaching, San Francisco, US: Jossey-Bass.

Brand, S. (1986) 'For God's Sake Margaret: A Conversation with Gregory Bateson and Margaret Mead', in *Ten Years of CoEvolution Quarterly: News That Stayed News* (eds) Kleiner, A. and Brand, S., San Francisco, US: North Point Press, pp. 26–46.

Briggs, J. and Peat, F. D. (1990) *Turbulent Mirror: An Illustrated Guide to Chaos Theory and the Science of Wholeness*, New York: Harper & Row.

Brown, V. A. (2005) 'Leadership in the Local Government sector: working from the inside out', in (eds) Hargroves, K. and Smith, M., *The Natural Advantage of Nations: Business Opportunities, Innovation and Governance in the 21st Century*. London: Earthscan, pp. 289–98.

Brown, V. A. (2008) *Leonardo's Vision: A Guide for Collective Thinking and Action,* Rotterdam, Netherlands: Sense.

Brown, V. A. (2010) 'Collective Inquiry and Its Wicked Problems', in (eds) Brown, V. A., Harris, J. A. and Russell, J. Y., *Tackling Wicked Problems: Through the Transdisciplinary Imagination*, London: Earthscan, pp. 61–81.

Brown, V. A. (2010) 'Multiple Knowledges, Multiple Languages: Are the Limits of My Language the Limits of My World?', *Knowledge Management for Development Journal*, **6** (2), pp. 120–31.

Brown, V. A. and Lambert, J. A. (2013) *Collective Learning for Transformational Change: A Guide to Collaborative Action*, London and New York: Routledge.

Brown, V. A., Harris, J. A. and Russell, J. Y. (2010) (eds) *Tackling Wicked Problems: Through the Transdisciplinary Imagination,* London: Earthscan.

Browne, J. (1995) *Charles Darwin: Voyaging,* Princeton, New Jersey, US: Princeton University Press,

Browne, J. (2002) *Charles Darwin: The Power of Place,* London: Pimlico.

Bruner, J. (1960) *The Process of Education,* Cambridge, Massachusetts, US: Harvard University Press.

Bruner, J. (1966) *Toward a Theory of Instruction,* Cambridge, Massachusetts, US: Belkapp Press.

Bruner, J. (1986) *Actual Minds, Possible Worlds,* Cambridge, Massachusetts, US: Harvard University Press.

Bruner, J. (1990) *Acts of Meaning,* Cambridge, Massachusetts, US: Harvard University Press.

Bruner, J. (1996) *The Culture of Education,* Cambridge, US: Harvard University Press.

Buber, M. (1958/2000) *I and Thou* (tr.) Ronald Gregor Smith (2nd edn), New York: Scribner Classics.

Buchanan, M. (2000) *Ubiquity: The Science of History ... or Why the World is Simpler than We Think,* New York: Crown.

Canetti, E. (1960/1984) *Crowds and Power* (tr.) Carol Stewart, New York: Farrar, Straus and Giroux.

Caplow, T. (1982) 'Christmas Gifts and Kin Networks', *American Sociological Review,* 1982, pp. 383–92.

Capra, F. (1982) *The Turning Point: Science, Society and the Rising Culture,* New York: Simon & Schuster.

Capra, F. (1996) *The Web of Life: A New Scientific Understanding of Living Systems,* UK: HarperCollins.

Capra, F. (2004) *Hidden Dimensions: A Science for Living Sustainably,* New York: Anchor Books.

Carey, J. (1995) *The Faber Book of Science,* Boston, US: Faber and Faber.

Carson, R. (1962) *Silent Spring,* Boston, US: Houghton Mifflin.

Chodron, P. (1012) *Living Beautifully with Uncertainty and Change,* Boston, US and London: Shambhala.

Clark, K. (1971) *Civilization: A Personal View,* London: BBC and John Murray.

Clark, R. W. (1973) *Einstein: The Life and Times,* London: Hodder & Stoughton.

Clastres, P. (1974/1989) *Society Against The State* (trs Hurley, R. and Stein, A.), New York: Zone Books.

Cole, H. S. D., Freeman, C., Jahoda, M. and Pavitt, K. L. R. (eds) (1973) *Thinking About The Future: A Critique of 'The Limits to Growth',* London: Sussex University Press.

Cumming, F. (2010) 'Exploring the Doctoral Interface', in (eds) Brown, V. A., Harris, J. A. and Russell, J. Y., *Tackling Wicked Problems: Through the Transdisciplinary Imagination,* London: Earthscan, pp. 233–39.

Cummings, S., Regeer, B. L., Ho, Wenny W. S. and Zweekhorst, Marjolein, B. M. (2013) 'Proposing a fifth generation of knowledge management for development: investigating convergence between knowledge management for development and transdisciplinary research', *Knowledge Management for Development Journal,* **9** (2), pp. 10-36.

Daley, H. E. and Cobb, J. B. (1989/1994) *For the Common Good: Redirecting the Economy towards Community, the Environment and a Sustainable Future,* Boston, US: Beacon Press.

Damasio, A. (1994) *Descartes' Error: Emotion, Reason and the Human Brain,* New York: Penguin.

Darwin, C. (1859) *On the Origin of Species by Means of Natural Selection or the Preservation of Favoured Races in the Struggle for Life,* UK: John Murray.

Darwin, C. (1871) *The Descent of Man,* UK: John Murray.

Darwin, C. (1872) *The Expression of the Emotions in Man and Animals,* UK: John Murray.

Darwin, C. (1881) *The Formation of Vegetable Mould, through the Actions of Worms, with Observations on Their Habits,* UK: John Murray.

Darwin, C. and Wallace, A. R. (1858) 'On the Tendency of Species to Form Varieties; and On the Perpetuation of Varieties and Species by Natural Means of Selection', *Proc. Linn Soc. Zool.,* **3** (9), pp. 45–62.

Darwin, E. (1794–96) *Zoonomia; or the Laws of Organic Life* (illustrated version), Teddington, UK: Echo Library.

Dawkins, R. (1986) *The Blind Watchmaker,* UK: Longman.

Dawkins, R. (2006) *The God Delusion,* London: Bantam.

Descartes, R. (1637/1946) *A Discourse on the Method of Rightly Conducting One's Reason* (tr.) Veitch, J., London: Everyman's Library 570.

Dewey, J. (1916) *Democracy and Education: An Introduction to the Philosophy of Education,* New York: McMillan.

Diamond, J. (1991) *The Third Chimpanzee: The Evolution and Future of the Human Animal,* London: Hutchinson Radius.

Doidge, N. (2007) *The Brain That Changes Itself: Stories of Personal Triumph from the Frontiers of Brain Science,* Melbourne, Australia: Scribe.

Drysek, J. (2010) *Foundations and Frontiers of Deliberative Governance,* UK: Oxford University Press.

Dyball, R. (2010) 'Human Ecology and Open Transdisciplinary Inquiry', in *Tackling Wicked Problems: Through the Transdisciplinary Imagination* (eds) Brown, V. A., Harris, J. A. and Russell, J. Y., London: Earthscan.

Edgeworth, F. (1881) *Mathematical Physics,* London: C. Kegan Paul & Co.

Ehrlich, P. and Ehrlich, A. (1968) *The Population Bomb,* London: Ballantine.

Ehrlich, P., Ehrlich, A. and Holden, J. (1977) *Ecoscience: Population, Resources and Environment,* San Francisco, US: W. H. Freeman.

Einstein, A. and Infeld, L. (1966) *The Evolution of Physics: From Early Concepts to Relativity and Quanta,* New York: Touchstone.

Eldredge, N. and Gould, S. J. (1972) 'Punctuated Equilibria: An Alternative to Phyletic Gradualism', in (ed.) Schopf, T. J. M., *Models in Paleobiology,* San Francisco, US: Freeman, Cooper and Co., pp. 82–115.

Falk, R. (1999) *Predatory Globalization: A Critique,* Cambridge, UK: Polity Press.

Feez, S. (2010) *Montessori and Early Childhood: A Guide for Students,* London: Sage.

Fine, C. (2010) *Delusions of Gender: How our Minds, Society, and Neurosexism Create Difference,* New York: W.W. Norton & Company.

Fishkin, J. and Luskin, R. C. (2005) 'Experimenting with a Democratic Ideal: Deliberative Polling and Public Opinion', *ActaPolitica,* **40,** pp. 284–98.

Flannery, T. (1994) *The Future Eaters: An Ecological History of the Australasian Lands and People.* Chatswood, Australia: Reed Books.

Flannery, T. (2005) *The Weather Makers: The History and Future Impact of Climate Change,* Melbourne, Australia: Text Publishing Company.

Foucault, M. (1969/2002) *The Archaeology of Knowledge* (tr.) Sheridan Smith, A. M., London and New York: Routledge.

Freeman, D. (1983) *Margaret Mead in Samoa: The Making and Unmaking of an Anthropological Myth,* Canberra: Australian National University Press.

Freire, Paulo (2006) *Pedagogy of the Oppressed*, (30th Anniversary edn.), New York: Continuum.

Funtowicz, S. O. and Ravetz, J. R. (1993) 'Science for the post-normal age', *Futures*, **25** (7), pp. 739–55.

Gardner, H. (1983) *Frames of Mind: The Theory of Multiple Intelligences*, New York: Basic Books.

Gardner, H. (1993) *Multiple Intelligences: The Theory and Practice,* New York: Basic Books.

Ghiselin, M. T. (1972) *The Triumph of the Darwinian Method*, Berkeley and Los Angeles, US: University of California Press.

Ginsburg, H. and Opper, S. (1969) *Piaget's Theory of Intellectual Development: An Introduction*, Englewood Cliffs, New Jersey, US: Prentice-Hall.

Gleick, J. (1987) *Chaos: Making a New Science,* UK: Penguin.

Golding, W. (1954) *Lord of the Flies,* UK: Faber & Faber.

Goodwin, B. (1994) *How the Leopard Changed Its Spots: The Evolution of Complexity*, New York: Scribner's Sons.

Gopnik, A. (2011) *Winter: Five Windows on the Season*, Toronto: Anansi.

Gore, A. (2007) *An Inconvenient Truth: The Crisis of Global Warming*, London: Bloomsbury.

Gould, S. J. (1972) 'Punctuated Equilibria: An Alternative to Phyletic Gradualism', in (ed.) Schopf, T. J. M., *Models in Paleobiology*, San Francisco, US: Freeman, Cooper and Company, pp. 82–115.

Gould, S. J. (1977) *Ever Since Darwin: Reflections in Natural History*, New York: Norton.

Gould, S. J. (2002) *The Structure of Evolutionary Theory*, Cambridge, US: Belknap Press.

Gould, S. J. (2004) *The Hedgehog, The Fox and the Magister's Pox: Mending and Minding the Misconceived Gap between Science and the Humanities*, London: Vintage.

Gribbin, J. (1985) *In Search of The Double Helix: Quantum Physics and Life*, New York: McGraw-Hill.

Hamilton, C. (2013) *Earth Masters: Playing God with the Climate,* Sydney: Allen & Unwin.

Hardin, G. (1968) 'The Tragedy of the Commons', *Science*, **162**, 1243–48.

Hardin, G. and Baden, J. (1977) (eds) *Managing the Commons*, San Francisco, US: W H Freeman.

Hare, P. (1973) 'Group Decision by Consensus: Reaching Unity in the Society of Friends', *Sociological Inquiry,* **43** (1), 75–84.

Harris, J. A. (2009) *The Change Makers: Stories from Australia's first environmental studies graduates,* Canberra: University of Canberra: self-published.

Hawking, S. W. (1988) *A Brief History of Time: From the Big Bang to Black Holes*, New York: Bantam Books.

Hill, J. S. (1972) *Imagination in Coleridge*, London: MacMillan.

Hobsbawm, E. (1994) *Age of Extremes: The Short Twentieth Century 1914–1991*, Michael Joseph, London: Penguin.

Honderich, T. (ed.) (1995) *The Oxford Companion to Philosophy,* New York: Oxford University Press.

Hopkins, R. (2008) *The Transition Handbook: From Oil Dependence to Local Resilience*, UK: Green Books.

Hopkins, R. (2012) *The Transition Companion: Making Your Community More Resilient in Uncertain Times*, UK: Green Books.

Huxley, A. (1962) *Island*, New York: Harper & Row.

Hyde, L. (1983/2007) *The Gift: How the Creative Spirit Transforms the World*, Edinburgh: Canongate Books.

Isaacs, W. (1999) *Dialogue and the Art of Thinking Together*, New York: Currency.

Ison, R. L. and Russell, D. B. (2000) *Agricultural Extension and Rural Development: Breaking Out of Traditions*, Cambridge, UK: Cambridge University Press.

Jacobs, J. (1972) *The Death and Life of Great American Cities*, Harmondsworth, UK: Penguin.

Jevons, W. (1871) *Theory of Political Economy*, London: Macmillan.

Jevons, W. (1905) *Principles of Economics*, London: Macmillan.

Jungk, R. (1958) *Brighter than a Thousand Suns: A Personal History of the Atomic Scientists*, Boston, US: Houghton Mifflin Harcourt.

Keen, M., Brown, V. A. and Dyball, R. (2005) (eds) *Social Learning in Environmental Management: Towards a Sustainable Future,* London: Routledge.

Keller, E. F. (1983) *A Feeling for the Organism: The Life and Work of Barbara McClintock,* New York: Freeman.

Kelly, A. (2008) *Changing Software Development: Learning to Become Agile*, Chichester, UK: Wiley & Sons.

Kelly, G. A. (1965) *Theory of Personality: The Psychology of Personal Constructs,* New York: Norton.

Keynes, J. M. (1936) *General Theory of Employment, Interest and Money*, London: Macmillan.

Kickbusch, I. and Gleicher, D. (2012) *Governance for Health in the 21st Century*, World Health Organization.

Knowles, M. (1973) *The Adult Learner: A Neglected Species*, Houston, Texas, US: Gulf Publishing Company.

Koestler, A. (1964/1989) *The Act of Creation*, London: Arkana.

Koestler, A. (1967) *The Ghost in the Machine*, London: Arkana.

Koestler, A. (1978) *Janus: A Summing Up*, Victoria, Australia: Hutchinson of Australia.

Kolb, D. A. (1984) *Experiential Learning: Experience as the Source of Learning and Development*, New Jersey, US: Prentice Hall.

Kuhn, T. (1962/1970) *The Structure of Scientific Revolutions*, Chicago, US: University of Chicago Press.

Lackoff, G. and Johnson, M. (1999) *Philosophy in the Flesh: The Embodied Mind and Its Challenge to Western Thought*, New York: Basic Books.

Lakoff, G. (1994) *Don't Think of an Elephant! Know your Values and Frame the Debate*, Vermont, US: Chelsea Green.

Lash, J. P. (1980) *Helen and Teacher: The Story of Helen Keller and Anne Sullivan Macy*, New York: Delacorte Press.

Leopold, A. (1949/1981) *A Sand County Almanac and Sketches Here and There*, London: Oxford University Press.

Lewin, K. (1951) *Field Theory in Social Science: Selected Theoretical Papers* (ed.) Cartwright, D., New York: Harper & Row.

Lewin, R. (1993) *Complexity: Life at the Edge of Chaos*, London: Orion Books.

Lewis, M. and Woodhull, J. (2008) *Inside the No: Five Steps to Decisions that Last*, self-published in South Africa.

Lorenz, E. N. (1963) 'Deterministic Nonperiodic Flow', *J. Atmospheric Sciences*, **20** (2), 130 41.

Lovelock, J. (1979) *Gaia: A New Look at Life on Earth*, Oxford: Oxford University Press.

Lovelock, J. (1991) *Gaia: The Practical Guide of Planetary Medicine*, Sydney: Allen & Unwin.

Lovelock, J. (2000) *Homage to Gaia: The Life of an Independent Scientist*, New York: Oxford University Press.

Lovelock, J. (2009) *The Vanishing Face of Gaia: A Final Warning*, New York: Allen Lane.

MacDonald, R. (1998) *Mr. Darwin's Shooter: A Novel*, Sydney: Random House.

Malcolm, N. (1984) *Ludwig Wittgenstein: A Memoir*, New York: Oxford University Press.

Malouf, D. (1978/1999) *An Imaginary Life*, London: Vintage.

Mandelbrot, B. (1982) *The Fractal Geometry of Nature*, San Francisco, US: W. H. Freeman & Co.

Marden, O. S. (1908/2007) *He Can Who Thinks He Can*, Stilwell, Kansas, US: Digireads. com Book.

Margulis, L. (1998) *The Symbiotic Planet: A New Look at Evolution,* New York: Basic Books.

Margulis, L. and Sagan, D. (1995) *What is Life?*, New York: Simon & Schuster.

Masani, P. R. (1990) *Norbert Wiener 1894–1964*, Basel, Switzerland: Birkhauser.

Massy, C. (2011) *Breaking the Sheep's Back: The Shocking True Story of the Decline and Fall of the Australian Wool Industry*, St Lucia, Australia: Queensland University Press.

Mathews, F. (1991) *The Ecological Self*, London: Routledge.

Maturana, H. and Varela, F. (1980) *Autopoiesis and Cognition*, Dordrecht, Holland: D. Reidel.

Maturana, H. and Varela, F. (1987) *The Tree of Knowledge*, Boston, US: Shambhala.

Mauss, M. (1950/1990) *The Gift: Forms and Functions of Exchange in Archaic Societies*, (tr.) Halls, W. D., London: Routledge.

Maynard, W. B. (2004) *Walden Pond*, New York: Oxford University Press.

McElheny, V. K. (2010) *Drawing the Map of Life: Inside the Human Genome Project,* New York: Basic Books.

McLuhan, M. (1962) *The Gutenberg Galaxy: The Making of Typographic Man*, Canada: University of Toronto Press.

McLuhan, M. and Fiore, Q. (1967) *The Medium is the Massage: An Inventory of Effects*, UK: Penguin.

McMahon, A. M. S. (1994) *Understanding Language Change*, Cambridge, UK: Cambridge University Press.

Mead, M. (1928) *Coming of Age in Samoa: A Psychological Study of Primitive Youth for Western Society*, New York: William Morrow and Company.

Mead, M. (1978) *Culture and Commitment: The New Relationships between the Generations in the 1970s*, New York: Columbia University Press.

Meadows, D. H. and Meadows, D. L. (1972) *The Limits of Growth: A Report for the Club of Rome's Project on the Predicament of Mankind*, London: Potomac.

Meadows, D. H., Meadows, D. L. and Randers, J. (1992) *Beyond the Limits: Global Collapse or a Sustainable Future,* London: Earthscan.

Medawar, P. B. (1967/1915) *The Art of the Soluble*, London: Methuen.

Merchant, C. (1980) *The Death of Nature*, New York: Harper & Row.

Mesarovic, M. and Pestel, E. (1974) *Mankind at the Turning Point,* London: E. P. Dutton.

Methuen, A. (1921) *An Anthology of Modern Verse*, London: Methuen & Company.

Mill, J. S. (2002/1859) *On Liberty*, New York: Dover Publications.

Mindell, A. (1992) *The Leader as Martial Artist: An Introduction to Deep Democracy. Techniques and Strategies for Resolving Conflict and Creating Community*, San Francisco, US: HarperCollins.

Mindell, A. (2002) *The Deep Democracy of Open Forums: How to Transform Organizations into Communities: Practical Steps to Conflict Prevention and Resolution for Family, Workplace and World*, Charlottesville, US: Hampton Roads.

Mitroff, I. I. and Linstone, H. A. (1993) *The Unbounded Mind: Breaking the Chains of Traditional Business Thinking*, New York: Oxford University Press.

Mollison, B. (1988) *Permaculture: A Designers' Manual*, Tyalgum, Australia: Tagari Publications.

Monk, W. H. (1861) *Hymns Ancient and Modern*, London: Novello and Company.

Moore, C. (2013) *Margaret Thatcher: The Authorized Biography, Volume One: Not for Turning*, London: Allen Lane.

More, T. (1530/1995) *Utopia* (trs. Logan, G. M., Adams, R. M. and Miller, C.), Cambridge, UK: Cambridge University Press.

Mumford, L. (1961) *The City in History: Its Origins, its Transformations and its Prospects*, New York: Harcourt, Brace and World.

Murdoch, I. (1970) *The Sovereignty of Good*, London: Routledge & Kegan Paul.

Nettleship, R. L. (1955) *The Theory of Education in Plato's Republic,* London: Oxford University Press.

Newton, J. L. (2006) *Aldo Leopold's Odyssey: Rediscovering the Author of a Sound County Almanac*, Washington, DC: Island Press, a Shearwater book.

O'Riorden, T. (1971) *Perspectives on Resource Management*, London: Pion.

Odum, E. P. (1971) *Fundamentals of Ecology,* Philadelphia, US: W.B. Saunders.

Odum, H. T. (1971) *Environment, Power and Society*, New York: Wiley.

Odum, H. T. (1994) *Ecological and General Systems: An Introduction to Systems Ecology,* Colorado, US: Colorado University Press.

Oppenheimer, S. (2003) *Out of Eden: The peopling of the world*, London: Robinson.

Orwell, G. (1946/1962) *Animal Farm*, New York: Signet Classics.

Ostrom, E. (1990) *Governing the Commons: The Evolution of Institutions for Collective Action*, Cambridge, UK: Cambridge University Press.

Paine, T. (1776/2004) *Common Sense*, London: Penguin.

Paine, T. (1791–92) *The Rights of Man*, Dover.

Palmer, P. J. (2011) *Healing the Heart of Democracy: The Courage to Create a Politics Worthy of the Human Spirit*, San Francisco, US: Jossey-Bass.

Palmer, P. J. and Zajonc, A., with Megan Scribner (2010) *The Heart of Higher Education: A Call for Renewal*, San Francisco, US: Jossey-Bass.

Patel, Raj (2009) *The Value of Nothing: How to Reshape Market Society and Redefine Democracy*, New York: Picador.

Pels, D. (2003) *Unhastening Science: Autonomy and Reflexivity in the Social Theory of Knowledge*, Liverpool, UK: Liverpool University Press.

Piaget, J. (1951) *The Child's Conception of the World*, London: Routledge.

Plimer, I. (2009) *Heaven and Earth – Global Warming: The Missing Science*, Ballan, Victoria, Australia: Connor Court.

Plotnitsky, A. (2013) *Niels Bohr and Complementarity: An Introduction*, New York: Springer, Springer Briefs in Physics.

Plumwood, V. (2002) *Environmental Culture: The ecological crisis of reason*, London and New York: Routledge.

Polanyi, M. (1958) *Personal Knowledge: Towards a Post-Critical Philosophy,* Chicago, US: University of Chicago Press.

Pope, A. (1902) *The Complete Poetical Works of Alexander Pope* (ed.) Boynton, H. W., Boston, New York: Houghton, Mifflin and Company.

Popper, K. (1963) *Conjectures and Refutations: The Growth of Scientific Knowledge*, London: Harper & Row

Popper, K. (1972) *Objective Knowledge: An Evolutionary Approach*, Oxford, UK: Oxford University Press.

Poteete, A. R., Janssen, M. A. and Ostrom, E. (2010) *Working Together: Collective Action, the Commons, and Multiple Methods in Practice*, Princeton, New Jersey, US: Princeton University Press.

Poundstone, W. (1992) *Prisoner's Dilemma*, New York: Doubleday.

Prigogine, I. (1967) 'Dissipative Structures in Chemical Systems', in (ed.) Claesson, S., *Fast Reactions and Primary Processes in Chemical Kinetics*, New York: Interscience.

Prigogine, I. and Stengers, I. (1984) *Order out of Chaos*, London: Fontana.

Putman, R. (2000) *Bowling Alone: The Collapse and Revival of American Community*, New York: Simon & Schuster.

Ralston Saul, J. (1992) *Voltaire's Bastards: The Dictatorship of Reason in the West*, New York: Simon & Schuster.

Ravetz, J. (1971) *Scientific Knowledge and its Social Problems*, London: Oxford University Press.

Ravetz, J. (1999) 'What is Post-Normal Science?', *Futures*, **31** (7), pp. 647–53.

Ravetz, J. (2005) *A No-Nonsense Guide to Science*, UK: New Internationalist.

Rittle, H. and Webber, M. (1973) 'Dilemmas in a general theory of planning', *Policy Sciences*, **4**, pp. 155–69.

Roberts, R. M. (1989) *Serendipity: Accidental Discoveries in Science*, London: Wiley.

Ronan, C. A. (1982) *Science: Its History and Development among the World's Cultures*, New York: Hamlyn.

Rose, H. and Rose, S. (1970) *Science and Society*, Harmondsworth, UK: Pelican.

Rose, S. (1997) *Lifelines: Life beyond the gene*, London: Oxford University Press.

Roszak, T. (1968/1995) *The Making of a Counterculture: Reflections on the Technocratic Society and Its Youthful Opposition*, Berkeley and Los Angeles, US: University of California Press.

Roszak, T. (1972) *Where the Wasteland Ends: Politics and Transcendence in Post Industrial Society*, New York: Doubleday.

Roszak, T. (1975) *Unfinished Animal: The Aquarian Frontier and the Evolution of Consciousness*, New York: Harper & Row.

Roszak, T. (1979/1981) *Person/Planet: the Creative Disintegration of Industrial Society*, New York: Granada.

Roszak, T. (1992) *The Voice of the Earth: An Exploration of Ecopsychology,* New York: Simon & Schuster.

Russell, B. and Whitehead, A. N. (1910–13) *Principia Mathematica*, Cornell, US: Cornell University Library.

Russell, J. (2010) 'A Philosophical Framework for an Open and Critical Transdisciplinary Inquiry', *in Tackling Wicked Problems: Through the Transdisciplinary Imagination*, (eds) Brown, V. A., Harris, J. A. and Russell, J. Y., London: Earthscan, pp. 31–60.

Sacks, O. (1985) *The Man Who Mistook His Wife for a Hat*, New York: Summit Books.

Sahlins, M. (1972) *Stone Age Economics*, Chicago, US: Aldine-Atherton.

Schmidt, E. and Cohen, J. (2013) *The New Digital Age: Reshaping the Future of People, Nations and Business*, New York: Alfred A. Knopf.

Schneider, S. H., Miller, J. R., Crist, E., and Boston, P. J. (2004) (eds) *Scientists Debate Gaia: The Next Century*, Cambridge, Massachusetts, US: MIT Press.

Schon, D. (1987) *Educating the Reflective Practitioner*, San Francisco, US: Jossey-Bass.

Schuler, D. (2008) *Liberating Voices: A Pattern Language for Communication Revolution*, Massachusetts, US: MIT Press.

Schumacher, E. F. (1974) *Small is Beautiful: A Study of Economics as if People Mattered*, London: Abacus.

Schümmer, T. and Lukosch, S. (2007) *Patterns for Computer-Mediated Interaction,* Chichester, UK: Wiley & Sons.

Senge, P. M. (1990) *The Fifth Discipline: The Art and Practice of the Learning Organization*, New York: Currency Doubleday.

Sheldrake, R. (1990) *The Rebirth of Nature: The Greening of Science and God*, London: Century.

Shermer, M. (2002) *In Darwin's Shadow: The Life and Science of Alfred Russel Wallace*, New York: Oxford University Press.

Shiller, R. J. (2008) *The Subprime Solution: How Today's Global Financial Crisis Happened and What to Do about It*, New Jersey, US: Princeton University Press.

Shiva, V. (1991) *The Violence of the Green Revolution: Third World Agriculture, Ecology and Politics*, London: Zed Books.

Shorto, R. (2008) *Descartes' Bones: A Skeletal History of the Conflict between Faith and Reason*, New York: Doubleday.

Skolimowski, H. (1994) *The Participatory Mind: A New Theory of Knowledge and of the Universe*, London: Arkana.

Smith, A. (1776/1986) *The Wealth of Nations, Books I–III*, New York: Penguin Classics.

Smithson, M. (2010) 'Ignorance and Uncertainty', in *Tackling Wicked Problems: Through the Transdisciplinary Imagination* (eds) Brown, V. A., Harris, J. A. and Russell, J. Y. London: Earthscan, pp. 84–97.

Snow, C. P. (2012) *The Two Cultures*, Cambridge, UK: Cambridge University Press.

Speaight, R. (1967) *Teilhard de Chardin: A Biography*, London: Collins.

Stone, C. D. (1975/2010*) Should Trees Have Standing? Law, Morality and the Environment*, (3rd edn), New York: Oxford University Press.

Stringer, C. and Andrews, P. (2005) *The Complete World of Human Evolution,* London: Thames & Hudson.

Sussman, B. (2010) *The Great Coverup: Nixon and the Scandal of Watergate*, Santa Ana, California, US: Seven Locks Press.

Sykes, B. (2001) *The Seven Daughters of Eve: The Science that Reveals our Genetic Ancestry*, New York: Norton.

Teilhard de Chardin (1955/1975) *The Phenomenon of Man*, (tr.) Wall, B., New York: Harper & Row.

Teilhard de Chardin, P. (1966) *Man's Place in Nature* (tr.) Hague, R., St James's Place, London: Collins.

*The Holy Bible, King James Version*, 'Genesis', Cleveland and New York: The World Publishing Company.

Thoreau, H. D. (1844/1960) *Walden and Civil Disobedience*, Boston, US: Houghton Mifflin.

Toulmin, S. (1958) *The Uses of Argument*, Cambridge, UK: Cambridge University Press.

Toulmin, S. (1972) *Human Understanding: Vol.1: The Collective Use and Understanding of Concepts*, Princeton, US: Princeton University Press.

Uhr, J. (1998) *Deliberative Democracy in Australia: The Changing Place of Parliament*, Cambridge, UK: Cambridge University Press.

van Kerkhoff, L. (2010) 'Global Inequalities in Research: A Transdisciplinary Exploration of Causes and Consequences', in *Tackling Wicked Problems: Through the Transdisciplinary Imagination* (eds) Brown, V.A., Harris, J.A. and Russell, J.Y. London: Earthscan, pp. 130–38.

Varela, F. J., Thomson, E. and Rosch, E. (1991) *The Embodied Mind: Cognitive Science and Human Experience*, Cambridge, US: MIT Press.

Varma, R. and Alomes, A. (2012) *Towards a Nonviolent Mind,* Dharamsala, India: Library of Tibetan Works & Archives.

Voltaire (François Marie Arouet), 'Candide or Optimism', in *Candide and other stories* (tr.) Pearson, R., London: Oxford University Press.

Von Bertalanffy, L. (1976) *General Systems Theory: Foundations, Development and Applications*, New York: George Braziller.

wa Goro, W. (2007) 'Translating Africa and leadership: what is Africa to me?', in (ed.) Wambu, O., *Under The Tree of Talking: Leadership and Change in Africa*, London: Counterpoint.

Ward, B. and Dubos, R. (1972) *Only One Earth: The Care and Maintenance of a Small Planet*, UK: Penguin.

Waring, M. (1988/1999) *Counting for Nothing: What Men Value and What Women are Worth*, Toronto: University of Toronto Press.

Watson, J. (1968) *The Double Helix: A Personal Account of the Discovery of the Structure of DNA*, Harmondsworth, UK: Penguin.

Whitehead, A. N. (1929/1978) *Process and Reality* (corrected edition) (eds) Griffin, D. R. and Sherbourne, D. W., New York: Free Press.

Whitman, W. (1819–92) *Walt Whitman: The Complete Poems* (ed.) Murphy, F., London: Penguin Classics.

Whorf, B. L. and Carroll, J. B. (1956) (eds) *Language, Thought, and Reality: Selected Writings*, Massachusetts, US: MIT Press.

Wiener, N. (1948) *Cybernetics: Or Control and Communication in the Animal and the Machine*, Massachusetts, US: MIT Press.

Wiener, N. (1950/54) *The Human Use of Human Beings: Cybernetics and Society*, Boston, US: Da Capo Press.

Wierzbicka, A. (2006) *English: Meaning and Culture*, New York, NY: Oxford University Press.

Winchester, S. (1999) *The Surgeon of Crowthorne: A Tale of Murder, Madness and the Oxford Dictionary*, Harmondsworth, Middlesex, UK: Penguin.

Woodford, J. (2000) *The Wollemi Pine: The Incredible Discovery of a Living Fossil from the Age of the Dinosaurs*, Melbourne, Australia: Text Publishing.

Woodward, B. and Bernstein, C. (1974) *All the President's Men*, New York: Simon & Schuster.

Worboys, M. (2000) *Spreading Germs: Disease Theories and Medical Practice in Britain, 1865–1900*, Cambridge, UK: Cambridge University Press.

World Commission on Environment and Development (1987), *Our Common Future*, New York: Oxford University Press.

Wright, J. A. (1975) 'Nature is much to wreck', in *Because I Was Invited*, Melbourne, Australia: Oxford University Press, p. 206.

# Index

232    *Index*